The Triangle Papers:

ENGAGING RUSSIA
A Return to Containment?

**A Report to
The Trilateral Commission**

PAULA DOBRIANSKY

ANDRZEJ OLECHOWSKI

YUKIO SATOH

IGOR YURGENS

Published by
The Trilateral Commission
Washington, Paris, Tokyo
2014

The Trilateral Commission was formed in 1973 by experienced private leaders from Europe, North America, and Japan to foster closer cooperation among these three democratic industrialized regions on common problems facing an increasingly interconnected and interdependent world. It seeks to improve public understanding of such problems, to support proposals for handling them jointly, and to nurture habits and practices of working together. The European group has widened since with the ongoing enlargement of the European Union. The Japanese group has widened into an Asian Pacific group including China and India. The North American group now includes members from Canada, Mexico and the United States.

© The Trilateral Commission, 2014. All rights reserved.

Library of Congress Cataloging-in-Publication Data

Dobriansky, Paula.
  Engaging Russia : a return to containment? : a report to the Trilateral Commission / Paula J. Dobriansky, Andrzej Olechowski, Yukio Satoh, IgorYurgens.
     pages cm
  ISBN 978-0-930503-95-6 (pbk.)
  1. Russia (Federation)--Politics and government--21st century. 2. Russia (Federation)--Foreign relations--21st century. 3. World politics--21st century. I. Olechowski, Andrzej. II. Satoh, Yukio. III. IUrgens, I. IU. (Igor☐ IUr☐evich) IV. Trilateral Commission, issuing body. V. Title.
  DK510.763.D636 2014
  947.086--dc23
                    2014046100

The Trilateral Commission

www.trilateral.org

1156 15th Street, NW   5, rue de Téhéran
Washington, DC 20005   75008 Paris, France

Japan Center for International Exchange
4-9-17 Minami-Azabu
Minato-ku
Tokyo 106-0047, Japan

Contents

The Authors v
The Trilateral Process 1
Acknowledgements 4
Foreword by Carl Bildt 5

I. **Introduction** 7
          The Crisis in Ukraine 8
          Areas of Consensus 14
          Areas of Disagreement 18
          Joint Recommendations for Governments and Civil Society 19

II. **Regional summaries:** 23
    i.   Summary of North American Chapter 23
    ii. Summary or European Chapter 38
    iii. Summary of Asia Pacific Chapter 48
    iv. Summary of Russian Chapter 58

III. **A North American Perspective** 67

IV. **A European Perspective** 127

V. **An Asian Perspective** 187
    i.   A Retired Chinese Diplomat's View of the Ukraine Crisis 220
    ii. Russia and the Eurasian Balance: An Indian Perspective 224

VI. **A Russian Perspective** 233
          The West and Russia: An Outlook to 2020 and Beyond 257
                      (Drafted in June 2013)

Annex: Uniting for Ukraine Independence, *The Wall Street Journal Europe,* July 21, 2014 275

The Authors

Paula Dobriansky is a Senior Fellow at Harvard University's JFK Belfer Center for Science and International Affairs and Chair, National Board of Directors of the World Affairs Councils of America. Over 25 years, she served in senior government positions, including: Under Secretary of State for Global Affairs, USIA Associate Director for Policy and Programs, Deputy Assistant Secretary of State for Human Rights and Humanitarian Affairs, Deputy Head U.S. Delegation to the 1990 Copenhagen Conference on Security and Cooperation in Europe, and Director of European and Soviet Affairs at the National Security Council, the White House. She was also Senior Vice President and Global Head of Government and Regulatory Affairs at Thomson Reuters and held the U.S. Naval Academy Distinguished National Security Chair. A Council on Foreign Relations (CFR) member and Trilateral Commission Trustee, Ambassador Dobriansky served as Senior Vice President and Director of the CFR Washington Office and was the Council's first George F. Kennan Senior Fellow for Russian and Eurasian Studies. She received a B.S.F.S. *summa cum laude* in international politics from Georgetown University School of Foreign Service and an M.A. and Ph.D. in Soviet political/military affairs from Harvard University.

Andrzej Olechowski is Chairman of the Supervisory Board of Bank Handlowy, a Director of Euronet and a Member of the Supervisory Board of P4. He sits on the International Advisory Board of Macquarie European Infrastructure Funds. He is Chairman of the Polish Group in the Trilateral Commission and a member of European Council on Foreign Relations. A former Minister of Foreign Affairs (1993-95) and Minister of Finance (1992), he was a candidate in Presidential elections (2000 and 2010) and a founder of the Civic Platform. His previous positions include Chairman of the City Council in Wilanów (1994-98), Economic Advisor to President Lech Wałęsa (1992-93; 1995), Secretary of State for Foreign Economic Relations (1991-92), Deputy Governor, National Bank of Poland (1989-91). Educated at the Central School of Planning and Statistics (Ph.D., 1979), he is a professor at Vistula University and the author of a number of publications on international trade and foreign policy.

Yukio Satoh is Vice Chairman of the Japan Institute of International Affairs in Tokyo and is an accomplished Japanese diplomat, having served as the permanent representative of Japan to the United Nations. He also served as the ambassador of Japan to the Netherlands from 1994 to 1996 and to

Australia from 1996 to 1998. Satoh entered the Foreign Service in 1961 from the University of Tokyo's Faculty of Law and studied history at Edinburgh University from 1961 to 1963. He has written numerous articles on security issues both in English and Japanese.

Igor Yurgens is the Chairman of the Management Board of the Institute of Contemporary Development in Moscow, a member of the Presidential Council for the Development of the Information Society in Russia, a member of the Presidential Council for Civil Society Institutions and Human Rights, a member of the Academic Council of the Security Council of the Russian Federation, a member of Russian Council on International Affairs and a member of the Presidium of the Council for Foreign and Defence Policy. He graduated from the Economics Department of Moscow State University and is a professor of the Higher School of Economics and author of numerous articles and monographs. Igor Yurgens is Honorary Consul General of Monaco in Moscow.

The Trilateral Process

"Engaging Russia: A Return to Containment?" is the third in a series of reports on Russia that the Trilateral Commission has undertaken since 1995. In addition to the contributions from the Trilateral co-chairs, the Commission, for the first time, solicited a chapter from a group of Russian experts led by a Russian co-chair. The report reveals areas of agreement and disagreement among the four groups (Europe, Russia, North America and Asia Pacific) on where Russia is today, domestically and internationally, and what policy approaches the Trilateral countries should pursue toward Moscow. The collegial partnership among the co-chairs led to their publishing a joint op-ed, which advocates the establishment of a Friends of Ukraine task force.

The authors alone are responsible for this report's analysis and conclusions. They have been aided by extensive consultations with scholars, experts and business leaders from the Trilateral countries as well as Russia. Although their contributions and insights inform the contents of this report, the report's analysis and recommendations do not necessarily reflect the individual views of those consulted. These consultations included discussions during 2013 Trilateral Commission regional meetings in Krakow on October 25-27, in Mexico City on November 8-10, and in Manila on December 12-14. The authors also held a task force meeting at Harvard University on March 3-4, 2014 to prepare for the coming Washington plenary meeting and were graciously hosted by the Belfer Center for Science and International Affairs of the John F. Kennedy School of Government.

The authors are indebted to Trilateral Commission members, the Brookings Institution, Harvard University and business groups for their hospitality, assistance and encouragement in researching and preparing the report. The authors also wish to thank Sweden's Ambassador Bjorn Lyrvall for hosting a dinner with members of the diplomatic corps at which the report was discussed. On April 24, 2014, prior to the formal presentation of the report at the plenary meeting of the Commission two days later, the authors briefed U.S. officials from the National Security Council (The White House) and Department of State, and presented the report at the Center for Strategic and International Studies and the Council on Foreign Relations. Each of these sessions in Washington D.C. was a source of new ideas and questions for which the authors are grateful.

The authors particularly wish to thank the scholars who contributed to or reviewed various drafts of the report and attended meetings to discuss them.[1]

In North America, the following experts attended a June 25, 2013 consultation session at the Brookings Institution in Washington, D.C., and/or a similar September 24, 2013 session at the John F. Kennedy School of Government at Harvard University: Graham Allison, Leon Aron, Anders Åslund, Samuel Charap, Ariel Cohen, Timothy Colton, Fiona Hill, David Kramer, Joseph Nye, Thomas Pickering, Steven Pifer, David Rivkin, Kevin Ryan, Simon Saradzyhan, Paul Saunders, Stephen Sestanovich, Angela Stent, Strobe Talbott, and Richard Weitz. Gabriel Guerra Castellanos and John Sloan offered their views on a panel at the Trilateral Commission North America regional meeting in Mexico City on November 8-10 and provided comments on draft chapters throughout the process. A meeting with business leaders was held in New York City on October 8, 2013.

---

[1] The scholars who contributed to the report do not necessarily agree with the report's analysis, conclusions, or recommendations.

In Europe, the following Trilateral Commission members prepared individual essays -- some updated to reflect momentous changes in Ukraine over the recent months and weeks – which were subsequently consolidated into one report: Vladimir Dlouhy, Wolfgang Ischinger, Dominique Moïsi, Ursula Plassnik, and Franco Venturini. A special thanks is extended to Roderic Lyne -- the European author of the 2006 report to the Commission on *Engaging with Russia* -- for his two extensive contributions to this exercise.

In the Asia Pacific, the following Trilateral Commission Members convened a regional task force: Barry Desker, Robert F. de Ocampo, Han Sung-Joo, Hong Seok-Hyun, Shotaro Oshima and Jusuf Wanandi. In addition, thanks are extended to Japanese scholars and experts Shigeki Hakamada, Chikahito Harada, Hitoshi Kimura, Nobuo Shimotomai, Seiichiro Takagi and Hideki Uyama, as well as to Fiona Hill who graciously read the Asian draft.

In Russia, Alexei Kudrin and his collaborators Pavel Demidov, Sergei Gabulev and Ekaterina Malofeeva from the Civic Initiatives Foundation worked with Dmitri Trenin, Director of the Moscow Carnegie Center, and the Institute of Contemporary Development INSOR team with Sergei Kulik and Nikita Maslennikov.

The report was finalized prior to the shooting down of Malaysia Airlines Flight MH17 over Ukraine on July 17, 2014.

Acknowledgements

The authors are indebted to **Paul Révay**, European director of the Trilateral Commission, and **Michael J. O'Neil**, North American director, who both oversaw and guided the thorough, comprehensive preparation of this report. Their constant attention to detail, superb coordination, and congenial manner ensured a smooth and most productive process. Significantly, their able leadership fostered a vibrant and lasting esprit de corps among the authors throughout what constituted a challenging exercise. Messrs. Révay and O'Neil were steadfastly assisted by **Karine Fargier** and **Mary Valder**, respectively. Amid unexpected developments in Russia and the region, particularly in Ukraine, the authors would not have been able to produce a timely, updated report without such a genuine team effort.

The authors would also like to recognize the thoughtful and extraordinary contributions of **Pratik Chougule.** His meticulous research, editing and drafting were invaluable to the completion of the report. Mr. Chougule's attentiveness was especially crucial to finishing the report against the backdrop of changing events in Russia.

Our immeasurable gratitude goes as well to **Ambassador Shotaro Oshima**. In addition to his considered contributions to the Asia Pacific deliberations, Amb. Oshima went above and beyond in providing the Asia Pacific perspective at a co-chairs' meeting at Harvard University and at the April plenary meeting.

Forward

CARL BILDT
Minister of Foreign Affairs of Sweden

"Engaging Russia: A Return to Containment?" is a thoughtful review of Russia policy as it has evolved over the past eight years. Identifying "Putinism" as a critical factor in Russia's strategy at home and abroad, the Trilateral Commission report provides timely perspectives both on immediate crises, such as the situation in Ukraine, as well as long-term challenges ranging from Russia's energy and demographic outlook to its political future after Vladimir Putin.

Significantly, all of the report's co-chairs call for the establishment of a *Friends of Ukraine Task Force*, underscoring how crucial it is to assist Kiev urgently in its economic reforms.

The report reflects the insights of renowned analysts from North America, Europe, Asia and Russia. Their assessments will certainly shape the deliberations of policy-makers spanning the globe. I believe that the report's analysis and recommendations merit serious consideration as the world contends with a resurgent Russia.

INTRODUCTION

"Engaging Russia: A Return to Containment?" is the third in a series of reviews on Russia that the Trilateral Commission has undertaken since 1995. In addition to the contributions from the Trilateral co-chairs, the Commission, for the first time, solicited a chapter from a group of Russian experts led by a Russian co-chair. The report reveals areas of agreement and disagreement among the four groups (Asia-Pacific, Europe, North America, and Russia) on where Russia is today, domestically and internationally, and what policy approaches the Trilateral countries should pursue toward Moscow.

Each group of the Trilateral Commission Russia Task Force contributed reports, along with summaries, of their deliberations. After the Russian invasion of Crimea on February 27, 2014, group co-chairs convened at Harvard University and agreed to prepare new drafts, discussing the developments in Ukraine insofar as they bear upon Russia's behavior and intentions. All of the reports were written before the downing of Malaysia Airlines Flight 17 on July 17, 2014. Besides events in Ukraine, each group offered comments on the following five issues:

- Russia's geopolitical significance
- Moscow's foreign policy
- The economic situation in Russia
- Human rights and democracy in Russia
- International engagement with Russia

Joint recommendations of the co-chairs are listed at the end of this introduction.

THE CRISIS IN UKRAINE

Re-Creation of the International Order

On March 16, 2014, following the Russian invasion of Ukraine, Crimea voted in a referendum to unify with the Russian Federation. The United Nations General Assembly, by a vote of 100 to 11, with 58 abstentions and 24 absent, deemed the referendum illegal. In the Security Council, thirteen countries voted in favor of a U.S.-sponsored Security Council resolution affirming Ukraine's territorial integrity. China abstained. Russia vetoed.

In April 2014, the Parliamentary Assembly of the Council of Europe suspended Russia's voting rights, citing the "contradiction" between Moscow's annexation of Crimea and its commitments to the body.

And the Group of Seven countries, after excluding Russia, reiterated their "strong condemnation of Russia's illegal attempt to annex Crimea and Sevastopol" and agreed to impose coordinated sanctions.

Condemnation from the international community has done little to change President Putin's strategy. Citing threats to Russian speakers in the country, Mr. Putin is moving decisively to secure three short-term objectives:

- Bring Crimea into the Russian Federation,

- Push for a federal system in Ukraine that guarantees a high degree of linguistic, cultural, political, and economic autonomy for eastern and southern Ukraine, and

- Prevent the central government in Kiev from

seeking NATO assistance.

Over time, President Putin would like to see central Ukraine, with Kyiv, join with the eastern and southern regions of the country in an interstate-state compact aligned with Russia. Alternatively, Moscow is willing to see western Ukraine break away.

Mr. Putin believes that Russia cannot allow Ukraine to emerge as a democratic state on its borders, and become part of Western institutions, without losing an essential part of itself. Some 17% of Ukraine's population – more than eight million people – is ethnically Russian. By population, Ukraine has the largest Russian diaspora in the world, though ethnic Russians constitute a greater share of the population in Latvia (27%) and Estonia (26%). Ethnic Russians constitute the majority of the population in the Crimea and a substantial percentage of the population in East and Southeast Ukraine next to the Russian border. For Putin, whose own authority rests in no small part on his reputation as a strong Russian patriot, "losing" Ukraine means abandoning the Kremlin's goal of reviving Russia as a great power.

Events in Ukraine mark a fundamental rupture in relations between Russia and the West. President Putin said as much in his "Crimea speech" of March 18. He accused the West of "crossing all thinkable limits of diplomatic behavior" and vowed that Russia, at its "last frontier…would not be surrendered." Russia, he affirmed, is equal in its rights and ambitions, but morally superior to its rivals in the West. While cognizant of how difficult the next few years will be for Russia, Putin is bracing for intense competition and even confrontation, which, to him, are normal if unpleasant elements of international relations.

More so than the customary ruthlessness he showed in Crimea, it is Mr. Putin's challenge to the existing global order, and the norms of conduct that undergird it, which alarms the international community. Russia's use of brute force to redraw its borders with Ukraine and illegally annex Crimea is an indisputable violation of the UN Charter and the norms that have guided global affairs since the end of the Second World War.

Instead of acting as a guardian of international order, Putin is seeking to change the consequences of the collapse of the Soviet Union, an event he has infamously called "a major geopolitical disaster of the century." Moscow has abandoned Mikhail Gorbachev's vision of Russia joining its "common European home," destroying years of efforts to bring Europe's two parts together. Gone are the days of a "Europe whole and free."

In Asia meanwhile, there is a broadly-shared concern that Russia's actions, if left unanswered, would embolden China to enforce territorial claims in the East and South China Sea.

Moscow's willful violation of its obligations to respect Ukraine's political and territorial integrity, featured most robustly in the 1994 Budapest Memorandum on Security Assurances, has dealt a blow to the cause of nonproliferation. Russia had agreed to provide security assurances to Ukraine as a means of inducing Kiev to abandon its formidable nuclear arsenal, at the time, the world's third largest nuclear force. This development not only threatens global stability and harms western interests, it also undermines Russia's interests. The global clout Moscow derives from its membership in a small, exclusive club of nuclear weapons states would not look as powerful with the arrival of new entrants.

Impact on Russia

President Putin can take solace in the fact that the United States and EU are unlikely to go to war with Russia over Ukraine. After a decade of wars in the Middle East, the American public is weary of foreign adventures – an important reason, as the Kremlin sees it, for why President Obama was elected in the first place. The EU has neither the capability nor the stomach to wage war on Russia. Nor will the substance of the first phase of sanctions in itself cause any "unacceptable damage."

Still, there is reason to doubt the view of many in the Kremlin and in the Russian expert community that the United States and EU will eventually "reset" relations with Russia after a certain period of time, even without any concessions from Moscow. Ebbs and flows notwithstanding, Western public opinion is unlikely to remain as averse to international engagement as is presently the case if Moscow continues it saber-rattling. But Putin's actions are certain to poison Russia's relations with Ukraine and virtually all of its other neighbors for decades to come.

The first steps that the United States and its allies have taken in retaliation to the Crimea invasion could be a harbinger of more serious sanctions to come in the future. The Ukraine situation has already sent shivers through the business community, obliging companies to rework their risk models for projects with and in Russia.

In the coming years, Russia will face *five major consequences*, each of which could exact a substantial toll:

First, international rating agencies will review Russia's sovereign rating as well as ratings for Russian corporate borrowers. This automatically complicates the issue of refinancing debt assumed earlier; approximately $100 billion is up for refinancing in 2014. The conditions for IPOs and Eurobond placements will worsen. Any money coming from external sources will become more expensive – by 150-200 basis points according to some estimates -- which in turn will change the pricing conditions for the domestic debt market and exert pressure on the financial system.

Second, sanctions will set off further attacks on the Ruble, increasing the likelihood of a crisis in the banking sector. As both individuals and corporations seek cover in foreign currency, inflation expectations will accelerate. Capital flight will rise as well -- by some estimates, up to $200 billion -- which could lead to a negative balance of payments this year.

Third, sanctions, particularly if they disrupt arms and military equipment export contracts, could trigger a general economic downturn. Although immediate and abrupt moves in the energy sector are not expected – the EU depends on Russia for 31% of natural gas and 27% of oil – the current situation has already spurred the recalibration of global markets. The next 3-5 years will see, among other things:

- Successful efforts by the United States to become a global exporter of liquid hydrocarbons;
- Significant substitution of Russian gas with supplies from Qatar, Algeria, and Libya;
- Sizable investment projects among alternative suppliers of the EU in areas such as the North Sea deposits as well as major fields in the Persian Gulf, which have tenfold or more reserves than in Russia's Novy Urengoy region;
- The emergence of a global LNG market with its

own oil-based pricing mechanisms, in which Russia has a relatively minor market position of 5% among APEC countries; and
- Coordinated international efforts to ensure Ukraine's independence from Russian gas such as energy efficiency programs and reverse flow supplies at spot-market prices via Poland, Hungary, Slovakia, Bulgaria, Romania and Croatia.

In order to react to these structural changes, Russia will need to adapt its current energy policy through 2030.

More generally, the configuration of international trade flows could change in ways detrimental to Russia. Moscow's political and economic relations with Europe will remain impaired, and Russia will not be able to draw certain benefits from European markets until it changes its approach to Ukraine and other issues of dispute with the West. With regard to the WTO, Moscow, on the bilateral level, should be prepared to see new claims, confirmations of old claims, such as the utilization fee on imported cars, and antidumping cases against Russian companies. Russia's implementation of WTO rules will be scrutinized more closely. There will be negotiations on eliminating several dozen old trade restrictions that remain in place. And progress on the Transpacific Trade Partnership (TPP) and the Transatlantic Trade and Investment Partnership (TTIP) is likely to accelerate.

Fourth, growing tensions over the Crimea issue could produce higher risks for Russian companies, which have $30 billion worth of assets in Ukraine. These risks could manifest themselves through substantial impediments in the business environment, for example, nationalization, or measures such as tariffs, customs and tax policy, and the application of EU technical standards and regulations.

Finally, Moscow's plans to pursue the socio-economic development of Eastern Siberia and the Far East will become more difficult. Russia's isolation could result in the stagnation of the entire Russian economy, leaving the country without enough foreign investment to follow through on its agenda for the region. The development of Russia's eastern regions would increasingly depend on China, a trend with problematic consequences both for Russia as well as many Asian countries.

AREAS OF CONSENSUS

Russia's Geopolitical Significance

Russia remains a significant world power that affects the vital and important interests of states across North America, Europe, and the Asia Pacific. Four main factors account for Russia's sustained geopolitical influence: Russia's geography, capabilities and resources, stature in international institutions, and global ambitions.

Geography

Russia's landmass and location make the country a critical actor in the global balance of power. Russia is a European power, but one with values that preclude its membership as a genuine stakeholder in the continent's security architecture. Russia's already low profile in Asia-Pacific diplomacy is further overshadowed by the rise of China. And with a southern border that reaches down through Central Asia, Russia will impact the outcomes of Middle East conflicts ranging from the civil war in Syria to the U.S. withdrawal from Afghanistan.

Capabilities and Resources

Russia's capabilities and resources -- notably its strategic arms and energy reserves – give Moscow the ability to impact international stability, whether positively or negatively. Russia is pursuing an ambitious program of military modernization. Moscow has little intention of forgoing its nuclear arsenal, which it sees as a hedge against Euro-Atlantic missile defense as well as the growth and modernization of China's conventional and nuclear forces. On the energy front, Russia exerts global influence through its domestic resources and its control of vital transport routes.

Stature in International Institutions

Russia can unilaterally decide whether major international institutions respond or stand gridlocked in the face of global governance challenges. Moscow is a permanent member of the UN Security Council, and remains, even after the invasion of Ukraine, a member of the Council of Europe, Organization for Security and Cooperation in Europe (OSCE), G-20, and Asia's major multilateral institutions. Moscow is attempting to forge new regional groupings through its leadership in initiatives such as the Commonwealth of Independent States (CIS) and Eurasian Economic Union.

Global Ambitions

Russia aspires to superpower status and seeks a regional order in Eurasia that is no longer underwritten by the United States. Moscow considers its response to international events based on how it will impact Russia's standing vis-à-vis the United States, China, and European Union. Moscow's penchant for intransigence and unilateralism reflects a domestic consensus in Russia that the country should assume its rightful place as a great power on the world stage.

Russian Foreign Policy

Russia's approach to international institutions is not contributing to global stability. Rather than making practical investments in existing multilateral mechanisms for regional cooperation, Moscow is seeking to build new security architectures as part of an effort to challenge U.S.-backed orders in Europe and the Asia Pacific. In Europe, Russia is using all facets of its national power to ensure that CIS states neither join NATO nor pursue EU integration. In the Asia-Pacific, Russia is forgoing opportunities to contribute to the Asia-Pacific Economic Cooperation, the mechanisms for regional cooperation led by the Association of Southeast Asian Nations, and the East Asia Summit (EAS). Instead, Russia is pursuing a "polycentric system of international relations" that, with the notable exception of China, enjoys little support among countries in the region.

Economic Situation in Russia

Russia faces serious economic challenges that will affect Moscow's relations with the countries of North America, Europe, and Asia. Among the most pressing are depopulation, social instability, corruption, capital flight, and excessive dependence on natural resource revenues. President Putin's administration is not implementing the structural reforms necessary to improve the country's business environment.

Human Rights and Democracy in Russia

Respect for democracy and human rights has

deteriorated in Russia. President Putin's domestic repression is at odds with Russia's commitments as a signatory to the Universal Declaration of Human Rights, member of the OSCE and Council of Europe, and ratifier of international human rights instruments such as the International Covenant on Civil and Political Rights, International Covenant on Economic, Social and Cultural Rights, and the European Convention of Human Rights. Russia's record on democracy and human rights is undercutting Moscow's ability to forge constructive relationships abroad.

Democracies throughout Europe, North America, and the Asia-Pacific are concerned about the rollback of human rights in Russia. Yet, external pressure on Moscow regarding its domestic practices is most likely to come from the West rather than Asia. In the West, concern over Russian domestic policy remains a source of discontent that will influence western countries' policies toward Russia.

In the Asia-Pacific, by contrast, Russia's domestic policy is not a particular interest. The concept of "universal values" remains politically delicate in some Asian countries. Leaders in the Asia-Pacific, consistent with their general approach to foreign policy, are disinclined to include Russian domestic politics on the official agenda with Moscow. Prospects for a unified approach between Asian and Western countries are also complicated by the confusion in Asian-Pacific states as to why the West, in its advocacy of democracy and human rights, adopts a harder line against Russia than it does with China.

International Engagement with Russia

The future of international engagement with Russia depends largely on how the situation in Ukraine evolves.

The Ukrainian government does not recognize the illegal annexation of Crimea, an impediment to improved relations between Russia and the West. The entry of Russian troops into eastern Ukraine would incite major clashes and revert U.S.-Western relations to a full-fledged Cold War mode. Western governments, particularly the United States, would be inclined to punish Russia without considering fully the long-term effect of isolating Russia.

AREAS OF DISAGREEMENT

External Pressure on Moscow Regarding its Domestic Practices

Two broad views emerge from the reports on the question of how much pressure outside powers should exert on the Russian government regarding its domestic policies.

One considers external intervention in Russian domestic politics to be counterproductive and impractical. Western criticism and actions, from this perspective, will undermine efforts by Russian reformers to transform the country's politics.

The other maintains that Western calls for democracy and human rights carry authority, which can produce transformational change in Russia over the long-term. Downplaying Moscow's transgressions at home, from this standpoint, improves neither the domestic situation in Russia nor the state of relations with Moscow.

State Relations with Moscow

At the state-to-state level, Western experts, more so than their Asian and Russian counterparts, discount the feasibility of anything more than a *transactional relationship* between the Putin government and key members of the international community.

Moscow's Initiatives in the Asia-Pacific

Russian and Asian contributors have a more benign view of Moscow's activities in the Asia-Pacific than their counterparts in the West. The former believe that Moscow's shift toward the Asia-Pacific is primarily a response to the region's economic dynamism. Northeast Asian countries consider that the socio-economic development of Eastern Siberia and the Far East would be a difficult, long-term venture for which Russia would need their cooperation. They nevertheless think that the development of the eastern regions would help expand the Asia-Pacific economic space. Western experts, by contrast, are more inclined to interpret Russia's growing interest in Asia as a reaction to Moscow's diminishing interest in Russia's "European choice," lack of friends in the West, and competitive outlook toward Washington and Brussels.

JOINT RECOMMENDATIONS FOR GOVERNMENTS AND CIVIL SOCIETY

- **Promote an international agenda to uphold Ukraine's sovereignty**

Defending Ukraine's sovereignty and the right to make its own domestic and foreign policy choices should be at the center of our policy. It is vital that we work to maintain the widest international support. The world should not acknowledge a Russian zone of influence that limits the sovereignty of other post-Soviet states. Nor should the international community accept a settlement in which Moscow dictates terms to Kyiv, or, in which the West negotiates the future of Ukraine over the heads of the

Ukrainian government.

- **Ensure support for Ukraine by establishing a "Friends of Ukraine" Task Force**

The situation in Ukraine calls for the urgent creation of an international contact group, comprised of civil society, with the aim of providing real assistance to the people of Ukraine. Bolstering the Ukrainian economy, particularly in the areas of finance and market access, will lower the risk of an economic downturn for both Russia and the European Union. A "Friends of Ukraine" task force should also support Ukrainian requests for additional political and military assistance. Through enduring support for the private sector, the Task Force can help ensure that the Ukrainian government has the expertise and capacity to uphold its sovereignty, conduct free and fair elections, and implement necessary reforms.

- **Identify trusted intermediaries who can articulate to Moscow that it is fundamentally misreading long-term trends in western private and political attitudes toward Russia, and underestimating the costs that it will incur as a consequence of its aggressive actions.**

Western responses to events in Crimea have cast doubt on the West's ability and will to enforce its security commitments. Moscow appears to be underestimating the West's long-term resolve in dealing with Russia's aggressive moves, and overestimating the extent to which western hesitation in confronting Russia will endure. Uncertainty regarding NATO Article 5 commitments, in particular, could invite Russian interventions in the Baltic States, which would precipitate war and create a demonstration effect that could embolden China. With distrust permeating official relations between Moscow and the West, the United States and its allies should identify intermediaries *outside* the government with whom President Putin is willing to engage forthrightly. In private meetings with the Kremlin, and in forums with senior Russian officials, the intermediaries should communicate western positions and the consequences that would ensue from further Russian aggression in a wide range of scenarios.

- **Make concerted efforts to strengthen ties with Russian civil society**

Normalizing relations between Russia and its neighbors will ultimately require the emergence of a new leadership in Moscow that is more committed to constructive international engagement. The international community can support those who feel isolated by the current government by promoting the cross-fertilization of ideas between Russian citizens and the outside world. The process of visa liberalization, in this context, should continue, and private sector cooperation in fields such as science and policy research should be preserved. The international community should also monitor the status of democracy and human rights in Russia and speak out publicly when the Kremlin is violating international norms and/or agreements to which Moscow is a signatory.

REGIONAL SUMMARIES

SUMMARY OF NORTH AMERICAN CHAPTER

U.S. Interests

Russia's aggression against Ukraine is a frontal challenge to perhaps the most enduring priority of the United States' post-Cold War strategy: preserving a Europe "whole and free." Putin's Russia is an adversary, bent on pursuing regional hegemony and challenging the western-led international system.

Russia's reach, however, affects an array of U.S. interests beyond the Eurasian theater. Russia is a major power no longer experiencing the "decline" of the 1990s. Russia's nuclear weapons make it the only nation that can annihilate the United States within a matter of minutes. For countries that challenge American interests, Russia is an arms supplier and reliable source of military and diplomatic support. At the same time, Russia is among the most important potential U.S. partners in countering threats ranging from terrorism to proliferation. Advancing global counterterrorism efforts and moving toward a more stable nuclear order would be easier accomplished with Moscow's cooperation. In this regard, Moscow's failure to honor its commitments under the 1994 Budapest Memorandum, which provided guarantees of Ukraine's territorial and political integrity in exchange for Kiev's prompt denuclearization, have dealt a blow to the cause of nuclear nonproliferation.

Russia's international stature, economy, and geography, give Moscow a voice on pressing global issues. Russia is a veto-wielding, permanent member of the U.N.

Security Council, as well as an influential participant in other international organizations. Economically, Russia is the top global energy producer and the world's sixth largest economy; Russia draws greater foreign direct investment than rising powers such as India and Brazil. The location and sheer size of Russia's land area impacts the disposition of issues ranging from the selection of transport routes for energy and other trade to the maintenance of supply lines for NATO forces in Afghanistan.

In sum, Russia impacts a wide range of American national interests.[2]

Above all, Russia affects the United States' ability to advance six vital and important national goals:

- Ensure a favorable balance of power in critical regions that enables continued U.S. global leadership
- Prevent the proliferation of weapons of mass destruction
- Combat terrorism and radical Islamist networks
- Stabilize the international economy and promote global trade
- Ensure energy security
- Advance liberal democracy and human rights

Assessing the Reset

Until the Ukraine situation erupted, the Reset elicited three main responses among U.S. experts. One group saw the Reset as a misguided policy of unilateral U.S.

---

[2] See Graham Allison and Robert Blackwill, "10 reasons why Russia still matters" *Politico*, 30 October 2011, available at:
http://www.politico.com/news/stories/1011/67178.html

concessions. A second group saw the Reset as a worthwhile effort, but one that contributed little in terms of a new agenda to move bilateral relations forward. A third group, which included proponents of the policy in the Obama Administration, maintained that the Reset could advance U.S. interests by putting U.S.-Russia relations on a more cooperative footing.

The more ambitious goals of the Reset did not materialize. Although the Reset entailed significant U.S. compromises, the accomplishments of the Reset were largely limited to developments that Moscow perceived to be in its own best interest. While senior administration officials continue to defend the Reset, President Obama has effectively repudiated the approach.

Domestic Situation in Russia

Putinism

Putinism -- the assumptions, worldview, ideas and strategies of Vladimir Putin -- have become the most important political force in the country and a major factor in troubled U.S.-Russia relations. Since Putin's formal return to the presidency, the Kremlin has embarked on the most systematic political crackdown it has pursued since the Cold War. Putin's repression has provoked challenges from numerous factions within Russian society – particularly the Moscow-based creative and urban classes. The Ukraine crisis, however, bolstered Putin's approval ratings to 80%. Sixty-four percent of Russians indicated in a March 2014 poll by VCIOM (Russia Public Opinion Research Center) that they would re-elect Putin. The political climate surrounding Russia's 2018 presidential elections will depend on Putin's ability to manage domestic political challenges and sustain his image as a determined, nationalistic leader.

Economic Policy

The Kremlin is using economic policy to shore up its domestic political base. The redistributive emphasis in Moscow's economic policy has caused Russia's growth rate to dwindle toward stagnation. Sound fiscal balances, including over $400 billion of international reserves, are unlikely to protect Russia from financial instability due to the imposition of Western sanctions. According to Russia's Central Bank, the first quarter saw over $50 billion in capital leave the country, a period during which Russia's Micex Index plummeted by more than 10%. Former Finance Minister Alexei Kudrin predicted that capital flight will reach $160 billion by the end of the year, while the World Bank foresees scenarios in which Russia's economy contracts by 1.8% in 2014 due to geopolitical instability. With political objectives superseding economic goals, stagnation could become much worse if oil prices drop. Russia is likely to face intensified WTO disputes in the near future.

Corruption

Endemic corruption undergirds a web of informal networks across constituencies, at all levels of Russian society. Corruption in Russia does not consist simply of bribes and rent distribution, but also includes noncompetitive procurement, nepotism and organized criminal networks. Under Putin, key economic assets have come under the control of "private" owners with close ties to the Kremlin. This arrangement allows the Kremlin to maintain heavy oversight even if ownership structures are technically private. The fact that corruption serves as its foundation makes the Putin system resilient and resistant to evolutionary change. Government spending works to limit the political opposition by keeping unemployment numbers low and functioning as an employment tax of sorts. Yet corruption represents a major threat to Russia's national security, as acknowledged in the 2013 Public Security Concept approved by Putin. Massive and palpable corruption has engendered anger among many Russians that may exceed even their dissatisfaction over the lack of political pluralism.

Demographics

In 2012, Russia experienced its 20th straight year of natural population decrease. According to the government's medium-term forecast, the Russian population will decline further from 143.3 million in 2013 to 141.6 in 2031. During this period, Muslims, 80% of whom currently reside in two of seven federal districts, will comprise nearly 15% of the entire Russian population. And by 2050, the United Nations Development Programme projects that Russia's population will drop below 110 million.

Russia's demographic squeeze could have negative consequences for U.S. national interests. Even if Russia can turn around its exceptionally high male mortality rate – a figure worse than Haiti's and lower than 33 of the 48 countries that the United Nations designates as "least developed countries" -- the sharp decline in the Russian population from 148.3 million in 1991 to 143.7 million today has left the country in a position in which there are not enough women of child-bearing age to reach population replacement levels. The Russian Labor and Social Security Ministry is expecting a drop in the labor force of one million people annually in 2013-2015. Longer term, according to a recent forecast by secretary of Russia's

Security Council Nikolai Patrushev, the working-age population will see a decline of ten million by 2025. With the population stabilizing around a shortage of working adults, Eastern Siberia could become a zone of conflict if population declines generate a demand for Chinese labor beyond what national and regional governments can manage.

Russian Foreign Policy

Domestic Politics

Russia's foreign policy is largely driven by political considerations at home. The Putin regime cites foreign "dangers" to justify its consolidation of power at home. Never before in post-Communist Russia's history has the Kremlin's need to shore up domestic support impacted Russia's policy toward the United States as much as it has since Putin's 2011 decision to seek a third presidential term. Putin's opposition to U.S. foreign policy and his anti-American rhetoric resonate with a sizable segment of the public, which, after the perceived humiliation of the 1990s, accepts nationalist ideas and condones a strong state resisting the United States.

Reassertion of an Independent Russia

There is a national consensus that Russia should regain its status as a serious geopolitical player. Putin is trying to create a geopolitical and geo-economic demand for Russia. Having moved in the direction of interdependence in the 1990s and 2000s, with mixed results, the Kremlin now believes that a more unilateralist foreign policy is necessary to defend against the negatives of an interdependent world. Insofar as Putin has advanced a comprehensive strategic vision that outlines what Russia wants the world to look like in critical respects and how Russia can help deal with global challenges, he has downplayed Western values and collective security goals. Instead, Putin is emphasizing nationalistic ambitions and Russia's aspirations to create a sphere of influence encompassing Russian-speakers beyond the boundaries of the Russian Federation. Reassertion of influence in post-Soviet Eurasia is a particular priority of Russian foreign policy. The Putin regime seeks Russian political, economic, and military supremacy, if not hegemony, in the post-Soviet space.

Worsening Relations with Europe

Moscow's failure to attract broad diplomatic support for its agenda is apparent in Russia's worsening relations with Europe. For most of his two presidential terms, Putin was a proponent of Russia's integration with the EU. He remains interested in developing Russia-EU economic ties, but no longer believes in Russia's "European choice." European attitudes toward Russia, in turn, have hardened, not only amid the Ukraine crisis, but also due to Russia's human rights violations and manipulation of energy exports.

Russia's Energy Future

Energy issues play an outsized role in both Russia's foreign and domestic policy. Russia's leaders recognize that energy, which provides nearly 20% of its GDP and over half of its federal government's revenue, is critical to the country's future. Nevertheless, they have been slow to implement policies needed to maximize and sustain its contributions. Russia's oil production and exports have grown steadily over the last decade, though sustaining the industry will require significant and continuing investment.

Russia's economic dependence on its energy sector is an important point of leverage as Western-Russian relations continue to deteriorate. The Ukraine crisis has underscored to Western policymakers the potential for LNG exports to reduce Europe's dependence on Russia. Russia's oil production is particularly vulnerable given that Russian firms need not only investment, but also access to high-tech services provided by oil-field services firms. Russian attempts to reorient its energy exports toward Asia will necessitate considerable infrastructure financing to build pipelines to China or LNG terminals for exports by sea to Japan, South Korea, and other more distant markets.

U.S. Business in Russia

U.S business interests in Russia beyond energy have remained underdeveloped since the end of the Cold War, and now, with the imposition of Ukraine-related sanctions, are bound to decline even further. Trade between the United States and Russia totaled $38.12 billion in 2013. Compared to the United States' $14 billion, European countries such as France and Germany account for a far greater percentage of foreign direct investment into Russia.

U.S. business leaders are concerned about anemic growth and the economic climate in the country. Angst about the Russian economy among the U.S. business community is informed by low investor confidence and political risk emanating from the Kremlin's foreign and domestic policy.

Before the Ukraine crisis, U.S. business leaders, notwithstanding their concerns about Russia's economic climate, were investing in Russia on a long time horizon. With scheduled talks on the Bilateral Investment Treaty cancelled, trends are moving in the opposite direction.

U.S. Goals vis-à-vis Russia

While the fulcrum of U.S.-Russia relations has shifted toward Eurasian issues in light of the Ukraine crisis, Moscow remains a factor in Washington's ability to achieve important goals around the world. In formulating a post-Crimea strategy, Washington should work toward a paradigm in which Moscow does not prevent the United States from achieving key goals in seven areas: regional issues; non-proliferation and arms control; democracy and human rights; terrorism and radical Islam; international trade, global energy markets, and global governance. Some of these goals are untenable at this time and some are vocally and robustly opposed by Moscow. But articulating them would help ensure that Russia appreciates the full range of U.S. concerns and objectives.

U.S. Strategic Options

The United States faces an increasingly aggressive Russia that acts as an adversary on key international issues. While Russia cannot compete with the United States at a global level, it can exacerbate virtually any international problem that Washington is trying to address.

Before the invasion of Crimea, U.S. experts generally proposed one of three strategic alternatives toward Russia: comprehensive containment, selective engagement with selective containment, and deep engagement. Momentum has shifted toward advocates of containment. Consensus, however, is unlikely to jell behind any one of these approaches unless Russia continues with its aggressive policy toward Ukraine, or, Moscow's conduct toward Ukraine, even if it doesn't escalate further, portends a new status quo in which Russia becomes uniformly hostile and/or significantly more repressive at home.

Comprehensive Containment

Like the original containment, comprehensive containment assumes: that the problem is in the nature of the Russia side, not in the interaction between the two sides; that the relationship cannot change fundamentally until the Russian side changes fundamentally; and that while there are a few issues on which Washington must do business with Russia, the United States' primary interest is in blocking Russia's problematic foreign policy and in pressing Moscow to retreat from its illiberal ways domestically.

Selective Engagement with Selective Containment

Selective engagement with selective containment assumes that the issues on which the United States and Russia need to cooperate are significant, but so too are the areas where Washington needs to stand its ground and counter Russian *foreign* policy. The relationship is consequential but should be understood as limited. Russia, viewed broadly, is neither an adversary nor a potential partner. Washington should pursue transactional deals when possible and necessary, but otherwise stand its ground and counter current Russian foreign policy.

Deep Engagement

Deep engagement starts from the premise that common interests considerably outweigh the issues that divide the United States and Russia. Without ignoring the obstacles to a durable strategic partnership, or suggesting that Washington "give away the store" to achieve it, the strategy would seek cooperation across the many areas where U.S. and Russian interests intersect.

Should the United States Promote Democracy and Human Rights in Russia?

The question of how, if at all, Washington should promote democracy and human rights in Russia is among the most contentious issues dividing experts. Some fundamentally question the thesis that a more democratic Russia will serve U.S. interests given how hostile public opinion is toward the United States. Only a few measures -- liberalizing visa regimes and expanding exchanges with academics and younger Russians, for example -- enjoy broad support among the U.S. foreign policy establishment. There is little consensus on how receptive Russians are to U.S. intervention, and to what extent Moscow's intransigence is influenced by U.S. policy. Nor do experts agree on how much influence the United States has in legitimizing the Russian regime domestically and internationally, or on what level of pressure would be effective to improve human rights in Russia. These differences are premised on varying assessments of the anti-Putin opposition.

Advocates of containment are most inclined to support robust democracy promotion efforts in Russia. They argue that pro-democracy rhetoric and actions from Washington carry a great deal of authority, even if U.S. solidarity with Russian liberals does not yield visible gains in the short-term.

Those experts, by contrast, who question the feasibility and wisdom of U.S.-led democracy promotion, cite Putin's popularity and the amount of control he wields in Russia. U.S. attempts to support Russian reforms, they argue, are counterproductive and jeopardize cooperation on areas of mutual interest. Undermining Putin, critics warn, could open the door to an even more hostile Russian leadership.

Policy Recommendations

Our core recommendation is that a fundamental reassessment of all aspects of U.S. policy toward Russia is in order. In the short-term, the United States must consider how its response to the aggression in Crimea, and Russia's ongoing efforts to weaken the Ukrainian central government will affect:

- **Regional issues in Eurasia, and**
- **U.S. vital interests around the world**

Even if Moscow seeks "normalization" with the West, the nature of Putin's regime permits little more than a transactional U.S.-Russia relationship on a narrow range of issues. Putin's departure from office, however, may produce a transformational moment that portends real systemic change in the Russian system. Russian politics will have to be invented almost from the ground-up, perhaps creating possibilities for a rapprochement.

The following are additional, specific policy recommendations that should be taken in the short-term and factored into the overarching reassessment of our policy.

Ukraine

- *Maintain a non-recognition policy of the illegal Russian annexation of Crimea.*
- *Uphold Ukraine's sovereignty* and right to make its own domestic and foreign policy choices, free from intimidation by Russia.
- *Intensify support for Ukraine by establishing a*

"Friends of Ukraine" Task Force. This international group, comprised of civil society, should focus on the urgent need to stabilize Ukraine through economic assistance in areas such as finance and market access.
- In steering international assistance and support, *prioritize goals that will facilitate a successful political transition in Ukraine.* As Ukraine holds parliamentary elections, forms a new government, and reviews its constitution, Washington, working with our allies, should assist Kiev in its efforts to rid the country of corruption and establish independent institutions and the rule of law.
- *Respond promptly and positively to Ukraine's request for military assistance.* Determine how much assistance to provide based on a comprehensive assessment of the country's needs in the event of a Russian invasion.
- *Enhance Ukraine's ability to maintain law and order* by providing training to the country's police force.
- *Strengthen ties between Ukraine and NATO* in the context of the existing Partnership for Peace.

Regional Issues

- *Respond to the requests of the Central European and Baltic States to bolster their defenses* and enhance deterrence by forward deploying significant NATO assets on their territories.
- *Exercise U.S. leadership in convincing NATO* to adopt the Membership Action Plan for *Georgia.*
- *Preserve NATO-Russia cooperation on Afghanistan* while lessening U.S. dependence on the Northern Distribution Network. Propose a multilateral regional dialogue regarding Afghanistan's post-2014

security environment, but develop work-around options to the Northern Distribution Network such as airlift deliveries and Central Asian routes that bypass Russia.

Economics/Business

- *Task the United States Trade Representative* with redoubling efforts to ensure Russian compliance with its WTO commitments. Prepare to undertake appropriate steps if compliance is not achieved.
- In response to Russia's aggression, expand sanctions to *shut down credit and other types of access to financial markets*.

Energy

- Communicate to Russian officials at a high level that *unfair treatment of U.S. energy companies* and other American investors in Russia risks pushing the President and Congress toward even tougher policies against Moscow.
- Develop a *coordinated strategy with Europe to establish a 20-30% target for U.S LNG energy exports*.
- *Revise the law on U.S. natural gas exports*, which simplifies export licensing procedures for gas shipments to U.S. free trade partners by presuming that such exports serve the U.S. national interest, but does not extend the same presumption to U.S. allies.
- *Warn Moscow that further aggression and other hostile policies would mean sanctions on Russia's hydrocarbon extraction industry*, which would restrict Russia's access to advanced Western technologies.

The Arctic

- *Accelerate U.S.-Canada maritime cooperation* and diplomatic coordination in the Arctic Council to contain Russian ambitions in the region.

Democracy and Human Rights

- *Accelerate support* to those organizations advancing rule of law, greater transparency, and press freedoms in Russia.
- *Work closely* with civil society organizations, as well as the Organization for Security and Cooperation in Europe (OSCE) and Office for Democratic Institutions and Human Rights (ODIHR), on election monitoring and other Ukraine and Russia-related human rights issues.

Demographics/Civil Society/Cultural Exchanges

- *Expand exchange programs* focused on mayors and city council members in an effort to strengthen Russia's local governance. Seek to pair cities/regions facing similar challenges (e.g., Alaska and Siberia, industrial cities, agricultural regions, border towns, etc.)
- *Engage Russian citizens beyond the capital cities of Moscow and St. Petersburg*, and beyond any single ethnic group, to become more sensitized to Russian diversity.
- *Encourage American corporate, civil society, and government leaders* to regularize discussions and exchanges with Russian youth, academics, and other groups that are generally disenchanted with the Putin regime and inclined toward cooperation with the West.

SUMMARY OF EUROPEAN CHAPTER

Europeans are less divided on Russia than at any time in the last two decades.

Gone are good intentions and overblown aspirations, divisions between western enthusiasts and eastern skeptics, between naïve hopes and excessive fears. Europeans are - east and west - disappointed and disheartened with Russia. That feeling has been greatly enhanced by the Russian brutal intervention in Ukraine.

When 35 Heads of states and governments convened at the November 1990 Conference on Security and Cooperation in Europe in Paris, proclaiming a "New Era of Democracy, Peace and Unity," their aspiration was to construct the much-sought "One and United Europe." Europeans were hoping that Russians would join them in a common endeavor to reshape the continent. They believed that Russia was going to embrace common European values and transform into a society based on those values; a country at peace with its neighbors, working to build sustainable relationships on the basis of mutual trust, acting constructively in the UN Security Council, and carrying its fair share of the burden in securing international peace; a country with a fast growing, competitive market economy. In sum, a European country that had finally found its place in the "common European home" envisioned by Mikhail Gorbachev.

Today's "real" Russia, however, keeps distancing herself from a "Europe liberating itself from the legacy of the past" as heralded in the 1990 Charter of Paris for a New Europe. One wonders whether the past has not surged back with a Russia moving ever closer to authoritarian Asia.

Russia is at best a semi-democracy with little apparent appetite for further reforms. Looking back at the 2006 Trilateral Commission Report on *Engaging with Russia,* what is striking is how much has *not* changed over the past seven years. Trends discernible then have been accentuated: the manipulation of elections and impediments on political activity; the control of the principal media (especially central television); "the resurgence of the ... FSB and the other successor agencies to the KGB, operating outside the confines of law and accountability"; the growth of the bureaucracy and the dependence on a single institution, the Presidency, asserting "control over the legislature, the judiciary, regional institutions, the commanding heights of business in the private as well as the public sector, the media and civil society." "Phase Two" of Vladimir Putin's presidency is mainly characterized by repression.

Russia's economy is no less dependent on hydrocarbons and other extractive industries now than it was a decade ago. Well over half of GDP is in the State sector. The number of small and medium enterprises – already low by comparison with other emerging economies – has been falling. Efforts by the State to promote and invest in innovation have produced only a few success stories. Research in science and technology has declined. Many highly educated and talented young Russians have left the country over the past two decades. Russia lags badly in the global competition for investment.

No structural reforms are being undertaken to address these and other acute problems, including a looming demographic crisis (epitomized by a still lacking pension reform), pervasive corruption, and massive capital flight, not to mention growing competition from shale gas and oil.

As a result, economic growth has fallen far short of the ambitious targets set by President Putin in his first term: from nearly 7% annually in the years before the 2008 crisis to a rate of 1.3% in 2013, significantly less than the projected 3.7%. The World Bank forecasts two growth scenarios in 2014: a low-risk scenario assuming a limited short-lived impact of the Crimea/Ukraine crisis, and a high-risk scenario were the geopolitical situation to worsen. In the former case, the rate is estimated at 1.1% and in the latter at -1.8%. For 2015, the respective growth rates are 2.1% and 1.3%. These worrisome growth figures, much more than electoral frauds, epitomize the breakdown of the "social pact" that had characterized Vladimir Putin's first two terms.

In international affairs, Russia, a veto-welding permanent member of the UN Security Council and one of the world's five recognized nuclear states, remains a global power. In spite of that status and potential, Russia functions mainly as the country that says "No." More importantly, it resorts to the bankrupt patterns from the past centuries of political and military intervention in the affairs of its sovereign neighbors to keep them in its orbit "and oppose the gravitational pull of other powers." (Refer to 2006 Trilateral Commission Report).

Strangely however, Russia has no friends in Europe, although relations had improved before the current crisis in and over Ukraine, notably with Poland. Former allies and partners have more or less openly turned their back on Russia and Russia has failed to win them back. The Russian leadership seems to focus primarily on the United States and China as powers of reference, if only to preserve its global status. "Eye-to-eye" relations are restricted to these two big powers. Russia has little to no understanding and a definite lack of positive attention for smaller partners.

Europe, in particular, appears to be of little interest and the EU's "soft power" profile is often ridiculed. The contemporary European concept of shared sovereignty finds no appeal in Russia, engrossed as it remains in classical security interests. Hence Russia's playing of one EU member country against the others with a notable attention given to Germany as the single most important partner in Europe.

Given the above picture, do Europe and Russia have a common future?

Many dismiss this possibility outright. History and intellectual tradition push Russia towards Asia more than toward democratic Europe. This despotic temptation (see Karl Wittfogel's definition of "Oriental Despotism"), which ignores any concern for the rule of law, has never been stronger than today, although it has been going on for the last two decades. Given its Tsarist and Soviet legacies, Russia will always retain super-power ambitions. The gap between smaller urban, middle aged and successful groups in society on the one side and, on the other side, the much larger segment of Russia's population that accepts the authorities' conservative, Orthodox and nationalistic values, will continue to exist in the decades ahead and, together with present and future Russian governments' geopolitical ambitions, will be a permanent source of tension between Russia and the West. "Democracy" as we would like to see it will not prevail in Russia.

In short, Russia always was and will remain different. Acceptance of that "otherness" should be a premise for forming our views on Russia's future and our relations with her.

Others, however, argue that Russians are clearly

dissatisfied with the way their country is governed – with the concentration of political and economic power in very few hands; with rampant corruption; with the highly uneven distribution of wealth; with the weak judicial system; and with the absence of separation of powers and independent institutions. There is a strong desire for better governance. It is particularly pronounced among the urban middle class, as demonstrated in the protests against electoral frauds and in the vote for Mayors and Governors. Which will prevail in the years ahead – the ideology of conservatism, the visceral opposition of the Orthodox Church to liberalism, and the entrenched interests of beneficiaries of the status quo, or the strive for the modernization of society -- is an open question.

Change, however, will not come without a change of leadership.

Most of Russia's current powerbrokers are in their fifties or sixties, their careers have roots in the Soviet Union, and after – thus far – 13 years in power their strategic objectives do not appear to extend beyond retaining power for as long as they can. But despite the present hiatus, a window will open for a future Russian leadership to create – if it so wishes – an entirely different set of relationships.

The first view has been dramatically supported by the Russian intervention in Ukraine and ensuing eruption of Russian "patriotic" propaganda. The Russia that has emerged from these developments is not only a country that is pursuing a different economic and political course from the rest of Europe, but also a country that is actively working against European values and EU interests: neither a friend or a fellow traveller, but a challenger. It seeks to revise the current European order, and beyond that, the global order. It strives to establish a Eurasian Union for which Ukraine would provide needed demographic, industrial and agricultural potential. Its domestic inspiration, a beacon, the new "Russian idea," is a mixture of nationalism based on Russian ethnicity and language, an imperial notion of "Eurasia," a socially conservative values agenda, and contempt for western values and their way of life. One only needs to read President Putin's Kremlin address to the Russian Parliament on March 18 upon Crimea's "accession to the Russian Federation" to better understand Russia's motives and grievances.

In the words of Norbert Röttgen, Chairman of the Bundestag Foreign Affairs Committee: "The foreign policy of President Vladimir Putin's Russia seems to be writing a new chapter in a book we thought we had closed a long time ago".

The second view, however, draws support from the assumption that the Ukrainian intervention is not an element of a broad, long-term strategy, but a desperate and opportunistic attempt by President Putin to shore up his position. Indeed, politically, he has "boxed himself in." He has no succession plan. He cannot institute the structural reforms that might begin to turn the country around: these would only threaten his and his associates' grip on power. Putin didn't invade Ukraine to bring it back into the fold, but to stop it from escaping. He established a patriarchal-oligarchic police state in Russia; the now universally despised Ukrainian president-in-exile was well on his way to establishing one in Ukraine. Putin's great fear is that the people of a better Ukraine might inspire an entirely different unification with their East Slav brethren on his side of the border – a common cause of popular revolt against him and other leaders like him. The revolution on Maidan is the closest script to date for his downfall. In that sense, the invasion is a counter-revolution by Putin and his government against Russians and Ukrainians alike – against East Slav resistance as a whole.

By December 2013, President Putin's poll ratings had fallen to their lowest level, and a large majority of Russians were opposed to his standing for another term in 2018. But Crimea boosted his popularity rate to over 80%!

SO WHAT SHOULD WE DO?

"Engagement" or "estrangement?" Only a few months ago, calls were made to treat Russia as a partner, not as a threat. While it sounded minimalistic, the prospect of a partnership was a historic achievement of the last two decades since the time when the Soviet Union was a mortal threat to Europe and the West at large. In this new light, three steps are necessary:

First, *the most immediate task is to assist with Ukraine's political and economic recovery.*

The West does not seek to "capture" Ukraine, nor does it have strategic designs on the country: it wants to uphold Ukraine's sovereign right to determine its own future. The challenges facing Ukraine are huge: electing credible political leaders, writing up a new constitution, and fundamentally overhauling its economic and social system, among others. Ukraine will require tremendous help from its neighbours. EU assistance should be particularly comprehensive and generous in the areas of finance, market access and in integrating Ukraine into the European energy market. Persistent efforts, using both persuasion and sanctions, should be made to solicit Russian cooperation in assisting Ukraine. Moscow's refusal to help, and its continuing policy of pressure and blackmail, will bring additional suffering and loss to millions of people, many of them of Russian origin. EU institutions should learn lessons from the flawed and ultimately failed "Eastern Partnership," exemplified in Vilnius last November.

Second, *we must stand firm in refusing to recognize the annexation of Crimea, for as long as it takes, until Ukraine is able to normalize relations with Russia on an equal basis.*

Crimea has to be treated as an outlaw territory. Not only because Russia violated basic international principles and laws, but also because, unpunished, Crimea risks becoming an inspiration for all who think, "Why should I be a minority in your country if you could be a minority in mine?" Nationalists and extremists in EU member countries to the north and west are already referring to the "Crimean option" in their statements.

EU relations with Russia have to rest on greater distance, discipline and caution. Western governments should continue to deal with the Russian government on a selective and transactional basis, where it is in their interests to do so. Europe's energy market must be integrated rapidly. EU authorities should monitor the behaviour of Russian enterprises on our markets and European investors must be warned about the risks of excessive engagement in Russia. Russia's implementation of WTO rules should be scrutinized far more closely.

Russia must be warned that its political and economic relations with Europe will remain impaired and, that it will not be able to draw benefits from European integration and globalization, so long as it fails to normalize relations with Ukraine.

Third, *we can't ignore the fact that the EU and Russia straddle the same continent: both must cope with many common issues.*

A permanently divided continent is too depressing a prospect to resign to it. While Russian behavior in Ukraine rules out a "business as usual" approach, we should not seek to deepen Russia's isolation. Thus the need for a **"keeping the door open" policy:**

- Severing non-defence-related trade with Russia is neither in the Western interest, nor will it contribute to the long-term development of a more cooperative Russian state. In particular business links which give Russia an incentive to conform to international norms should be developed;

- Joint work should continue to overcome dysfunctional and costly doctrines and postures of the past. Who would lose if Washington and Moscow reduced the number of missiles on ready alert or dismantled at least parts of their nuclear arsenals?

- For similar reasons, personal travel by ordinary Russians and educational, cultural and professional links should be sustained and developed. Bridges to ordinary Russians, civic society, and the next generation of policymakers must be multiplied. The EU should develop a special scholarship program similar to ERASMUS for students from Russia, the Ukraine and Belarus.

- Phasing out visa restrictions is the most effective way for the EU to use its soft power to the benefit of the whole continent;

A "keeping the door open" policy is perhaps the only realistic choice. But it is a second-best approach, incapable certainly of addressing Europe's long-term needs and interests. Thus, after years of neglect, **crafting a Russia strategy must become Europe's highest priority**.

What is needed is *a strategy* based not on lofty aspirations, but *on a realistic assessment of common interests and goals;* a strategy that will describe a place for Russia in the European architecture that would both satisfy Moscow and be useful for Europe.

Without such a concept, Europe will have little to offer to Russians, who in turn will be unable to conceive of a different role for their country than that of a separate power without any allies.

It is not at all certain that Russia would react to such a strategy the way we want. However, there is now much for Russians to reflect upon. And much will depend on the younger, well-educated generation. A European Union principled, strategic and open for partnership with Russia will help this important country choose cooperation over confrontation.

Summary of Asia Pacific Chapter

The Asians' Perceptions of Russia

To countries in the Asia-Pacific region, except for those in Northeast Asia, Russia is a remote country even though its territory covers the northern part of Asia and reaches the Pacific Ocean. Even people in the Northeast Asian countries bordering Russia regard Russians as European. Asians generally are not well informed on Russia's domestic situation. Nor are they interested in Russia's evolution except as it affects their countries.

This makes the Asians' attitude towards Russia fundamentally different from the European and North American approach.

The Ukrainian Crisis

Many countries in the Asia-Pacific region are critical of Russia's annexation of Crimea and alarmed that this development might lower the threshold for similar attempts to change borders in their own region. At the UN Security Council, South Korea voted in favor of the resolution to deny the validity of the referendum on the status of Crimea. Russia vetoed, and China abstained. Japan joined the G7 condemnation of Russia's violation of international law. Major ASEAN countries voted, together with Japan and South Korea, for the UN General Assembly resolution calling upon states, international organizations, and agencies not to recognize any alteration of the status of Crimea and Sevastopol. China and India abstained. Asians are concerned that there could be a demonstration effect on countries such as China, whose choice between solidarity with Moscow and relations with the West has been sharpened as a result; a distractive effect on the United States with its "rebalancing to Asia" policy; and that it might diminish East Asian countries' opportunities for economic and regional cooperation with Russia.

From China's perspective, the Ukrainian crisis is the product of residual Cold War mentalities. President Putin is perceived as being defiant in the face of sanctions imposed by the West. Ukraine is seen not only as a link among East European countries but also as a region of immense importance for Russia's security in the south. What western media call "a new Cold War," triggered by the Ukraine crisis, is in no one's interest. If Ukraine is forced to choose between the West and Russia, the situation will be further destabilized. The country risks another round of disintegration after the loss of Crimea. And if the EU breaks with Russia over Ukraine, resulting in a new Cold War, the interests of both sides will be jeopardized, with the costs far outweighing the gains.

With this in mind, a Chinese member of the task force argues that the solution to the Ukrainian crisis should strike a balance between the interests of all sides, in which both the West and Russia give the other side an out. Furthermore, the international community should urge Ukraine to set up a new government acceptable to all parties; one that may be a friend of Western Europe but not an enemy of Russia. The people of Ukraine should be allowed to decide by themselves whether or not to join the EU. To balance the interests of the U.S., Europe and Russia, Ukraine's membership in NATO should be considered a red line that shall not be crossed. An ultra-nationalist government in Ukraine will not be in the interest of peace and stability in the country.

On the other hand, India's apparent tilt towards Russia throughout the Ukraine crisis underscores Delhi's enduring political ties with Moscow notwithstanding the significant improvement in India's relations with the United States and Western Europe. From a mid-term perspective, focused on the Asian balance of power, an Indian member of the task force concludes that enduring tensions between Russia and the West in Europe will work to the advantage of China and to the disadvantage of India. The strategic priorities of the West and Asia may be diverging, and the gap is reflected in the way they look at Russia. If Europe and America see Russia's assertiveness as a major threat, Asia worries about Moscow's lack of strategic ambition in the East.

Russia's Low Profile

Russia's profile in the Asia-Pacific region has remained low since the end of the Cold War. Moscow's foreign policy has prioritized Euro-Atlantic and Eurasian relations over engagement in Asia-Pacific diplomacy. More significantly in the regional context, the post-Cold War economic decay and the consequent depopulation of Eastern Siberia and the Far East (with the exception of Sakhalin) have deprived Russia of the means to expand its presence in the region, where economic interdependence has been the primary focus of international relations.

Moreover, Russia is being overshadowed by China, economically as well as in terms of political influence. The rapid growth of China's economy has drastically transformed geopolitical dynamics in the region, giving Beijing increased weight in regional diplomacy. The expansion of Chinese military power has made the U.S.-China strategic balance the focus of the Asia-Pacific geopolitics, while the U.S.-Russia balance, at least so far, has not been relevant to regional security.

China's increased military power, together with Beijing's attempts to enforce its territorial claims, adds to security concerns in the region. Although countries in the region, including the United States, regard China as an indispensable economic and, to a lesser extent, political partner, U.S. allies and friends in the Asia-Pacific region support the United States' strategic rebalance toward the region.

Diverse Relations

Relations between Russia and Asia-Pacific countries are diverse.

President Vladimir Putin's Executive Order of 2012 elaborates Moscow's country-wise foreign policy priorities in the region according to the following order: "deepening equal, trust-based partnership and strategic cooperation with China", "deepening strategic partnership with India and Vietnam", and "developing mutually beneficial cooperation with Japan, South Korea, Australia, New Zealand and other key countries in the Asia-Pacific region."

Asia-Pacific countries' relations with Russia also differ from each other, particularly in the political agendas they are pursuing. China is trying to strengthen its partnership with Moscow as part of a strategy to replace what Beijing sees as a unipolar world dominated by the United States with a "multipolar" world order. Japan, on the other hand, is pursuing the goals of recovering its "Northern Territories" under Russian control and concluding a peace treaty with Moscow, which has not been signed since the end of World War II.

South Korea needs Russian cooperation in denuclearizing North Korea and reunifying the divided Korea. But, Seoul, like Washington and Tokyo, counts more on Beijing than Moscow for political influence on Pyongyang. The proposed plans to connect Russia and South Korea through by rail, grid and gas pipelines seem to be far-fetched. But if realized, they would add to Moscow's influence on the future of the Korean Peninsula.

ASEAN countries, except for Vietnam, do not seem to have any near-term political agenda in their relations with Russia. For better or worse, they are preoccupied with the rise of China in their immediate vicinity. Vietnam, too, is concerned about China and is seeking closer relations with the United States, while continuing military ties and deepening energy cooperation with Russia.

India's partnership with Russia remains politically viable, if increasingly limited, given Russia's closer relations with China and the improvement in India's relations with the United States and Europe. In the future, it will be significantly influenced by Moscow's approaches towards two important bilateral relations: Pakistan and China.

Given all these issues, cooperation between Russia and the Asia-Pacific countries would be better pursued bilaterally rather than multilaterally, at least in the near future.

Russia's New Overtures towards Asia

During the first two years of his renewed presidency, President Putin took diplomatic steps to underscore Russia's new overtures to Asia. In 2012, he visited Beijing and New Delhi and hosted the APEC Summit in Vladivostok. In

2013, he received the Chinese and Japanese leaders in Moscow, visited Hanoi and Seoul, and attended the APEC Summit held in Jakarta. This year, he visited China in May, and plans to visit Japan in the fall. This new approach seems to be aimed at expanding Russia's presence in the economically thriving Asia while promoting the socio-economic development of the country's long-ignored regions of Eastern Siberia and the Far East. To this end, Moscow created the Ministry for the Development of Russian Far East.

The development of Eastern Siberia and the Far East is essential to solidify Russia's position in the Asia-Pacific region, economically connect Russia with Asia, and sustain the growth of Russia's economy as a whole. Without the development of the eastern regions, it would be difficult for Russia to enhance its profile in Asia-Pacific diplomacy. Military power, including nuclear weapons, would not strengthen Moscow's "soft power" in its relations with Asian countries.

But given the harsh natural conditions of the eastern regions, the legacy of ill-planned Soviet-era infrastructure, and workforce shortages, it would be difficult and costly to develop these long-neglected regions. Moscow's firm and sustained commitment would be essential for moving the difficult project forward. Foreign investment and cooperation would no doubt be indispensable to the end.

China is a natural partner for the development of Russia's eastern regions. Russia's isolation following the Crimea annexation might lead to increased dependence on Beijing. But there are concerns in Russia about relying too much on China. For example, the influential Valdai Discussion Club warned in 2012 of the "threat" that Russia would develop a one-sided dependence on China in important sectors of the economy, and ultimately in politics.

Japan, equipped with advanced technology, finance and business expertise, would be an ideal "another" partner for the socio-economic development of Russia's eastern regions. So would be South Korea. Japan agreed at the Moscow meeting between Prime Minister Shinzo Abe and President Putin in 2013 to vitalize trade and economic cooperation with Russia's Eastern Siberia and Far East, with a particular focus on "energy, agriculture, infrastructure and transportation."

Need of New Approach after a Setback

It remains to be seen how the Ukrainian crisis will be resolved diplomatically. The degree to which Russia responsibly upholds the principles of international law in dealing with the situation will have defining consequences not only for the Euro-Atlantic, but also for the Asia-Pacific dimension of Moscow's diplomacy. The annexation of Crimea is a diplomatic setback for Moscow in the Asia-Pacific region.

It would be advisable for Russia to do the following **to engage productively in the Asia-Pacific region:**

> *First, enhance the credibility of Moscow's pronounced commitment to uphold international law.*

> *Second, remove obstacles to the prospect of sustained economic growth.*

These measures take on added importance in the wake of the Crimea annexation. Russia is facing dim economic prospects due to an increase in capital flight, diminished foreign investment, and strained relations with the West. Sustaining the growth of Russia's economy as a whole is a precondition for the socio-economic development of Eastern Siberia and the Far East.

> ***Third, cultivate improved relations with Japan, South Korea and other democracies in the Asia-Pacific region.***

This would help Russia to establish its own identity, distinct from China. Russia's decision to hold security consultations with Japan and South Korea -- particularly the "Two Plus Two" meeting with Japan involving Foreign and Defense Ministers -- are significant to the end.

It is natural for Russia to seek strategic partnership with China. Moscow shares with Beijing the strategic goal of creating a "multipolar" world order and, like China, abhors the West's interference in its domestic affairs. But if Moscow increases its reliance on Beijing as part of a confrontation with the West, Russia's identity would be further blurred in the eyes of other Asian powers.

> ***Fourth, participate in existing mechanisms for regional dialogue and cooperation more earnestly than before.***

The evolutionary process of consensus building has already put in place a complex of multilateral mechanisms for regional cooperation, including: the ASEAN-led dialogue forums, such as the ASEAN Post-Ministerial Conference (ASEAN-PMC), the ASEAN Regional Forum (ARF), and the ASEAN Defense Ministers Meeting Plus (ADMM Plus); as well as the APEC process and the East Asian Summit (EAS). All of them include Russia. Nevertheless,

Russia's role in these institutions has hitherto been seen to be ineffective by many Asians. It would be advisable for Moscow to engage in them more positively before proposing alternatives, such as a new security architecture.

> ➤ *Fifth, cooperate with countries in the region on issues of common interest.*

Such issues could range broadly, from energy supply and development to maritime, space and cyber security; from counterterrorism, piracy, drug and human trafficking to disaster relief and pandemics prevention; and from promotion of science and education to cultural exchanges and tourism.

> ➤ *Sixth, promote universal values, such as democracy, the rule of law and human rights, both at home and abroad.*

Progress in these areas is more important than ever in order to reassure an Asia that is becoming increasingly democratized.

Unlike their North American and European counterparts, *Asian countries have been reluctant to put these issues on the agenda of official discourse with Russia.* Apart from the Asians' general inclination to refrain from meddling in other countries' domestic affairs, the so-called "universal values" are still politically delicate issues for some Asian countries. Nevertheless, Moscow's autocratic politics, often pursued at the cost of basic human rights, have put doubts in the minds of many Asians about whether Russia has changed from its Soviet past.

Conclusion

From the perspective of the Asia-Pacific, the Trilateral Commission's review on Russia is particularly timely, given that **Russia is increasingly interested in engagement with Asia-Pacific countries.**

It is thus important for Trilateral Commission members to understand the **contextual differences between Asia-Pacific and Euro-Atlantic geopolitics**. In an increasingly globalized world economy and political system, Russia's future relations with countries in the two regions inevitably affect each other.

Summary of Russian Chapter

The Ukrainian situation has changed Russian-Western relations drastically.

Even as late as December 2013, it seemed that globalization of the economic, information and cultural ties between us strengthened our interdependence. Tough rhetoric notwithstanding, even cooperation in defence and security areas, including on cyber security, did not meet with insurmountable barriers for further interaction: almost six hundred activities within the framework of the NATO-Russia Council were accomplished.

A common conceptual vision of the developments in New Eastern Europe, including Ukraine, and in Central Asia, was long overdue.

In this respect, sharp criticism of the Customs Union and Eurasian integration in the West does not seem reasonable. We view this project as a pragmatic continuation of the idea of a "Common economic space from Lisbon to Vladivostok."

The West was seriously disappointed with Russia's abrupt change of course, timidly pursued by then President Medvedev. The manner in which Vladimir Putin staged his comeback caused a dramatic showdown, both domestically and internationally.

We, Russians, are also disappointed and do not mince words. But Western analysts' fixation on Vladimir Putin and his immediate entourage is superfluous. The majority of paternalistically-minded Russians support the

President as their legitimate leader. If he were not present in the political arena, a leader with very similar if not tougher post-imperial views would emerge.

Russia will always seek an independent global position with her own perception of national interests and rules of fair play. Russia's size and history will not allow for a seamless external behavior, as proved these days by the Ukrainian case.

The crisis in Ukraine began with Kiev's reversal on the anticipated signing of an association agreement with the European Union. This was followed by wave of confrontation and resulting casualties that swept the president of Ukraine and his team out of power.

Russia thinks that it cannot allow Ukraine to become part of the Western system without losing an essential part of itself and without abandoning President Vladimir Putin's goal of reviving Russia as a great power. And Mr. Putin's own authority rests in no small part on his reputation as a strong Russian patriot.

Some 17% of Ukraine's population – more than eight million – is ethnically Russian, the largest Russian diaspora in the world. Ethnic Russians constitute the majority of Crimea's population. There are also substantial numbers in East and Southeast Ukraine next to the Russian border, as well as in the major cities. Indeed, the origin and heart of Russia's Slavic culture lies in the mediaeval kingdom of Kievian Rus, centered in modern Ukraine, not Moscow.

Ukraine was and remains deeply divided over the question of closer association with the EU, opinions generally mirroring ethnic divisions. It was reckless of the post-Yanukovych government to abolish, as its very first act, Russian as Ukraine's second language. This move aroused the worst fears of Russia and Russian Ukrainians. It is estimated that almost 700,000 Ukrainian citizens, most believed to be ethnic Russians, fled to Russia in January and February of this year. It was inevitable that Moscow would move decisively. And so it did, with a customary ruthlessness that caught the West flat-footed.

Russia's endgame in Ukraine is to follow up on the March 16 referendum by securing Crimea as part of the Russian Federation; making sure that the rest of Ukraine is federalized to give Russian speakers in the eastern and southern regions a high degree of linguistic, cultural and economic autonomy; and preventing the central government in Kiev from seeking NATO membership. Over time, Putin would like to see central Ukraine, with Kiev, join the eastern and southern regions of the country in a compact aligned with Russia. Putin has no illusions, of course, as to how difficult the next few years will be for Russia and for him personally, and he is no doubt bracing for intense competition, even confrontation, which to him are normal, if unpleasant, elements of international relations.

The United States and the EU do not intend to go to war with Russia over Ukraine, as Putin well knows. After a decade of wars in the Middle East, the American public is weary of foreign adventures. That was among the reasons that Obama was elected in the first place. The EU has neither the capability nor the stomach to wage war on Russia.

Before the events in Crimea, representatives of Western governments were advocating shared responsibility for Ukraine's future with Russia. Russia remains one of Ukraine's most important markets and financial and energy donors. These ties cannot be severed instantaneously.

But in his "Crimea speech" in the Kremlin on March 18, President Putin took the conflict to a much higher level. He accused the West of "crossing all thinkable limits of diplomatic behavior" and announced Russia at its "last frontier, which would not surrender." The ruling group has taken the stance that Russia is equal in its rights and ambitions to the consolidated West, but, at the same time, is morally superior to it.

In the view of many in the Kremlin and in the Russian expert community, Russia -- as a nuclear weapon state, a permanent member of the UN Security Council and a major energy supplier -- cannot simply be ostracized forever.

With regard to **the short-term consequences of the crisis in Ukraine**, we see the picture as follows.

The substance of the **first phase of sanctions** (visa restrictions; halting negotiations across a wide range of trade, economic, financial and investment issues; blocking accounts and assets of officials and other "involved" individuals; freezing assets of state companies; and targeted measures against state banks) in itself will not cause any "unacceptable damage" to the Russian economy.

At the same time, *the consequences of even these first steps*, which in essence are a declaration to enact more serious sanctions in the future, *will be much more painful than the preliminary calculations of the direct damage incurred:*

> *First,* this will serve as a formal reason for international rating agencies to review Russia's sovereign rating and ratings for Russian corporate borrowers. This automatically raises the issue of refinancing debt assumed earlier (approximately $100 billion is up for refinancing in 2014). The conditions for IPOs and Eurobond placements will get worse. Any money coming from external sources will become more expensive (according to some estimate, by 150-200 basis points), which in turn will change the pricing conditions for the domestic debt market and exert greater pressure on the financial system.

> *Second,* the announced sanctions will set off further attacks on the ruble. The ruble has already fallen by 10% since the start of the year. Meanwhile, since the beginning of February, the capital adequacy of Russian banks has declined by 10-50 basis points, increasing the probability of a crisis in the banking sector. As both individuals and corporations seek cover in foreign currency, inflation expectations will accelerate and capital flight will rise (estimates range from $80 billion to $200 billion), which could lead to a negative balance of payments this year.

> *Third,* sanctions, particularly if they disrupt arms and military equipment export contracts, could trigger a general economic downturn. Continued stagnation (at last year's level), growth decreasing to 1%, or a slide into a mild recession with GDP declining by 1-2%, are scenarios that are roughly equally likely to play out.

Immediate and abrupt moves in the **energy sector** are not expected.

The EU's dependence on Russian natural gas (31%) and oil (27%) remains very strong. Nonetheless, the current situation has already spurred the recalibration of global markets.

In the next 3-5 years this will be expressed in the following ways:

1. An increase in practical measures by the United States to become an exporter of liquid hydrocarbons;

2. Attempts to substitute Russian gas with supplies form Qatar, Algeria, Libya and possibly even Iran;

3. Major investment projects among alternative suppliers of the EU, notably deposits in the North Sea as well as major fields in the Persian Gulf, which have reserves tenfold or more than that in Russia's Novy Urengoy region;

4. The emergence of a global LNG market with its own oil-based pricing mechanism, where Australia is one of the leaders and Russia has a relatively minor market position (only 5% of the market among APEC countries);

5. Coordinated international efforts to ensure Ukraine's independence from Russian gas, including energy efficiency programs and reverse supplies at spot-market prices via Poland, Hungary, Slovakia, Bulgaria, Romania and Croatia.

In order to react to these structural changes, Russia will need to adapt its current energy policy through 2030.

With regard to the WTO, Russia, on the bilateral level, should be prepared to see new claims, confirmations of old claims (for example, the utilization fee on imported cars), and antidumping cases against Russian companies. There will be negotiations on eliminating the several dozen old trade restrictions that remain in place. And the configuration of international trade flows could change in ways unfavourable to Russia in light of the progress on the Transpacific Trade Partnership and the Transatlantic Trade and Investment Partnership.

It is also important to keep in mind that the assets of Russian companies in Ukraine face would higher risks in the event of growing tensions over the Crimean issue. The total volume of assets at risk is no less than $30 billion. These risks could manifest themselves either through substantial impediments in the business environment -- tariffs, customs and tax policy, and application of EU technical standards and regulations -- or through nationalization.

Russia and the West have to start de-escalation

In order to avoid direct confrontation and find a mutually acceptable solution to the situation, *Russia and the West must de-escalate rhetoric and actions that are* reminiscent of the worst periods of the Cold War.

Option Number 1 was the Russian plan: disbanding the irregular groups; adopting a new Ukrainian constitution, which, among other things, would stipulate elected governors; providing official status for the Russian language; affirming Ukrainian neutrality in the U.N. Security Council; and respecting the new status of Crimea.

The Geneva Agreements [3] embraced all of these conditions in principle, but proved meaningless because no side in the conflict really wanted to "de-escalate" tensions. This is why it is critical to convene a "Geneva-II" conference, with far more concrete mechanisms and enforcement procedures.

To straighten all of this out, **we call for the *urgent creation of a Contact Group* to provide real assistance to the people of Ukraine**, the economy of which is on the verge of national catastrophe.

The Contact Group should avoid political squabbling and grandstanding, and immediately begin addressing specific issues in this process. It could also discuss measures to lower the risk of an economic downturn, triggered by sanctions, for both Russia and the European Union. This, in turn, should pave the way for negotiations to avoid military escalation on the Eurasian continent.

As Henry Kissinger highlighted in his *Washington Post* op-ed on March 6, 2014:

> Far too often the Ukrainian issue is posed as a showdown: whether Ukraine joins the East or the West. But if Ukraine is to survive and thrive, it must not be either side's outpost against the other – it should function as a bridge between them.

He concludes his article with this thought:

"The test is not absolute satisfaction but balanced dissatisfaction."

---

[3] Quadrilateral talks between Ukraine, Russia, the U.S., and the EU were held in Geneva on April 17, 2014

A NORTH AMERICAN PERSPECTIVE

Introduction

"To the extent that there were any illusions left in Washington, and it is hard to imagine there were by this point, they were finally and irrevocably shattered by Mr. Putin's takeover of Crimea and the exchange of sanctions that has followed. As Russian forces now mass on the Ukrainian border, the debate has now shifted from how to work with Mr. Putin to how to counter him." – Peter Baker, *The New York Times*, March 2014

The Trilateral Commission's last task force report on Russia was released in 2006. Even after Russia's invasion of Georgia in 2008, two American presidents espoused the feasibility, and desirability, of integrating Russia with the West. In this regard, a conventional wisdom prevailed: Moscow, for all its bluster, had not abandoned its aspirations to join what President Gorbachev called Russia's "common European home." This view is credible no longer. When Ukraine made a civilizational choice to move westward, Moscow responded with the unprovoked and unlawful invasion of Ukraine and illegal annexation of Crimea.[4] Washington accepted that Russia, at least under Vladimir Putin, is an adversary bent on pursuing regional hegemony and challenging the western-led international system. Twenty-five years after the fall of the Berlin Wall, containment is back.

Shifts in Russian domestic politics have been less dramatic, but may portend far-reaching change in the

---

[4] For a discussion on the Crimea annexation's implications for international law and the Geneva Conventions, see David Rivkin and Lee Casey, "The Outlaw Vladimir Putin," *Wall Street Journal*, 8 April 2014; David Rivkin and Lee Casey, "Russia's actions in Ukraine clearly violate the rules of war," *Washington Post*, 6 May 2014.

coming years. Vladimir Putin remains the dominant figure in Russian politics. But the type of stability that Putin provided from 2000-2008 is no longer sufficient to meet the aspirations of Russian society, particularly those of its urban elite. The unprecedented demonstrations of 2011-2012 will not easily dissipate despite the Kremlin's efforts to stifle dissent.

Russia's Significance to U.S. Interests[5]

"No one wants a new Cold War, much less a military confrontation. We want Russia to be a partner, but that is now self-evidently not possible under Mr. Putin's leadership. He has thrown down a gauntlet that is not limited to Crimea or even Ukraine. His actions challenge the entire post-Cold War order, including, above all, the right of independent states to align themselves and do business with whomever they choose. – Robert Gates, *The Wall Street Journal*, March 2014

Russia's aggression against Ukraine is a frontal challenge to perhaps the most enduring priority of the United States' post-Cold War strategy: preserving a Europe "whole and free." Russia's reach, however, affects a variety of U.S. interests beyond the Eurasian theater.

Russia is a major power no longer experiencing the "decline" of the 1990s. Russia's nuclear weapons make it the only nation that can annihilate the United States within a matter of minutes, although the growth in Chinese nuclear forces would give Beijing the same capability in the not too distant future. For countries that challenge American interests, Russia is an arms supplier and reliable source of military and diplomatic support. At the same time, Russia

---

[5] This report was written before the downing of Malaysia Airlines Flight 17 and does not factor the incident into its analysis.

is among the most important potential U.S. partners in countering threats ranging from terrorism to proliferation. Advancing global counterterrorism efforts and moving toward a more stable nuclear order would be easier accomplished with Moscow's cooperation. In this regard, Moscow's failure to honor its commitments under the 1994 Budapest Memorandum, which provided guarantees of Ukraine's territorial and political integrity in exchange for Kiev's prompt denuclearization, have dealt a blow to the cause of nuclear nonproliferation.[6]

Russia's international stature, economy, and geography, moreover, give Moscow a voice on pressing global issues. Russia is a veto-wielding, permanent member of the U.N. Security Council, as well as an influential participant in other international organizations. The country is the world's top global energy producer and sixth largest economy; Russia has drawn greater foreign direct investment than rising powers such as India and Brazil. Meanwhile, the location and sheer size of Russia's land area impacts the disposition of issues ranging from the selection of transport routes for energy and other trade, to the maintenance of supply lines for NATO forces in Afghanistan.

In sum, Russia impacts a wide range of American national interests.[7]

Above all, Russia affects the United States' ability to advance six vital and important national goals:

---

[6] Paula Dobriansky and David Rivkin, "Ukraine a victim of weak Western allies," *USA Today*, 6 March 2014

[7] See Graham Allison and Robert Blackwill, "10 reasons why Russia still matters" *Politico*, 30 October 2011, available at:
http://www.politico.com/news/stories/1011/67178.html

- Ensure, in critical regions, a favorable balance of power that enables continued U.S. global leadership
- Prevent the proliferation of weapons of mass destruction
- Combat terrorism and radical Islamist networks
- Stabilize the international economy and promote global trade
- Ensure energy security
- Advance liberal democracy and human rights

Assessing the Reset

"For all the ways that the United States and the European Union blundered into the current crisis, it is Moscow that now worries that it has overplayed its hand. Even if the end result of its gamble is a pliant regime in Kiev, the global balance of power will emerge completely unaltered. Indeed, Moscow is no longer a global power capable of threatening key American interests. The reset's failure is Russia's problem, not Washington's." – Daniel Nexon, *The Washington Post*, March 2014

In the period between the Trilateral Commission's last review of Russia in 2006 and the invasion of Crimea, U.S. policy toward Russia was largely defined by the Obama Administration's "Reset." The administration formulated the Reset against the backdrop of a rupture in U.S.-Russia relations that deepened following the August 2008 war in Georgia. The Obama Administration's Reset, as the scholar Angela Stent notes in her recent book *The Limits of Partnership*, marked the fourth major U.S. attempt since the end of the Cold War to improve relations with Russia through engagement and integration in international institutions. Although each of their strategies differed in significant ways, all three of President Obama's predecessors watched their outreach efforts falter before their first terms in office came to a close.[8] While senior administration officials continue to defend the Reset, President Obama has effectively repudiated the approach.[9]

Until the Ukraine situation erupted, the Reset elicited three main responses among U.S. experts. One group saw the Reset as a misguided policy of unilateral U.S. concessions that ignored concerns about Russia's internal governance as well as the hostile aspects of Russian foreign policy. A second group saw the Reset as a worthwhile effort, but one that emphasized continuity with past U.S.-Russia relations, and thus, contributed little in terms of a new agenda to move bilateral relations forward. A third group, which included proponents of the policy in the Obama Administration, maintained that the Reset could advance U.S. interests by putting U.S.-Russia relations on a more cooperative footing.

While the more ambitious goals of the Reset plainly did not materialize, the policy was not without achievements. Most came in the area of arms control and international security issues. In addition to the New

---

[8] Angela Stent, *The Limits of Partnership: U.S.-Russian Relations in the Twenty-First Century*, Princeton: Princeton University Press, 2014, pp. 250-51

[9] Deputy National Security Adviser Tony Blinken defended the Reset in a March 19 interview, in which he said, "It wasn't a failure, because the reset was premised on two things: first, that there were areas where out of mutual self-interest it made sense to cooperate with Russia…But, second, there would be areas where we would not cooperate because our differences were too stark, like the issue of spheres of influence, which we reject." See Jay Solomon and Carol Lee, "How Putin Parried Obama's Overtures on Crimea," *The Wall Street Journal*, 19 March 2014.

President Obama, after calling for a "pause" of U.S.-Russia relations in 2013, threatened Moscow with further isolation in his March 26 Brussels speech: "…the United States, Europe and our partners around the world…have isolated Russia politically, suspending it from the G-8 nations and downgrading our bilateral ties. Together, we are imposing costs through sanctions that have left a mark on Russia and those accountable for its actions.

And if the Russian leadership stays on its current course, together, we will ensure that this isolation deepens. Sanctions will expand, and the toll on Russia's economy, as well as its standing in the world, will only increase."

START treaty, which limits offensive strategic arms, the United States and Russia entered into an agreement on civil-nuclear cooperation under Section 123 of the U.S. Atomic Energy Act, and accelerated joint efforts to secure fissile materials. On Iran, Russia supported a new round of sanctions under U.N. Security Council Resolution 1929 and banned the sale of S-300 anti-aircraft missiles to the country. During a period of worsening relations with Pakistan, greater cooperation from Russia has allowed the United States to deliver supplies for operations in Afghanistan as it draws down forces. Finally, the Reset enabled developments such as Russia's membership in the WTO, Russia's abstention on U.N. Security Council Resolution 1973 authorizing efforts to protect civilians in Libya, and progress on easing visa requirements.

With the possible exceptions of the Iran sanctions and the Libya resolution however, the accomplishments of the Reset consisted, not of Russian compromises, but rather, of developments that Moscow perceived to be in its own best interest. In the case of arms control, for example, successful negotiations were more consequential for Russia than they were for the United States. Moscow continues to see reductions in nuclear and offensive strategic arms as a cost-effective means of pursuing strategic stability and inducing missile defense accommodations by the United States. Although Moscow claims that missile defense, in the long run, could undermine the paradigm of mutually assured destruction, there is a more plausible explanation for Moscow's palpable hostility toward American missile defense efforts: The Russian leadership opposes the presence of anti-ballistic missiles on its borders, and understands that even a modest deployed U.S. defense capability would buttress Washington's position vis-à-vis rogue states that have deployed rudimentary offensive capabilities, thereby enhancing the U.S. foreign policy prowess. Moscow's concerns are exacerbated by U.S. plans for non-nuclear strategic weapons such as Prompt Global Strike – a system to launch conventional strikes around the world with unprecedented speed.

The Reset's achievements also came at a cost. The policy entailed a passive approach to Russia's domestic crackdown. Compromises on missile defense in Eastern Europe, aside from adverse global consequences, have harmed U.S. relations with key NATO countries. The Reset signalled, in perception if not reality, that Washington was scaling back bilateral relations with allies in post-Soviet Eurasia and was prepared to condone Moscow's hegemonic policies in the near abroad. By forgoing a policy of linkage, the Obama Administration left Moscow with the impression that it could take hostile steps against the United States without paying a commensurate price.

Influential critics now blame the Reset for contributing to the crisis in Ukraine. Putin, they contend, interpreted the Reset as a sign of weakness, particularly when combined with other signs of American global disengagement, and felt emboldened to assert Russian power with insufficient fear of American pushback. This insight will, and should, inform ongoing U.S. deliberations over Russia policy.

Domestic Situation in Russia

"Citizens rally round the flag during crises, and propaganda works. But Mr. Putin's nationalism is fuelled primarily by a crude, neo-Soviet anti-Americanism. To continue to spook Russians about American encirclement and internal meddling will be hard to sustain. They are too smart." -- Michael McFaul, *The New York Times*, March 2014

Putinism

Moscow's reaction to the Reset is symptomatic of the broader domestic situation in Russia. The unique phenomena seen in Russia today can be summarized in one word – Putinism. The assumptions, worldview, ideas and strategies of Vladimir Putin have become the most important political force in the country and a major factor in troubled U.S.-Russia relations. The highly personal "vertical power" Putin is consolidating has come at the price of Russia's institutional development at home, including that of its civil society, and Moscow's relationships and standing abroad.

Domestic Crackdown

Putin's imprint is evident in the erosion of democratic institutions and weakened rule of law in Russia. Since his formal return to the presidency in 2012, the Kremlin has embarked on the most systematic political crackdown since the Cold War.[10] The crackdown extends beyond anti-Kremlin political groups to ordinary Russians and apolitical organizations within Russian civil society that are self-organized and independent of the government. Among the crackdown's most visible components is a "foreign agents" law that places tighter controls on NGOs receiving foreign financial assistance, as well as an expanded definition of treason, which could be used against domestic NGOs. In its near paranoia over the "color" revolutions, the Kremlin has publicly accused these groups of cooperating with the United States to overthrow Russia's government. Highly-visible raids and investigations have

---

[10] Even after the dissolution of the Congress of People's Deputies in 1993, all the key political opponents of the government were able to participate in national and local politics without restrictions. Many were elected to the Duma or became governors. Opposition media, both print and television, remained free.

stigmatized the opposition and deterred its leaders from making contact with western officials. Putin took small steps in the direction of liberalization during the Sochi Olympics, releasing, for example, prominent Kremlin-critic Mikhail Khodorkovsky from prison. But having waged aggression against Ukraine, the upper strata of the political system are taking extra precautions to maintain order.

While U.S. experts agree that Putin does not seek to create another totalitarian society, they differ as to whether Russia should now be considered an authoritarian state. On the one hand, strides that Russia made under President Boris Yeltsin toward a pluralistic political system have not been reversed entirely. Russians still enjoy personal freedoms, and, to a lesser degree, political freedoms, so long as they do not challenge the Putin regime. Nor is the Kremlin returning to the Soviet mold by restricting Russians from leaving the country. Yet as part of an effort to consolidate power, target perceived opponents, and perpetuate his regime, the executive under Putin has assumed substantial control over courts, broadcast media, and "strategic" parts of the economy.

Russian Opposition to Putin

Putin's repression has provoked challenges from numerous factions within Russian society. The heart of the opposition is Russia's creative and urban classes, largely based in Moscow, that were content with their new wealth in the mid-2000s, but are now frustrated with slowing economic growth and limits on political activity. Discontent with the regime has spread from urban areas into the rural regions, particularly as the government has become identified with the country's rampant corruption.

Before the invasion of Crimea, Putin's ability to manage domestic challenges to his presidency seemed to be eroding. Even now, he appears isolated from the emerging class of politically-active Russians and does not fully understand their wants, needs, and motivations. Putin has shown little inclination in gaining such an understanding, much less, in responding to the opposition's demands. There has been little dialogue between the top levels of the Putin administration and urban elites. Putin is opting instead to deal with the problem, as he sees it, by solidifying his political base through populism, anti-Americanism, and social conservatism. He forcefully points to a dichotomy between traditional Russian orthodox values and, as he characterizes it, the dysfunctional liberal values of the West.

From the standpoint of Russian domestic politics, the crisis in Ukraine has worked in Putin's favor. A February 2014 poll by the state-owned All Russia Center for the Study of Public Opinion showed that 73% of Russians opposed military intervention in Ukraine. Although thousands did turn out to protest the invasion of Ukraine, the successful annexation of Crimea overall has bolstered Putin's approval ratings, which hit 80% in March 2014.

Putin's nationalism and image as a determined leader may inspire sustained political support. Sixty-four percent of Russians indicated in a March 2014 poll by VCIOM (Russia Public Opinion Research Center) that they would re-elect Putin. But if opposition to Putin's run for reelection remains constant or grows in the intervening time, Russia could see an increasingly disaffected population and perhaps even mass protests coinciding with the 2018 presidential elections. Putin is facing increasing criticism from Russia's hardline nationalists for being too weak in Ukraine and failing to protect Russian speakers. And while their regimes are not comparable, many Russians have noted that Putin intends to stay in power as long as Stalin did. Another elite-orchestrated transfer of power within Putin's inner circle could produce renewed public outrage and instability.

Economic Policy

The Kremlin is using economic policy to shore up its domestic political base. Putin is providing large subsidies and arranging rents to bolster support among the groups that comprise "Russia II"—an older, more conservative segment of Russians, compromised largely of state-employed workers, pensioners, and rural dwellers. Investments in the defense industry have become a priority for the Kremlin. They allow Putin to maintain support among the working class as well as segments of the old Soviet intelligentsia like scientists and engineers at defense plants. Military reform has focused more on providing rents to elites and jobs to provincial middle and working classes than it has on achieving important policy outcomes. As a result, these investments have had limited impact on Russia's defense capabilities.

The redistributive emphasis in Moscow's economic policy has led Russia's growth rate to dwindle toward stagnation. Russia has a dynamic small business sector in areas such as import/export, food processing, restaurants, advertising and public relations, which is overshadowed by corporations such as Gazprom, Rosneft and Sberbank. But given that Russia works at full capacity, increased productivity will require more competition. The opposite is happening. Large, poorly-managed state corporations are buying up big private companies, which in turn buy smaller private companies. The consequence is a declining number of companies, less competition, and less growth.

Investment remains low. And top businessmen and ambitious professionals are leaving the country.

Realizing that Russia's current model of economic growth, dependent on rising oil prices, is exhausted, Putin took a number of steps in the second half of 2013 to encourage competition and boost efficiency in the energy sector. He signed a law breaking Gazprom's monopoly on gas exports, and ordered Gazprom and other monopolies to freeze tariffs and slash expenditures by half. Even prior to the imposition of sanctions, however, these measures had failed to reverse Russia's flagging economic growth.

Before the Ukraine crisis, experts predicted that sound fiscal balances would protect Russia from the risk of financial instability even in the event of a drop in oil prices. Russia had maintained an almost balanced budget, a minor current account surplus, and over $400 billion of international reserves, although the country's non-oil budget deficit was over 10%. Whether these assessments hold up amid the imposition of sanctions against Moscow, and the resulting uncertainty in the Russian economy, remains to be seen. According to Russia's Central Bank, the first quarter of 2014 saw over $50 billion in capital leave the country, a period during which Russia's Micex Index plummeted by more than 10%. Former Finance Minister Alexei Kudrin predicted that capital flight could reach $150-$160 billion by the end of the year, while Central bank governor Elvira Nabiullina projected that capital flight will reach a more modest $85 to $90 billion by the end of the year.[11] The return of the MICEX index to pre-Crimea levels, however,

---

[11] "Kudrin projects capital outflow from Russia at USD 150-160 bln in 2014", *Itar-Tass*, 27 March 2014, available at: http://www.eabr.org/e/press_center/news-region/?id_4=37584; "Russia's Central Bank sees capital outflow at $85-$90 billion in 2014", *Itar-Tass*, 23 March 2014, available at: http://en.itar-tass.com/economy/732979

may suggest that uncertainty stemming from Russian policy, more so than western sanctions, accounts for the decline in investor confidence.

Russia joined the World Trade Organization (WTO) in August 2012, but it is pursuing policies contrary to WTO governing principles. The Customs Union with Belarus and Kazakhstan is based on protectionist policies that lead to trade diversion. Yet the Customs Union has become the main focus of Russia's trade policy. Moscow's threats to sanction Ukraine were part of a gambit to coerce Kiev into joining the Customs Union. With political objectives superseding economic goals, Russia is likely to face intensified WTO disputes in the near future.

Corruption

Neither economic liberalism nor economic nationalism entirely captures the Kremlin's strategy. The Putin regime is distributing the country's wealth through a form of "trickle down corruption" in which elites are coopted by bribes and politically-motivated rent distribution. Escalating government spending works to limit the political opposition by keeping unemployment numbers low. In other words, the Putin system is willing to pay an employment tax of sorts. At the same time, a process of "trickle-up corruption" is prevalent in which lower-level officials send a share of bribes that they receive from the public to their superiors. It should be noted though that Russian authorities have respected the policies of certain Russian companies that publicly refuse to pay bribes under any circumstance.

Corruption in Russia does not consist simply of bribes and rent distribution, but also includes noncompetitive procurement, nepotism and organized criminal networks. Endemic corruption undergirds a web of informal networks across constituencies, at all levels of Russian society. The fact that corruption serves as its foundation makes the Putin system resilient and resistant to evolutionary change. Yet, massive and palpable corruption has engendered anger among many Russians that may exceed even their dissatisfaction over the lack of political pluralism – a reality manifested in the rise of Alexei Navalny and the anti-corruption bloggers. If the networks of pro-regime forces snap, the system could prove more brittle than many expect.

Corruption represents a major threat to Russia's national security. Putin has acknowledged this in the 2013 Public Security Concept. Corruption among law enforcement officials and the employees of government agencies remains a nationwide phenomenon that has allowed terrorist groups to strike Russian cities hundreds of miles from their bases in the North Caucasus.

The corrupt nature of the Putin system creates dilemmas for the Kremlin as it grapples with the demands of political and economic reform. Diversifying Russia's economy, currently reliant on commodity exports, will be difficult without strengthening the rule of law and improving the investment climate. Under Putin, key economic assets have come under the control of "private" owners with close ties to the Kremlin. This arrangement allows the Kremlin to maintain heavy oversight even if ownership structures are technically private. But it complicates efforts to impose greater accountability on Russian officials, as reform could weaken elites' loyalty to the system.

Risk of Political Instability

Economic mismanagement by the Kremlin could produce domestic political instability in the near future. Even before the leveling of sanctions, economic circumstances were making it difficult for Putin to honor his populist promises from the 2012 campaign – promises that extend beyond his political base and cannot be met within existing budget limitations. Even in a best-case scenario, in which Moscow improves the investment climate and enjoys another sustained rise in global oil prices, structural factors are likely to preclude much growth. A period of low energy prices could force the Kremlin to make unpopular spending cuts. The Russian finance ministry's budget strategy through 2030 predicts that, unless the federal government cuts expenditures, the country's funding gap could reach $300 billion between 2017 and 2020 and that its oil savings would be depleted in just three years.[12] Spending cuts would undermine the existing social contract in which poorer Russians expect to join the country's urban middle class.

The Kremlin has pursued limited reforms to increase its own effectiveness. The regime has removed some corrupt officials and has taken steps to combat lower-level corruption. To improve transparency and prevent foreign financial firms from gaining leverage over Russian elites, the Kremlin has imposed new asset disclosure rules, placed limits on the foreign accounts of officials and parliamentarians, and established a special anti-corruption directorate to audit their income declarations.

During the remainder of his time in office, however, Putin is unlikely to pursue an energetic program of domestic

---

[12] Darya Korsunskaya and Lidia Kelly, "Russia faces budget shortfalls, risks erasing oil savings – document," *Reuters*, December 4, 2013.

reform. A push to impose far greater accountability for Russian officials could undermine the Putin system – a risk the current leadership is unwilling to take.

Consequences of Putin's Departure

Putin has failed to establish a reliable system of leadership succession. Even though he is expected to remain in office until the next election, his eventual departure from office will spark competition with unpredictable consequences.

The prospects for liberalization after Putin are uncertain. Putin's departure would not necessarily change the nature of Russia's political and economic system. There is a risk – the level of which is unclear – that the webs and networks on which Putin relies may simply produce another authoritarian leader, possibly one even more anti-American than the current leadership.

A key question is whether liberals will be able to capture wider public support than the statist, nationalist, xenophobic, and populist right. Putin fears the latter more than the liberal opposition. Liberals in Russia have been undermined not only by direct political repression, but also by economic trends that have worked to limit their ranks. The number of small enterprises for example has declined due to high taxes, prohibitive interest rates on loans, weak property rights, and pervasive corruption. Small enterprises form only about 20% of the Russian economy. In most Organization for Economic Cooperation and Development (OECD) economies by contrast, they account for 40-50%. Young, educated Russians, opposition figures, and civil society activists, generally concentrated in urban areas, are leaving the country in the face of economic and political hardships.

Prospects for the liberal opposition are further hampered by its inability to unify around an appealing message. Liberal economics remains discredited outside urban centers. Many of the liberals and youth who have made headway to date hold firmly patriotic, if not strongly nationalist foreign policy views.

Still, Putin's exit could be followed by a brief and limited "glasnost." Freedom to campaign during this period could benefit Russia's liberals. In Russia's past, liberal rulers have tended to follow reactionary ones. As in the "third wave" of democratization in Southern Europe and Asia, middle-class professionals and students are at the forefront of Russia's urban middle class protest movement. Up to 20,000 people participated in a January 2013 demonstration against the ban on American adoptions. The liberal opposition could come to power in the largest Russian cities, as it did in 1990.

Is Putin a Long-term Thinker?

The degree to which long-term challenges influence Putin's decision-making is a source of disagreement among experts. On the one hand, Putin has pursued short-term goals in ways that undermine the Kremlin's ability to pursue long-term reforms. At numerous junctures, Putin could have chosen alternate paths that would not have injected as much uncertainty into the system. Putin's victory in the last election was the culmination of a relentless effort since 1999 to prevent the emergence of any real political rivals. Had Putin won a free and fair election against a credible opponent in two rounds, he may have appeared weaker temporarily, but the election outcome would not have changed fundamental power dynamics in Russia and it may have bolstered Putin's long-term legitimacy. Nor has the Kremlin opted for limited change on the Chinese model – regular rotation of leaders and selective economic reform, without full political accountability -- even though such a model would likely drive modernization.

Others argue that Putin is a long-term thinker, but does not consider tradeoffs in ways similar to western governments and Russian liberals. In destroying alternate loci of power such as oligarchs, Putin has shown that he can set and achieve long-term goals. Putin also has long-term policies on energy and China, the prospects of which may become clearer now that Gazprom and China have signed a 30-year, $400 billion contract. Putin referred to the deal as "the biggest contract in the history of the gas sector of the former USSR," but questions remain on whether the agreement can be implemented and financed.[13]

Russia's aggression in Ukraine does little to resolve the debate. Putin demonstrated his ability to seize opportunities when presented with a power vacuum. Yet, the extent to which he considered the long-term repercussions of annexing Crimea, or acted as part of a preconceived campaign, is uncertain. In the run-up to Ukraine's May 25, 2014 elections, pro-Russian separatists incited unrest throughout the country's eastern provinces. But after 55% of Ukrainians turned out to vote and elected Petro Poroshenko in a landslide victory, Putin refrained from denouncing the election results, met with the newly-elected president, and returned Russia's ambassador to Ukraine to attend Poroshenko's inauguration.[14] To be sure,

---

[13] Paul Saunders, "The Not-So-Mighty Russia-China Gas Deal", *The National Interest*, 24 May 2014, available at: http://www.cftni.org/The%20Not-So-Mighty%20Russia-China%20Gas%20Deal%20%20%20The%20National%20Interest.htm

[14] Michael Birnbaum, Fredrick Kunkle and Abigail Hauslohner, "Vladimir Putin says Russia will respect result of Ukraine's presidential election," *Washington Post*, 23 May 2014

whether the benefits of Putin's gambit in Ukraine outweigh its costs depends, in part, on how the West responds.

Demographic Change, Long-Term Challenges

Whether the Kremlin's incremental approach to reform will be enough to prevent Russia's long-term decline remains to be seen. Among the country's most significant challenges is its demographic outlook. In 2012, Russia experienced its 20th straight year of natural population decrease.[15] According to the government's medium-term forecast, the Russian population will decline from 143.3 million in 2013 to 141.6 in 2031.[16] And by 2050, the United Nations Development Programme projects that the population will drop below 110 million.

Russia is making modest improvements in stimulating the birth rate by providing material perks and investing in health care and fertility. But these improvements are happening in the context of a declining base. Even if Russia can turn around its exceptionally high male mortality rate – a figure worse than Haiti and lower than 33 of the 48 countries the United Nations designates as "least developed countries" -- the sharp decline in the Russian population from 148.3 million in 1991 to 143.7 million today has left the country in a position in which there are not enough women of child-bearing age to reach population replacement levels. In 2012, Russia's birth rate of 1.7 per woman left the country 20% below replacement level.[17]

---

[15] Natalya Krainova, "Population Declines for 20th Straight Year, *The Moscow Times*, 07 February 2013.
[16] 'Change of the Population. Forecast Variants,' Federal Service of State Statistics of Russia. Available in Russian at:
http://www.gks.ru/free_doc/new_site/population/demo/progn1.htm
[17] Nicholas Eberstadt, "Putin's Hollowed-Out Homeland," *Wall Street Journal*, 7 May 2014

Even as Russian birth rates increase, the population is stabilizing around a shortage of working adults. The Russian Labor and Social Security Ministry is expecting a drop in the labor force of one million people annually in 2013-2015. Longer term, according to a recent forecast by secretary of Russia's Security Council Nikolai Patrushev, the working-age population will see a decline of ten million by 2025. And in 2030, Russia, according to the International Institute of Applied Systems Analysis in Austria, will account for just 3% of the world's working-age college graduates, down from 9% in 1990.[18] A combination of enhanced productivity and an influx of foreign specialists will be needed to overcome the labor shortfall.

It is an open question whether Russia can address its demographic challenges through immigration. Migration from the neighboring post-Soviet republics accounts for the growth in Russia's population by one million since 2009. But even if Moscow creates a vibrant economy that sustains long-term growth, it is unclear whether Russian resistance to immigration will ease. Implicated in the immigration debate is a package of issues surrounding national identity. As people from outside the Russian Federation fill jobs in the country, Russia will change in ways that challenge the Kremlin's attempt to foster a national identity around ethnicity and Orthodox Christianity.

Among the fastest growing populations within the Russian Federation are non-Russian ethnic groups. But for birth rates in Russia's tribal regions and historically Muslim areas like Chechnya and Dagestan, Russia would still be a net-mortality country.[19] By 2030, Muslims, 80% of whom currently reside in two of seven federal districts, will

---

[18] *Ibid*
[19] *Ibid*

comprise nearly 15% of the entire Russian population.[20] The search for a Russian state identity, therefore, must stand on an inclusive concept of citizenship. Xenophobic political rhetoric is pushing the Russian state in the opposite direction, as demonstrated by recent ethnic riots in the towns of Kondopoga, Pugachev, and Moscow's Biryulyovo district.

Russia's demographic squeeze could have negative consequences for U.S. national interests. One reason is the potential for population trends to change political dynamics in the Eurasian social and demographic space. The contradictory trajectories of diversity and xenophobic political rhetoric could complicate Russian efforts to promote economic development and maintain social stability. Eastern Siberia, for example, could become a zone of conflict if population declines generate a demand for Chinese labor beyond what national and regional governments can manage. While Central Asia can serve as a source of low-skilled immigrants, China is the most obvious source of the skilled immigrants needed to tap the region's resources, facilitate defense modernization, and fill the shortage of doctors. The Russian federal government estimated in 2008 that there are some 338,000 Chinese citizens legally residing in Russia, but that there could be a total of 1.5 million Chinese in Russia.[21] A large number of Chinese migrants in Siberia are seasonal workers with little interest in settling in Russia. The challenge is how to integrate non-Russians into a Russian state that embraces cultural and ethnic diversity.

---

[20] "The Future of the Global Muslim Population," Pew Research Center's Religion & Public Life Project, 27 January 2011, available at:
http://www.pewforum.org/2011/01/27/future-of-the-global-muslim-population-regional-europe/#russia

[21] "Information on number of Chinese citizens in Russia," *RIA Novosti*, January 2009, available in Russian at http://ria.ru/society/20090126/160113371.html

Russia's imperial history provides an intellectual framework in which Russians can at least understand, if not entirely accept, an influx of migrant workers from Central Asia. Russia's legacy of managing diversity can inform efforts to develop an inclusive Russian identity. Putin embraces Russia's multiethnic, multi-religious heritage, and sees little issue with the fact that Russia is already the second largest recipient of immigrants in the world after the United States.

Still, Chinese immigrants are likely to be greeted with a mixed degree of tolerance. Russians, particularly Moscovites, have difficulty seeing China as a potential market rather than a threat to Siberian development. High-level relations are superficially good, but competitive under the surface. Fears of a Chinese zone of influence in Russia are fueled by the reality that Russian authorities are facing challenges in governing the region.

Given that Russia's xenophobic political movements are among its most anti-American -- as seen by their voting patterns in the Russian parliament -- U.S.-Russia relations could face new tensions if ultranationalists rise to power on the immigration issue. Russian leaders could work toward a better scenario by drawing lessons from the American and Canadian experience in converting diversity into a national asset. Tatarstan, one of Russia's most successful regions, is already doing so, partnering with Canada on innovative approaches to integrate Islamic immigrants into the wider community.

Russian Foreign Policy

"In short, we have every reason to assume that the infamous policy of containment, led in the 18th, 19th and 20th centuries, continues today. They are constantly trying to

sweep us into a corner because we have an independent position, because we maintain it and because we call things like they are and do not engage in hypocrisy. But there is a limit to everything. And with Ukraine, our western partners have crossed the line, playing the bear and acting irresponsibly and unprofessionally." – Vladimir Putin, March 2014

An Extension of Domestic Politics

The Putin regime cites foreign "dangers" to justify its consolidation of power at home. Never before in post-Communist Russia's history has the Kremlin's need to shore up domestic support impacted Russia's policy toward the United States to the degree that it has since Putin's 2011 decision to seek a third presidential term. Putin's opposition to U.S. foreign policy and his anti-American rhetoric resonate with a sizable segment of the public, which, after the perceived humiliation of the 1990s, accepts nationalist ideas and condones a strong state resisting the United States. Large segments of Russian society are concerned about U.S. foreign policy, especially its use of force and its efforts to shape the internal politics of other states. NATO enlargement and perceptions of U.S. involvement in the "color revolutions" fuel these sentiments. There is a national consensus that Russia should regain its status as a serious geopolitical player.

Reassertion of an Independent Russia

Putin is trying to create a geopolitical and geo-economic demand for Russia. While Moscow understands that its goal of achieving parity with the United States is not attainable for now, Russia leaders believe that they should be an important part of major international issues, even when Russia ultimately lacks the capabilities and/or the will to contribute to solutions. Putin captured this sentiment in his 1999 acceptance speech to become Yeltsin's prime minister, remarking that, "Russia has been a great power for centuries. And it remains one."

Moscow is reasserting its global influence at a time when the country's leadership is increasingly resisting international interdependence. Having moved in the direction of integration in the 1990s and 2000s, with mixed results, the Kremlin now believes that a more unilateralist foreign policy is necessary to defend against the negatives of an interdependent world. Moscow's commitment to national sovereignty is hardened by western policies that affect the country's state-controlled strategic sectors. Moscow believes that strategic sovereignty is critical in a world in which the West does not welcome Russian engagement on fair terms.

Moscow no longer seeks to export a revolutionary, universalist ideology around the world. Instead, Putin portrays Russia as a status quo power resisting the United States' revisionist foreign policy. In this sense, events in Ukraine can be understood, in part, by Moscow's grievances – real and alleged – against Washington.[22]

Insofar as Putin has advanced a comprehensive strategic vision that outlines what Russia wants the world to look like in critical respects and how Russia can help deal with global challenges, he has emphasized nationalistic ambitions with little regard to Western values or collective security goals. Putin envisions a sphere of influence that encompasses Russian-speaking peoples beyond the boundaries of the Russian Federation. The national identity that Putin is trying to cultivate – one that is socially

---

[22] Address by the President of Russia, The Kremlin, Moscow, 18 March 2014, available at: http://eng.kremlin.ru/news/6889

conservative, Eurasian, and includes Russia's Islamic population in the national narrative – reinforces a foreign policy that prizes Russia's state sovereignty.

Post-Soviet Eurasia

The reassertion of influence in post-Soviet Eurasia is a particular priority of Russian foreign policy. While Moscow does not harbor ambitions to reconstruct the Soviet Union, it is attempting to reverse certain consequences of the Soviet collapse, an event that Putin has infamously called "a major geopolitical disaster of the century."[23] The Putin regime seeks Russian political, economic and military supremacy, if not hegemony, in the post-Soviet space. Russia wants to be surrounded by friendly, stable regimes that follow the country's lead on economic, defense, and security issues. When decisions are made in the post-Soviet states, Russian interests should prevail.

Washington and Brussels undermine Putin's objectives. The United States is pursuing trade negotiations with groups of partners in Europe and Asia that do not include Russia. The European Union is also deepening cooperation with some of Russia's post-Soviet members. Two of them, Georgia and Moldova, initialed Association Agreements and Deep and Comprehensive Free Trade Area Accords with the EU at a summit in November 2013. Ukraine was preparing to sign its Association Agreement and Deep and Comprehensive Free Trade Area Accords but backed away at the last minute due to Russian threats and energy sanctions, as well as concerns about the short-term economic consequences. The Ukrainian government's

---

[23] "Annual Address to the Federal Assembly of the Russian Federation,' The Kremlin, Moscow, 25 April 2005, available at:
http://archive.kremlin.ru/eng/speeches/2005/04/25/2031_type70029type82912_87086.shtml

decision triggered mass protests in Kyiv, culminating in the abdication of Russian-backed president Victor Yanukovych.

Moscow wants to create its own regional institutions and trading blocs. Ukraine is the most-desired target in terms of Moscow's policy to build Russian influence and Russia-dominated institutions in the post-Soviet space.

The Putin regime sees Eurasia as an arena of competition with the United States and Europe. This mindset informs Russian support for authoritarian regimes in the region. Unlike the United States, Moscow's notion of stability tends to emphasize a strong state and unified society rather than a resilient, dynamic system with outlets for dissent. While concerned about aging leaders in Central Asia, Moscow deems authoritarian regimes to be reliable partners in preventing threats such as Islamic extremism, terrorism, and drug trafficking from spilling over its borders. Transitions from authoritarianism to democracy in the region could undermine Russian interests in this respect.

Well before the invasion of Crimea, the conduct and rhetoric to which Russia resorted in order to press claims in post-Soviet Eurasia fell beyond the bounds of international norms. This approach has yielded some benefits for Moscow. Armenia succumbed to Russian pressure, agreeing to join the Moscow-led Customs Union, even though the country does not share a border with any current or prospective member. Before Yanukovych fled to Moscow, Ukraine bowed to Russia by suspending preparations for the signing of the agreements with Brussels. Yet, Russia's foreign policy is built upon a narrow self-interest that does little to encourage or inspire others to follow Moscow. Coercive, non-transparent tactics exacerbate Russia's challenge in attracting close allies. Even Belarus and the member states of the Collective

Security Treaty Organization are client states of varying reliability.

Experts disagree on whether Moscow's hostile policies toward its neighbors are motivated by the Kremlin's perception of its own strength or its own weakness. If Moscow felt stable and self-confident in its ability to project power, some argue, Russia would not bully states like Ukraine, Georgia, and Moldova. Others suggest that Moscow's behavior is consistent with its history. Russia, they note, has behaved aggressively toward its neighbors during past periods when the leadership felt emboldened by the Russian state's growing stature and ability to export Russian values in its neighborhood.

Worsening Relations with Europe

Moscow's failure to attract broad diplomatic support for its agenda is apparent in Russia's worsening relations with Europe. For most of his two presidential terms, Putin was a proponent of Russia's integration with the EU. Increasingly, he has lost interest in Russia's "European choice." Moscow is frustrated by EU policies that, in its view, interfere with the operations of Russian companies such as Gazprom. Weighing on the Kremlin's approach is a perception of Europe's decline – a view accelerated by the EU's response to the financial crisis, and its collectively weak foreign policy. An additional consideration is the fact that Moscow's effort to develop bilateral ties with EU members states, especially with the most influential countries -- Germany, Italy, France, and the UK -- has yielded few benefits in recent years, national leaders that had friendly relations with Putin have been replaced.

European attitudes toward Russia were hardening even before the invasion of Crimea. Amid concerns over

Russia's human rights violations and manipulation of energy exports, for example, the European Parliament passed the Magnitsky sanctions resolution.

But Ukraine is a game-changer in European relations with Russia. In April, the Parliamentary Assembly of the Council of Europe suspended Russia's voting rights, citing the "contradiction" between Moscow's annexation of Crimea and its commitments to the body.

Particularly notable is the shift in German policy. Before the Ukraine crisis, Berlin's actions in the Cyprus banking crisis and its criticism of the Putin regime's human rights abuses reverberated in the Kremlin. But Moscow could take solace in the fact that commercial relations between the two states remained strong and continuity, by and large, prevailed in the wider German-Russian relationship. Now, notwithstanding the continent's dependence on Russia's energy sector, European leaders agree that Russian aggression calls for sanctions, though the extent of their commitment to a broader containment strategy remains to be seen.

Eurasian Union

A prominent avenue through which Russia has pressed its interests vis-à-vis Europe is the Eurasian Union, the most significant economic integration project that Moscow has pursued since the Soviet collapse. The Eurasian Union is an economic project, but has a political motive and a political impact. More so than in the past, Moscow considers the EU to be a threat on par with NATO, and is using the Eurasian Union to foreclose EU integration for countries in the Commonwealth of Independent States. The rivalry between the Eurasian Union and the EU has become a focal point of tensions between Russia and the west.

The question for the United States is how Russia deals with potential new members of the Eurasian Union. Judging by how Russia coerced Ukraine not to pursue accession talks with the EU, and to join the Eurasian Union instead, Moscow is unlikely to relent in efforts to bring near abroad countries into the Russian fold. Even if the United States engages Russia's neighbors as independent, sovereign states, the Putin regime, locked in a mindset of competition with Washington and Brussels, is likely to resist western efforts to bolster relations with its neighbors.

China

While the Eurasian Union seeks to check Chinese influence as well, Russian officials have refrained from characterizing China as an adversary the way they increasingly do with the United States and the EU. Publicly, Putin says he wants to hitch Russia's sails to China's mast and ascend along with Beijing's rise. The Kremlin understands, among other things, how important Chinese investments are for the development of the Russian Far East.

Moscow believes however that China's rise is not without costs. China is making extensive economic inroads into Central Asia that undercut Russia's role in the region. Some Russian experts fear that growing inequalities in the Russia-China relationship, if unaddressed, may lead to a de facto loss of Russia's sovereignty over its far eastern regions. In 2010, the regional domestic products of all 27 provinces that comprise Russia's Urals, Siberian and Far East federal districts totaled roughly $372 billion. By comparison, four Chinese provinces that border Russia over the same period of time produced $538 billion worth of goods and services. There are fewer people living in all of those 27 regions of Russia than in Heilongjiang, just one of the four Chinese provinces bordering Russia.[24] According to the IMF's January 2014 forecasts, China's GDP will exceed Russia's by more than 4.5 times by 2018.

The risk of a Russia-China alliance emerging against the United States remains small, but cannot be discounted as a long-term threat. So far, Moscow and Beijing, even when pursuing similar goals, generally have chosen to work in parallel on key third-party issues, such as international financial institutions quotas in fora like the BRICS and the G20, rather than coordinating their policies. But a desire for more influence in the U.S.-led international system could form the basis of a tactical anti-American alignment between Russia and China. Individually, they are unlikely to overturn the existing Western-defined order; together they have a better chance at countering it. Both countries' foreign policies seek to prevent, as they see it, the U.S. drive for regime change, which contradicts their traditional views on state sovereignty and non-interference. Even if ultimately unsustainable, short-lived but close cooperation between Moscow and Beijing could have profound consequences for U.S. national interests.

In this sense, the western response to Russia's intervention in Ukraine has ramifications for China's long-term ambitions. China abstained from the Security Council resolution condemning Russia's move in Crimea, but joined a BRICS statement indicating support for Russia's participation in the G-20. Some analysts maintain that Moscow did not seek China's support over Crimea because the Kremlin was unwilling to offer, in exchange, support in

---

[24] Simon Saradzhyan, "Russia Needs to Develop Eastern Provinces as China Rises." *RIA Novosti*, March 5, 2013.

China's territorial disputes. These actions suggest that Moscow, for now, is not inclined toward an anti-American alliance with Beijing despite differing with the West's approach to international problems such as the Ukraine crisis. Weakening resolve by the United States however, could change their calculus. Russia's ability to invade and annex its neighbor with minimal punishment from the West could provide a precedent for China to act on historical grievances in its own territorial disputes. Without American reassurances regarding its commitments to extended deterrence, regional states could take destabilizing steps that would upset the balance of power in Asia.

Arctic

Moscow's approach to global governance can be seen in its Arctic policy. The melting of the polar icecap is opening up sea lanes and transit routes that introduce new commercial possibilities, but also new potential sources of conflict. Deep-water resources add to the region's importance.

Russia's leaders consider the Arctic to be a region of vital national interest due to the combination of its strategic location and extensive natural resources. Putin has called attention to Arctic geography, citing the threat that U.S. missiles would pose if deployed in the Arctic Ocean near Russia's shore. Russian Security Council officials have designated the Arctic as a "main strategic resource base" and Russian estimates suggest that the disputed territories may hold up to 10 trillion tons of hydrocarbon deposits. Receding ice will add to the region's significance, as the Northern Sea Route, an international shipping lane along Russia's northern coast, becomes available. By planting a Russian flag on the North Pole in 2007, Moscow was publicly pressing an ambitious 460,000 square mile territorial claim.

Moscow's intentions in the Arctic remain unclear. Russia has rebuilt military airfields, deployed aerospace defense units, and expanded strategic bomber flights, naval patrols, and icebreaker fleets in the north as part of a broader national security doctrine. More recently, a battalion of Russian paratroopers conducted a mass landing in the Arctic for the first time in the country's history. At the same time, Russia has worked actively through diplomatic channels. Russia, along with Canada, has stated that it will settle claims related to the continental shelf in the Arctic Council, which has proven a useful forum for engagement given the United States' absence from the UN Law of the Sea Process.

From a security perspective, Moscow sees real military risks in the region. As its "National Security Strategy of the Russian Federation until 2020" warns, "In case of a competitive struggle for resources it is not impossible to discount that it might be resolved by a decision to use military might. The existing balance of forces on the border of the Russian Federation and its allies can be changed." Defense Minister Sergei Shoigu promised that the Russian armed forces would form a dedicated group of forces in the Arctic in 2014. Notably, Moscow is not solely focused on Western rivals; senior Russian navy commanders have expressed particular concern over China's growing use of the Northern Sea Route. China has also recently gained observer status in the Arctic Council.

Discrepant views on the balance between environmental protection and economic development may exacerbate tensions over competing territorial claims. The United States and its allies have prioritized environmental stewardship, a consequence of tighter domestic regulations and political pressure at home -- considerations that have restrained their pursuit of territory and resources in the Arctic. Conversely, state-owned Russian companies have dumped nuclear waste in the Arctic and have pursued the region's minerals and untapped oil and natural gas reserves. Putin has bristled at suggestions that Russia relinquish Arctic territory to protect the environment.

Still, Russia's capacity to develop Arctic resources is limited at present, a reality that may mitigate disagreements over projects that are likely to remain hypothetical in the foreseeable future. Russia needs advanced foreign technology to develop offshore fields, which are technically demanding. More importantly, the shale oil/gas revolution may slow investment in capital-intensive projects by reducing potential returns and encouraging investors to pursue opportunities elsewhere.

Russia's Defense Policy

"We see what could be called 21st century revisionism. Attempts to turn back the clock. To draw new dividing lines on our maps. To monopolize markets. Subdue populations. Re-write, or simply rip up, the international rule book. And to use force to solve problems -- rather than the international mechanisms that we have spent decades to build.

We had thought that such behavior had been confined to history. But it is back. And it is dangerous. Because it violates international norms of accepted behavior. It exports instability. It reduces the potential to cooperate and build trust. And, ultimately it undermines our security. Not just NATO's or Ukraine's security, but also Russia's. If the rules don't apply, if agreements are not honored, certainly

Russia also stands to suffer the consequences. – Anders Fogh Rasmussen, The Brookings Institution, March 2014

The Russian armed forces have just undergone a major reorganization, shedding the anachronistic Soviet-era chain of command and replacing most divisions with more mobile and autonomous brigades. Russian submarines and strategic bombers have resumed global patrols. And Putin recently announced that as much as $755 billion will be allocated for re-armament of the Russian military through 2020.

Russia is modernizing its military at a time when Putin is expounding, and enforcing, new doctrines for intervention in the near abroad. Putin's stated commitment, notably in his March 18, 2014, Crimea speech, to "protect" Russian-speaking minorities has obvious implications for the Baltic States, each of which have sizable Russian minorities with grievances in their home countries. Latvia and Estonia, at 27% and 26%, respectively, have higher percentages of ethnic Russians than Ukraine, 17% of which is populated by ethnic Russians. The unresolved conflict in Transnistria, meanwhile, could provide a pretext for Russian aggression in Moldova, a state with a Russian population of 6% that does not enjoy NATO security guarantees.

For now, however, Russia's proposed defense build-up is a manageable threat to U.S. interests. Russia has a long track record of underfunding similar initiatives. Given the considerable slow-down of the Russian economy since the adoption of the procurement plan, Moscow is unlikely to allocate the proposed funds.

Even if Moscow follows through on its defense build-up, the United States' conventional superiority over

Russia will remain unchanged. Most of the funding will be allocated more toward replacing Soviet-era systems (some of which are so old they are unsafe), than to invest in new programs. Although Russia retains a formidable arsenal of nuclear weapons, Russia is not investing enough to maintain strategic nuclear parity with the United States. According to the New START aggregate numbers released in April 2014, Russia has 498 strategic delivery systems deployed compared to America's 778, and 1,512 warheads deployed on these systems compared to America's 1,585.

Russia could assuage concerns over its military modernization through defense cooperation with the United States in areas such as counterterrorism, where both countries face similar threats. The risks of "cooperation failures" between Russia and the United States can be seen in the failure to prevent the Boston marathon bombing of 2013 – risks that would have far more severe consequences if international terrorist organizations acquire weapons of mass destruction. The case for U.S.-Russia cooperation on counterterrorism will only increase as the United States and its allies scale down their presence in Afghanistan. The United States and Russia have already demonstrated their ability to conduct joint counterterrorism operations and have collaborated effectively in detecting and neutralizing narcotics labs in Afghanistan. Amid tensions over Ukraine, however, mutual interest may not be enough to sustain such cooperation.

Russia's Energy Future

"In a way, it all comes down to price. Europe's energy policies have taken cheap Russian gas for granted. Among many other things, the events of the last month make it clear: Russian gas isn't as cheap as it looks." – The Editors, *Bloomberg View*, March 2014

Energy issues play an outsized role in both Russia's foreign and domestic policy. Russia's leaders recognize that energy, which provides nearly 20% of its GDP and over half of federal government revenue, is critical to the country's future. Nevertheless, they have been slow to implement policies needed to sustain and maximize energy output. Russia's oil production and exports have grown steadily over the last decade, though sustaining the industry will require significant and continuing investment. By contrast, while natural gas production has grown consistently over the same period—except for a sharp drop after the 2008 financial crisis—exports have declined since 2010 due to growing competition in the European market, where America's shale gas revolution has made available liquified natural gas (LNG) originally intended for the United States. The Ukraine crisis has underscored to Western policymakers the potential for LNG exports to reduce Europe's dependence on Russia.

The shale boom has allowed the United States to replace Russia as the world's top gas producer. According to the International Energy Agency, the United States will overtake Russia to become the world's top oil producer in 2014. The Russian government has only recently acknowledged that the shale revolution is driving potentially dramatic changes in world oil and gas markets. The Russian government's "Forecast for Development of Energy Industry in Russia and in the World Until 2040," citing the shale boom, among other factors, warns of "big threats to the Russian economy resulting from deep transformation of world energy markets." The report's base scenario projects that exports of Russian oil will decline by 30 percent after 2015, causing the Russian economy to lose between $100 billion and $150 billion annually. In the same scenario, exports of gas will decrease by 15 to 20 percent after 2015, resulting in a loss of another $40 to $50 billion per year.[25]

Russia has sought to reorient its energy exports toward Asia, where it seeks high growth potential. Substantial new exports necessitate considerable infrastructure financing to build pipelines to China or LNG terminals for exports by sea to Japan, South Korea, and other more distant markets. To that end, after over a decade of negotiations, Gazprom signed and finalized an agreement in May 2014 to supply China with 38 billion cubic meters of natural gas.

Russia has had more success diversifying its oil exports. By 2012, some 20% of Russia's oil exports went eastward. Moscow's official goal is to increase the share of crude oil heading to Asia to 32% by 2035. Russia also aims to expand its nuclear power plant export business, especially in Asia and the Middle East, as well as mini-hydro stations in Siberia, which could be exported to developing countries.

Russia has imposed limits on foreign investment in its energy sector, which the government considers a strategic sector of the economy. The country's uncertain investment climate has also slowed foreign investment, particularly in the wake of the Ukraine crisis. However, Russia's vast resource wealth makes it an attractive destination for many energy investors, notwithstanding the challenges of doing business there. Structured public-private U.S.-Russia energy dialogues have repeatedly foundered, largely due to mismatched decision-making processes and expectations.

---

[25] *Ibid*.

Russia's energy sector will require considerable investment in the coming years to maintain its output. No less important, Russia would likely face significant obstacles in sustaining its oil and gas production and exports over time without access to Western technology. While Russia may be able to attract investment from China and elsewhere, pursuing new technically demanding sources such as offshore oil, shale, gas and tight oil poses a greater challenge.

Russia's economic dependence on its energy sector is an important point of Western leverage as relations with Russia deteriorate. Because of high taxes on Russia's oil industry, oil-related taxes provide a greater share of the federal budget than natural gas, which is subsidized inside Russia for the benefit of inefficient factories and home consumers. Russia's oil production is particularly vulnerable because Russian firms need not only investment, but also access to high-tech services provided by oil-field services firms, which would not be forthcoming if the West imposed targeted sanctions on Russia's hydrocarbon extraction industry.

Existing U.S. law on natural gas exports simplifies export licensing procedures for gas shipments to U.S. free trade partners by presuming that such exports serve the U.S. national interest, but does not extend the same presumption to U.S. allies. The law could be modified with relatively little effort. A coordinated U.S.-European strategy, meanwhile, could establish a target (starting with 20-30%) for U.S. LNG energy exports to replace Russian sources over time. In pursuing this goal, however, the United States and its allies will need to consider that higher prices and greater profit margins are redirecting U.S. shale gas from Europe to Asia. Replacing Russian sources may require

European subsidies to buy American gas, making up the difference for revenues in Asia.

Exploiting Russia's vulnerability on energy dependence through sanctions and other measures would not be entirely cost-free. For one thing, energy cooperation with Russia benefits Western companies and economies. Rosneft, for example, Russia's main state-owned oil company, is 19.75% owned by BP. Its name and headquarters notwithstanding, BP has become a heavily American company in many respects since it acquired Amoco. Furthermore, although Russia prefers the politically fragmented European market to the unified Chinese one, decoupling Europe from Russia by, for example, developing shale gas in Europe and exporting U.S. gas across the Atlantic could make Russia more accommodating vis-a-vis China. After demanding European-level prices, Gazprom, in its recent deal with the China National Petroleum Corporation, agreed to concessions on price and other issues amid European plans to reduce dependence on Russian gas exports.

U.S. Business in Russia

"Russia is an emerging market with growing incomes, and U.S. companies have been actively looking to increase their investment there in recent years. Companies, like Pepsi, Coke, and Ford will be reluctant to support any economic sanctions that dig into their bottom line, especially if the European Union refuses to implement their own sanctions. Since the U.S. and Russia do very little business together (only $30 billion in 2013), any unilateral sanctions from the U.S. will only have a marginal economic effect, although they may offer symbolic value as well." -- Danny Vinik, *The New Republic*, March 2014

U.S business interests in Russia beyond energy have remained underdeveloped since the end of the Cold War, and now, with the imposition of Ukraine-related sanctions, are bound to decline even further. Trade between the United States and Russia totaled $38.12 billion in 2013. Compared to the United States, European countries such as France and Germany account for a greater percentage of foreign direct investment into Russia. Direct American investment in Russia amounted to just $14 billion, though the United States was the leading investor in Russia in terms of the total number of FDI projects funded.[26] American exports were expected to double in the next five years due to the normalization of trade relations, a development rendered impossible by recent events in Ukraine.

U.S. business leaders are concerned about anemic growth and the economic climate in the country. Angst about the Russian economy among the U.S. business community is informed by low investor confidence and political risk emanating from the Kremlin's foreign and domestic policy. Unilateral, rigorous application of sanctions and potential retaliatory steps from Moscow could mean that U.S. firms suffer commercially for decades, while third country firms build relationships and lock in market positions that are all but impossible to win back.

A steep drop off in investor confidence currently poses the greatest threat to U.S. business in the country. Amid sanctions and declining commodity prices, capital flight has emerged as an immediate challenge that could have significant effects in Russia. A recent World Bank report projects that Russia, in a low-risk scenario, could see

---

[26] Warren Strobel, Arshad Mohamed and Anna Yukhananov, "U.S. and EU marshal economic tools to punish Russia," *Reuters*, 3 March 2014; "Russia 2013: Shaping Russia's Future," Ernst & Young's attractiveness survey, available at: http://www.ey.com/Publication/vwLUAssets/2013-Russia-attractiveness-survey-Eng/$FILE/2013-Russia-attractiveness-survey-Eng.pdf

1.1% growth; in a worst-case scenario, geopolitical volatility could lead to a contraction of 1.8%. Without robust growth in the short-term, investors are less able and willing to navigate challenges such as corruption, lack of rule of law, and bureaucratic intransigence, as well as Russia's isolation from the international community, especially when presented with opportunities in dynamic markets elsewhere.

Longer term, Russia faces challenges that originate from the Kremlin's debt for equity exchanges in the 1990s. One legacy is that a sizable percentage of capital outflows continue to come from oligarchs close to the Kremlin, contributing to perceptions in the U.S. business community that Russia is a kleptocracy with little more than a veneer of democracy.

Investors are also unsure how Russia will fare in the shale gas revolution – an important indicator in the country's long-term growth forecasts given the close relation between oil prices and Russia's GDP. Russia has large deposits of shale oil and gas. But without an investment environment and tax regime that facilitates the infrastructure investments needed for shale gas/oil production, Russia could have difficulty developing new oil and gas production.

The Putin government aspires to modernize Russia and turn the country into an attractive global financial center. Currently, Russia produces just over 1% of the world's service exports.[27] Some Kremlin initiatives have drawn favorable attention from U.S. investors. These include: reducing bureaucracy, relieving the administrative and tax burden, protecting intellectual property rights, and

---

[27] Nicholas Eberstadt, "Putin's Hollowed-Out Homeland," *Wall Street Journal*, 7 May 2014

creating enterprise zones. A business ombudsman has been appointed. And efforts to tackle health challenges such as alcoholism will improve the demographic outlook, and thus, investor attractiveness to the Russian market. The World Bank lauded Russia "among the most improved" in its 2013 Doing Business survey of 189 economies.

Yet Kremlin policies complicate U.S. business ventures. Privatization is not being implemented at a steady pace. The same is true of legislative initiatives to reform Russia's banking sector, consumer lending, and financial services industry. To the contrary, large state corporations are expanding the sphere of state ownership through enterprise purchases. The Kremlin is facilitating bilateral piecemeal deals with particular entities. But it is less proactive in improving the broader legal and regulatory environment. The government has not prioritized steps to enhance labor force participation and mobility, and reduce subsidies and trade protection for weaker sectors.

Putin's governing style adds to investor worries. Although Putin has established a Foreign Investment Advisory Council and meets actively with foreign CEOs doing business in Russia, his hostile rhetoric and tendency to aggregate power suggest that Russia is suffering from a lack of reform impetus. Investors are skeptical that they can deploy capital with certainty, fearful of future regulatory measures and arbitrary government confiscations. The political, social and court systems are neither fair nor transparent, and remain susceptible to intervention from the executive. And the absence of a post-Putin succession plan creates dilemmas for U.S. investors as they debate whether to wait out the Putin administration or accept the risk of political volatility in Russia.

U.S. business leaders, in general, are not inclined to collaborate with the U.S. government in promoting democracy and human rights. They resent accusations by Russian decision-makers that American business is a proxy for U.S. government concerns. But they do acknowledge the need for a cultural shift in Russia. Without greater emphasis on free will and independent thought, Russia will struggle to incubate talent and build a more diversified, innovative economy. Insofar as U.S. business tries to prod Russia toward the rule of law, it does not do so through direct coordination with Washington. Instead, U.S. business leaders refrain from corrupt practices that their foreign competitors are more inclined to pursue.. More so than preferred oligarchs, the U.S. business community sees promise in the expansion of Russia's urban, middle class.

Russia's foreign policy, especially in the wake of the Crimea invasion, is a source of concern for U.S. business. "Cold War hangover" among U.S. business leaders is reinforced by Russia's aggressive territorial ambition, as they characterize it, and weighs on their investment decisions. In a context in which negative impressions of Russia are rooted in the American historical consciousness, the 2008 war in Georgia confirmed investor perceptions that Russia is not a safe place to do business. Any progress Moscow made since then in changing these sentiments has been more than undone by the unlawful annexation of Crimea in March 2014. As in Iran and other states facing U.S. sanctions, the U.S. government is discouraging the private sector from embarking on new projects in Russia.

Before the invasion of Ukraine, the OECD was pursuing accession talks with Russia. At the request of the organization's 34 members, the accession process is now on hold. In the pre-Crimea debate, supporters of OECD accession argued that the Kremlin was more likely to liberalize the Russian economy if doing so would cement Russia's place in international institutions. They noted that Russia had already ratified the OECD Anti-Bribery Convention – an achievement toward improving the country's business climate. Russia would have been exposed to best practices and global standards, and would have had to meet the minimum standards set out in the OECD Acquis. Opponents warned that OECD accession would risk "commitment overload." Rather than pushing Russia to adopt institutionally-dominated reforms, they argued that the United States and its allies should identify the core goals for which the OECD is a proxy, and then press Moscow to move toward these goals with initial building blocks. Experts on both sides of the debate however drew cautionary lessons from Russia's failure to follow through on WTO commitments. Even optimists conceded that a strategy of encouraging economic reform through international economic institutions would be a slow, laborious process. Barring "real progress on the ground," in the words of OECD Secretary General Angel Gurría, the OECD accession for Russia is postponed indefinitely.

Although U.S. business leaders maintain that business-to-business dialogues are mutually beneficial regardless of the state of governmental relations between Washington and Moscow, the political atmosphere is not conducive to such dialogues and exchanges. The U.S. business community would like to expand exchanges, which would provide Russian professionals with opportunities to work in the United States, and then return home with a better understanding of American institutions. The Russian business community, however, is facing political pressure not to reciprocate to American overtures. According to U.S. business leaders, the Kremlin is urging Russian business to engage cautiously with the United States, and focus instead on developing economic ties in Asia. Even before the Ukraine crisis, Moscow rebuffed the Obama Administration's proposal to expand business-to-business links as part of the Reset. Reluctance among Russia's national and local politicians to embrace market-oriented models sends a similar message of disengagement from U.S. business.

Before the Ukraine crisis, U.S. business leaders, notwithstanding their concerns about Russia's economic climate, were investing in Russia on a long time horizon. Greater business-to-business ties, they anticipated, could serve as a catalyst for concluding a Bilateral Investment Treaty to protect American investments and encourage market-based reforms in Russia. Trends have moved in the opposite direction. The Obama Administration cancelled scheduled talks with trade officials on the Bilateral Investment Treaty in March 2014 and Senator John McCain has called for the "suspension of business" between American and Russian companies as "punishment" for the Putin regime's actions in Ukraine.[28]

U.S. Goals vis-à-vis Russia

"Russia is a regional power that is threatening some of its neighbors, not out of strength, but out of weakness….Russia's actions are a problem. They don't pose the number one national security threat to the United States. I continue to be much more concerned when it comes to our security the prospect of a nuclear weapon going off in Manhattan." – President Obama, News Conference in the Hague, March 2014

---

[28] Interview on Bloomberg Television's "Political Capital with Al Hunt," 28 March 2014, transcript available at: http://www.businessweek.com/news/2014-03-28/mccain-says-forcing-companies-from-russia-an-option-transcript#p1

While the fulcrum of U.S.-Russia relations has shifted toward Eurasian issues in light of the Ukraine crisis, Moscow remains a factor in Washington's ability to achieve important goals around the world. In formulating a post-Crimea strategy, Washington should work toward a paradigm in which Moscow does not prevent the United States from achieving the following goals. Some of these goals are untenable at this time and some are vocally and robustly opposed by Moscow. But articulating them would ensure that Russia understands the full range of U.S. concerns and objectives.

Regional Issues

- Support a Euro-Atlantic security community that accelerates the integration of post-Soviet states with the West;
- Contain Chinese hegemonic ambitions that could undermine the peaceful rise of the Asia-Pacific;
- Stabilize the greater Middle East by containing Iran and promoting political settlements in the Afghanistan-Pakistan and Syrian conflicts
- Secure U.S. rights to sea lanes, hydrocarbons and other interests in the Arctic

Non-Proliferation and Arms Control

- Prevent rogue, adversarial, and unstable states like Iran, North Korea, and Pakistan from developing and proliferating weapons of mass destruction

Democracy and Human Rights

- Consolidate liberal politics and the rule of law in key regions

- Gain international support for new norms of humanitarian intervention

Terrorism and Radical Islam

- Decimate al Qaeda and affiliated groups

International Economy and Trade

- Enforce the rules of international economic organizations such as the WTO
- Protect the rights of U.S. investors in foreign countries

Global Energy Markets

- Ensure that the United States and its allies develop greater self-sufficiency in energy

Global Governance

- Enlarge NATO to include like-minded, aspiring members
- Secure the support of key institutions like the United Nations Security Council and IAEA for U.S. foreign policy objectives

U.S. Strategic Options

"For its part, the United States needs to avoid treating Russia as an aberrant to be patiently taught rules of conduct established by Washington. Putin is a serious strategist – on the premises of Russian history. Understanding U.S. values and psychology are not his strong suits. Nor has understanding Russian history and psychology been a strong point of U.S. policymakers." – Henry Kissinger, *The Washington Post*, March 2014

The United States faces an increasingly aggressive Russia that acts as an adversary on key international issues. While Russia cannot compete with the United States at a global level, it can exacerbate virtually any international problem that Washington is trying to address.

Before the invasion of Crimea in February 2014, U.S. experts generally proposed one of three strategic alternatives toward Russia: comprehensive containment, selective engagement with selective containment, and deep engagement. Momentum has shifted toward advocates of containment. Consensus, however, is unlikely to jell behind any one of these approaches unless Russia continues with its aggressive policy toward Ukraine, or Moscow's conduct toward Ukraine, even if it doesn't escalate further, portends a new status quo in which Russia becomes uniformly hostile and/or significantly more repressive at home.

One group advocates comprehensive containment.

Like the original containment, comprehensive containment assumes: that the problem is in the nature of the Russia side, not in the interaction between the two sides; that the relationship cannot change fundamentally until the Russian side changes fundamentally; and that while there are a few issues on which Washington must do business with Russia, the United States' primary interest is in blocking Russia's problematic foreign policy and in pressing Moscow to retreat from its illiberal ways domestically.

Proponents of comprehensive containment believe that the Obama Administration has made Russia more relevant by engaging Moscow despite the gap between U.S. and Russian interests and values. The Putin regime, which does not share Washington's win-win mentality, now believes that the United States needs Russia more than Russia needs the United States. The authoritarian and corrupt nature of the Putin regime dooms prospects for sustainable cooperation and partnership. The Putin regime's anti-Americanism is symptomatic of this larger problem.

Instead of pressing Moscow for partnership, the United States ought to try a containment policy, which entails a set of sticks to go with the carrots. When Moscow violates human rights at home or commits foreign policy misdeeds that harm U.S. interests, the United States should punish Russia through both rhetorical and concrete policy steps.

Washington has tremendous leverage over Russia. The United States could use smart sanctions and anti-corruption laws, for example, to discipline Russian elites. It could even virtually destroy the Russian economy, the continued functioning of which depends on access to the global banking system. Economic disruption of Russia, in turn, could precipitate domestic unrest in Russia. The benefits of making Russia pay a price for anti-American antics would outweigh the costs of any retaliatory steps that the Kremlin is likely to take.

Experts in this camp are more inclined than their counterparts to accept the risks associated with destabilizing Russia. They reason that a weakened Russia would pose less of a threat to the United States and its allies.

Another group favors selective engagement with selective containment.

Selective engagement with selective containment assumes that the issues on which the United States and

Russia need to cooperate are significant, but so too are the areas where Washington needs to stand its ground and counter Russian *foreign* policy. The relationship is consequential but should be understood as limited. Russia, viewed broadly, is an adversary on some issues, but a potential partner on others. It is too big not to matter and too big to fail.

As long as Putin is in power, Washington should recognize that Moscow is not measuring the relationship with the United States by the deliverables that are negotiated. Indeed, the Kremlin seems to lack clarity on its own goals. Dysfunction within the decision-making structures in Moscow may account for the Kremlin's inconsistent statements and policies on some issues, silence on others, and general unwillingness to negotiate about anything specific, even on "win-win" issues.

Putin treats the United States as a threat, but also wants validation from Washington as an equal. Putin may not mind being disliked in Washington, but would not appreciate being ignored.

Changing circumstances either at home or abroad could make Moscow more amenable to partnership down the line. Until then, Washington should pursue transactional deals when possible and necessary, but otherwise stand its ground and counter current Russian foreign policy.

The final group is committed to deep engagement.

Deep engagement starts from the premise that common interests considerably outweigh the issues that divide the United States and Russia. Without ignoring the obstacles to a durable strategic partnership, or suggesting that Washington "give away the store" to achieve it, the strategy would seek cooperation across the many areas where U.S. and Russian interests intersect.

Washington should articulate what the substantial stakes are in the U.S.-Russia relationship and the goals towards which the two sides should work. Producing deliverables with Russia is difficult but not impossible. Recent events in Syria have demonstrated the importance of continuous U.S. engagement with Russia. Washington and Moscow would never have crafted a deal on Syria's chemical weapons if the White House heeded the advice of those advocating a 'strategic pause' in the bilateral relationship. In the short-term, expanded partnerships on win-win issues such as information technology, agriculture, environmental cleanup, northern development, railway modernization, and trade in metals and pharmaceuticals could give U.S. and Russian negotiators cover for dealing with divisive issues. At a minimum, these channels would hedge against worsening relations.

Given the huge advantage the United States enjoys over Russia, Washington can go the extra mile in engaging Russia and still negotiate from a position of strength. Indeed, a U.S. attempt at improving relations with Russia would deny Putin an external enemy, thus undercutting his strategy of coopting domestic support through anti-Americanism. In the current environment, Moscow will show limited initiative even if it ultimately wants a cooperative relationship.

The Kremlin does not want to destroy the U.S.-Russia partnership. But a provocative U.S. approach could end Moscow's engagement on issues of U.S. interest, along with any chance of achieving a durable strategic partnership across the many areas where the two countries' interests intersect.

Proponents of deep engagement may have modified their position as a result of Moscow's aggressive behavior vis-à-vis Ukraine.

Should the United States Promote Democracy and Human Rights in Russia?
-- A Divisive Issue

The question of how, if at all, Washington should promote democracy and human rights in Russia is among the most contentious issues dividing experts. Some fundamentally question the thesis that a more democratic Russia will serve U.S. interests given how hostile public opinion is toward the United States. Greater rule of law and the development of stronger institutions, they argue, is a better U.S. goal, as it would create the basis for a more predictable system in Russia. Only a few measures -- liberalizing visa regimes and expanding exchanges with academics and younger Russians, for example -- enjoy broad support among the U.S. foreign policy establishment. There is little consensus on how receptive Russians are to U.S. intervention, and to what extent Moscow's intransigence is influenced by U.S. policy. Nor do experts agree on how much influence the United States has in legitimizing the Russian regime domestically and internationally, or on what level of pressure would be effective to improve human rights in Russia. These differences are premised on varying assessments of the anti-Putin opposition. What percentage of Russian society sympathizes with the opposition? How likely is the opposition to topple the current leadership? How would it govern if it came to power?

Advocates of containment are most inclined to support robust democracy promotion efforts in Russia. They argue that pro-democracy rhetoric and actions from Washington carry a great deal of authority, even if U.S. solidarity with Russian liberals does not yield visible gains in the short-term. Particularly in times of crisis, U.S. leadership on democracy and human rights can shape the choices that Russian and international actors make. Skilled diplomats could navigate the demands of engaging the Putin system while assisting the opposition. Should the United States fail to defend Russian civil society, Washington could find itself in a situation in which the regime falls, and no liberal alternative exists to fill the vacuum. Russia is already a signatory to various human rights agreements. Advocates of this view believe, at a minimum, that Washington ought to wage a proactive diplomatic effort to ensure their enforcement.

Those experts, by contrast, who question the feasibility and wisdom of U.S.-led democracy promotion, cite Putin's popularity and the amount of control he wields in Russia. U.S. attempts to support Russian reforms, they argue, are counterproductive and jeopardize cooperation on areas of mutual interest. The United States does not serve as a powerful moral example to most Russians. Compared to the situation in the 1990s, the state-to-state context in U.S.-Russia relations is less conducive to pressuring Russia on human rights. Most human rights agreements to which Russia is a signatory are not legally binding and lack enforcement mechanisms. Washington, critics argue, does not understand how to pressure Russia on human rights in effective ways. Grants and statements of support to civil society have drawn unnecessary attention to U.S. efforts and have incited a backlash from the Putin regime. Even opponents of the Putin system question why the United States singles out Russia through legislation like the

Magnitsky Act instead of applying the same rules to other violators of human rights. Why the contrast, they ask, between the United States' "business-like" approach to China – which, after all, remains nominally communist – and its more assertive human rights policy directed at Russia? Despite its intentions, the United States has undermined the efforts of Russian groups and individuals working for change.

Policy Recommendations

"We don't need another visionary like Churchill to know what to do next. Today's democracies have enough experience; applied with common sense and a modicum of courage, we can avoid the worst." -- Mikheil Saakashvili, *The Washington Post*, March 2014

Russia invaded Crimea in February 2014 as an early draft of this report was being written. The Group of 7 countries boycotted the G-8 meeting to be held in Sochi, suspended Russia from the group, and agreed to impose coordinated sanctions. Thousands of Russian troops remain amassed on Ukraine's eastern border, resulting in the imposition of U.S. and EU sanctions. Even amid security challenges in Ukraine's two eastern regions, the National Democratic Institute found that over 60% of voters had the opportunity to cast a ballot in the May 25, 2014 elections. A preliminary statement by the OSCE determined that Ukraine held "a genuine election largely in line with international commitments and with a respect for fundamental freedoms in the vast majority of the country." The Obama Administration followed up with $48 million in additional aid to Ukraine. As of this writing, prospects for a political settlement of the crisis in eastern Ukraine remain uncertain.

Our core recommendation is that a fundamental reassessment of all aspects of U.S. policy toward Russia is in order. In the short-term, the United States must consider how its response to the aggression in Crimea, and Russia's ongoing efforts to weaken the Ukrainian central government's authority over its eastern provinces, will affect:

- *Regional issues in Eurasia, and*
- *U.S. vital interests around the world*

The reassessment should formulate and articulate, both in a presidential speech, and in a sustained public diplomacy strategy, a response to what constitutes the "broader strategic and moral dimensions of Moscow's behavior."[29] This approach would counter Putin's March 18th speech and, more fundamentally, the strategic doctrine that he laid out.

Even if Russia does not move beyond Ukraine and opts instead to seek "normalization" with the West, the nature of Putin's regime permits little more than a transactional U.S.-Russia relationship on a narrow range of issues. Putin's departure from office, however, may produce a transformational moment that portends real systemic change in the Russian system. Russian politics will have to be invented almost from the ground-up, perhaps creating possibilities for a rapprochement.

The following are additional, specific policy recommendations that should be taken in the short-term and factored into the overarching reassessment of our policy.

---

[29] Paula Dobriansky, "U.S. needs a strong moral narrative to combat Putin", *Washington Post*, 23 May 2014, available at: http://www.washingtonpost.com/opinions/us-needs-a-strong-moral-narrative-to-combat-putin/2014/05/23/dd56450c-e10e-11e3-9743-bb9b59cde7b9_story.html

While the recommendations do not necessarily reflect the views of the working group's individual participants, their opinions and analyses, offered before the invasion of Crimea, provided a basis for the report's recommendations. The recommendations below are not intended to be comprehensive.

Ukraine

- Maintain a non-recognition policy of the illegal Russian annexation of Crimea.
- Uphold Ukraine's sovereignty and right to make its own domestic and foreign policy choices, free from Russian intimidation.
- Intensify support for Ukraine by establishing a "Friends of Ukraine" Task Force. This international group, comprised of civil society, should focus on stabilizing Ukraine through economic assistance in areas such as finance and market access.
- In steering international assistance and support, prioritize goals that will facilitate a successful political transition in Ukraine. As Ukraine holds parliamentary elections, forms a new government, and reviews its constitution, Washington, working with our allies, should assist Kiev in its efforts to rid the country of corruption and establish independent institutions and the rule of law.
- Respond promptly and positively to Ukraine's request for military assistance. Determine assistance levels based on a comprehensive assessment of the country's needs in the event of a Russian invasion.
- Enhance Ukraine's ability to maintain law and order by providing training to the country's police force.
- Strengthen ties between Ukraine and NATO in the context of the existing Partnership for Peace.

- Encourage President Poroshenko to follow through on his promise to dissolve the Ukrainian parliament and convene early parliamentary elections before the end of 2014.

Regional Issues

- Respond to the requests of the Central Europe and Baltic States to bolster their defenses and enhance deterrence by forward deploying significant NATO assets on their territories.
- Exercise U.S. leadership in convincing NATO to adopt the Membership Action Plan for Georgia.
- Preserve NATO-Russia cooperation on Afghanistan, while lessening U.S. dependence on the Northern Distribution Network.
Propose a multilateral regional dialogue regarding Afghanistan's post-2014 security environment that includes Russia, but develop work-around options to the Northern Distribution Network such as airlift deliveries and Central Asian routes that bypass Russia.

Economics/Business

- Task the United States Trade Representative with redoubling efforts to ensure Russian compliance with its WTO commitments. Prepare to undertake appropriate steps if compliance is not achieved.
- Expand sanctions to shut down credit and other types of access to financial markets.

Energy

- Communicate to Russian officials at a high level that unfair treatment of U.S. energy companies and other

American investors in Russia could lead the president and Congress to adopt even tougher policies toward Moscow
- Develop a coordinated strategy with Europe to establish a 20-30% target for U.S LNG energy exports.
- Revise the law on U.S. natural gas exports, which simplifies export licensing procedures for gas shipments to U.S. free trade partners by presuming that such exports serve the U.S. national interest, but does not extend the same presumption to U.S. allies.
- Warn Moscow that further aggression and other hostile policies would mean sanctions on Russia's hydrocarbon extraction industry, which would restrict Russia's access to advanced Western technologies.

Arctic

- Accelerate U.S.-Canada maritime cooperation and diplomatic coordination in the Arctic Council to contain Russian ambitions in the region

Democracy and Human Rights

- Accelerate support to those organizations advancing rule of law, transparency, and press freedoms in Russia.
- Work closely with civil society organizations as well as the OSCE Office for Democratic Institutions and Human Rights (ODIHR) on election monitoring and other Ukraine and Russia-related human rights issues.

Demographics/Civil Society/Cultural Exchanges

- Expand exchange programs focused on mayors and city council members in an effort to strengthen Russia's local governance. Seek to pair cities/regions facing similar challenges (e.g., Alaska and Siberia, industrial cities, agricultural regions, border towns, etc.)
- Engage Russian citizens beyond the capital cities of Moscow and St. Petersburg, and beyond any single ethnic group, to become more sensitized to Russian diversity.
- Encourage American corporate, civil society, and government leaders to regularize discussions and exchanges with Russian youth, academics, and other groups that are generally disenchanted with the Putin regime and inclined toward cooperation with the West.

A EUROPEAN PRESPECTIVE

A Changed Global Context

The global context has changed markedly since the Trilateral Commission's last report on Russia in 2006.[30] The fragmentation of global power has become more pronounced, compounding the difficulty of achieving international agreements, whether on conflict, security issues, or trade. The relative power, influence and self-confidence of the G-7 countries and the "West", however defined, have declined amid the 2008 financial crisis and the long-running, unsuccessful conflicts in Afghanistan and Iraq. The Eurozone crisis has changed the European Union – albeit still the world's largest economic bloc - from a success story into an existential struggle. The notion of the BRICs, dating from 2003, has been exposed as bogus, but the rise of Asia – not only of China and India, but also of a slew of countries from ASEAN to South Korea – is no longer a projection, but a fact, as is the growing importance of other emerging economies, including Turkey, Poland, and a number of countries in Latin America and sub-Saharan Africa. The Middle East is in deep turmoil; conflict between Shia and Sunni casts a growing and dramatic shadow across the Islamic world as seen by the ISIS insurgency.

Freedom today means essentially the capacity of a state to adapt wilfully and confidently to the new rules of cooperative pooling and share influence in the global village. With different speeds, most of us are learning the lesson that the age of exclusive influence in any region of

---

[30] Roderic Lyne, Strobe Talbott, and Koji Watanabe, *"Engaging with Russia: The Next Phase,"* The Trilateral Commission, 2006.

the world is over for good. Those – big or small - who adapt more rapidly and pro-actively to this sea change in international relations will arguably do best in the future. They will turn out to be positive political standard setters and best economic performers.

Little Change in Russia

Looking back at the 2006 Trilateral Commission Report, what is striking is how much has not changed in Russia over the past seven years. Russia is at best a semi-democracy with apparently little appetite for reform. Trends discernible then have been accentuated: the manipulation of elections and impediments on political activity; the control of the principal media (especially central television); the "resurgence of the ...FSB and the other successor agencies to the KGB, operating outside the confines of law and accountability";[31] the growth of the bureaucracy; and the dependence on a single institution, the Presidency, asserting "control over the legislature, the judiciary, regional institutions, the commanding heights of business in the private as well as the public sector, the media and civil society."[32]

Russia's economy is no less dependent on hydrocarbons and other extractive industries now than it was a decade ago. Well over half of GDP is in the State sector. The number of small and medium enterprises – already low by comparison with other emerging economies – has been falling. Efforts by the State to promote and invest in innovation have produced only a few success stories. Research in science and technology has declined. Many highly educated and talented young Russians have

---

[31] *Ibid*, 147
[32] *Ibid*, 150

left the country over the past two decades. Russia lags badly in the global competition for investment.

In international affairs, Russia, a veto-welding permanent member of the UN Security Council and one of the world's five recognized nuclear states, remains an energy giant and global power. Russia is the world's largest single country, spanning a total of 9 time zones and 17,075,400 square kilometres. Its population of 143 million is about the same as that of Germany and France together, though its demographic outlook is troubled. Russia's GDP is roughly half of Germany's; per capita income in US$ is less than a quarter of Germany's. In spite of that status and potential, Russia functions mainly as the country that says "No." More importantly, it resorts to the bankrupt patterns from past centuries of political and military intervention in the affairs of its sovereign neighbors in order to keep them in its orbit and "oppose the gravitational pull of other powers."[33]

Russia has been more assertive since Putin began his second term in 2004. Buoyed by rocketing oil prices, Russia has reinvested in its armed forces over the past six years, and is certainly "resurgent" by comparison with the 1990s. However, after its growth spurt from 1999 to 2007, the economy is in poor shape, dipping into stagnation.

Indeed, the most significant change in Russia since 2006 has been the sharp fall in the rate of GDP growth. No structural reforms have been undertaken to address these and other acute problems, including a looming demographic crisis (epitomized by a still lacking pension reform), pervasive corruption and massive capital flight, not to mention growing competition from the shale gas and oil industries. In 14 years, with consistently high oil prices,

---

[33] *Ibid*, 159

Putin has failed to deliver on his promises to modernise the country and its infrastructure, promote innovation and diversification, bear down on corruption (the reverse has been the case), and join the advanced nations of the world. Russia has fallen far behind the more successful emerging and transitional economies.

Economic growth has fallen far short of the ambitious targets President Putin set in his first term: from nearly 7% annually in the years before the 2008 crisis to a rate of 1.3% in 2013 -- significantly less than the projected 3.7%. Some estimates show a growth rate below 1% for 2014. While that still compares favourably with growth rates in Western Europe, Russia is trying to catch up from a much lower baseline. Investments and consumes are sinking, too, while inflation nears 7%.

The World Bank forecasts two growth scenarios in 2014: a low-risk scenario assuming a limited short-lived impact of the Crimea/Ukraine crisis, and a high-risk scenario if the geopolitical situation worsens. In the former case, the rate is estimated at 1.1%, in the latter at -1.8%. For 2015, the respective growth rates are 2.1% and 1.3%. These worrisome growth figures -- much more than electoral fraud -- epitomize the breakdown of the "social pact" that characterized Vladimir Putin's first two terms. As Putin commented on 10 June 2013, economic growth is below the range necessary for sustainable development, resolving social problems, and narrowing the gap with the leading nations.

Clearly, the worst threat looming over the "Putin system" is the Russian economy. The concern expressed in the 2006 Trilateral Commission Report -- that the opportunity for growth was threatened by "bureaucratic state-corporatist stagnation," [34] the failure to combat corruption, and the abandonment of structural reforms – alas, has been borne out. The Report concluded that the current course would "lead toward stagnation, rising dissatisfaction at bad governance and at backward public services, and an underperforming economy, which will become increasingly uncompetitive and inefficient in the sectors now seized and occupied by the state."[35]

Of course, the global economic downturn has affected Russia's performance. The government cannot entirely be held responsible for the current predicament – although Putin does criticize Medvedev, more or less directly, implying that the two might be drifting apart. However, while global economic circumstances are indubitably negative, it is also true that – as economist and former finance minister Alexei Kudrin emphasized at the November 2012 Trilateral meeting in Helsinki – Russia has good reasons of its own to be worried about an economic crisis and possibly a recession: the demographic crisis that has been affecting the country for decades, and that is already creating recruitment problems; massive capital flight; the technology gap and de-industrialization process; and the arrival on the market of shale gas, a much cheaper solution than the current supply contracts.

Vladimir Putin should be fully aware that his country is going through a serious economic downturn: recession is on the way, with sanctions already resulting in an enormous capital flight. Andrey Klepach, Russia's deputy economy minister, estimates that $70 billion left the country in the first term of 2014, compared to $63 billion in

---

[34] *Ibid* 74

[35] *Ibid* 164

2013. Kudrin estimates that total outflow in 2014 will reach at least $150 billion.

European Disenchantment with Russia

Europeans are less divided on Russia than at any time in the last two decades. Gone are divisions between western enthusiasts and eastern skeptics, between naïve hopes and excessive fears. Europeans are, east and west, disappointed and disheartened with Russia – a feeling has been greatly enhanced by the brutal Russian intervention in Ukraine. Most Europeans believed that nationalistic propaganda, aggressive policy statements, and the use of military force were phenomena that, in the European context, ended in the late 20th century.

When 35 heads of state convened at the November 1990 Conference on Security and Cooperation in Europe meeting in Paris proclaiming a "New Era of Democracy, Peace and Unity," their aspiration was to construct the much-sought "One and United Europe." Europeans were hoping that Russians would join them in the common endeavor of reshaping the continent. They believed that Russia would embrace common European values and transform into a society based on those values; a country at peace with its neighbors, working to build sustainable relationships on the basis of mutual trust, acting constructively in the UN Security Council, and carrying its fair share of the burden in securing international peace; a country with a fast growing, competitive market economy. In sum, a European country that had finally found its place in the "common European home" Mikhail Gorbachev envisioned.

Since the end of communism and the collapse of Soviet Union, however, both Europe and the United States have mismanaged and misread Russia. We, "the West," naively believed that Russia would dissolve into our type of democracy. In other words, we expected Russia to transit through a period of transformation as the countries of Central and Eastern Europe had done. It was a mistake: Russia always was and will remain different. This is rendered by a different history. Among many historical facts, Russia neither witnessed the Ages of the Renaissance and Enlightenment nor the rapid expansion of capitalism; Parliamentary democracy lasted only for a short period; the role of the close relationship between the Orthodox Church and the Powers that be in cementing traditional values; geographical vastness; multi-ethnicity, and by many more factors.

Russia has always stuck to one long-term goal: to build a strong Russia, based on its own historical and cultural values, respected worldwide as a nuclear power. Given the Soviet legacy, Russia, despite its present relative weakness, will always have Super Power ambitions.

As time moved on, Russia felt more and more betrayed by the West; by a cavalier and patronizing approach immediately after the 1991 Soviet demise, by the greed of some western investors during Russia's economic chaos, by NATO enlargement to the Baltics, by floating the (irresponsible) idea of potential Ukrainian and especially Georgian NATO membership, by our alleged manipulation of the Ukrainian elections leading to and after the Orange Revolution, just to mention main events and Russian grievances.

With this mind-set, Russia and Vladimir Putin arrived at their undisputable conclusion: unless they do not defend Russia's interests by force, they will never achieve the above-mentioned long-term goal. Russia has apparently concluded that the consensus on European security, established by the CSCE Final Act and the 1990 Charter of Paris, does not bind it anymore. "Russia today," as Wolfgang Ischinger noted in a May 2014 speech at the Ahtisaari Symposium of the Wilson Center, "looks less like a partner in managing global and regional security, but more like an adversary."[36] Revisionism is the best description for Russia's new foreign policy. This is *their* reality today ("Living in another world" as mentioned recently by Chancellor Merkel) and it is endorsed by a large part of the Russian population.

It is certainly different from our perspective. But if we finally accept that Russia was, is, and will be different, then shouldn't we respect their reality more than we did in the past? Or, if respect is impossible because of diverging principles, shouldn't we be able to understand Russia better?

Most of the 2006 Report's chapter 9 -- *"How should the Trilateral Countries Respond"* -- remains sound as a methodological recommendation. On the other hand, the changes occurring in Russia lead to further remarks. We have argued against the very nature of the "Putin system" and its complexity. Now it is the West's turn to be reprehended: for apparently not being sufficiently willing to examine Russia's drawbacks in depth; for continuously wavering between silent Realpolitik and resonating human rights promotion in Russia; for finding it difficult to comprehend Russian foreign policy; and for pondering over alternatives that often do not even exist.

The past 20 years of Russo/Western European relations have been a graveyard of good intentions and

---

[36] Wolfgang Ischinger, 2014 Ahtisaari Symposium Keynote: The Crisis of Euro-Atlantic Security," Wilson Center, Washington, DC, 5 May 2014.

overblown aspirations – for a "strategic partnership" between Russia and the EU, for NATO/Russia Founding Acts and Councils, for G8s and bilateral love-ins. The question of Russian membership in NATO was actively discussed during the Clinton Administration. This now sounds like a song from a distant past. Even before the Ukraine crisis, all of this activity had come almost to naught. But at no time since the end of the Cold War, not even during the heated debate over the Kosovo intervention or the Iraq War, was the atmosphere between East and West as antagonistic as today.

Russia has become defensive and isolated. Russia's obvious strength is in blatant contrast with its own feelings of mistrust, suspicion and its felt lack of respect from others. Strangely, Russia has no equal level friends, although relations had improved before the Ukraine crisis, notably with Poland. Former allies and partners – with the exception of Serbia - have more or less openly turned their back on Russia, and Russia has failed to win them back as reliable partners. Even the Eurasian Economic Union Treaty (EaU) signed by Russia, Belarus and Kazakhstan on 29 May 2014 is taxiing due to lack of enthusiasm from potential partners. This will not change any time soon unless Russia learns to express, more credibly, a sincere wish to cooperate with partners on an eye-to-eye-level, rather than in terms of allegiance or thinly-veiled domination. An underlying feeling of exclusion and encirclement by potentially unfriendly neighbours, combined with bad historical experience, might account for the present Russian mental frame.

The 2014 crisis over Ukraine is not a blip. It should not be a surprise. It is still possible for the crisis to further escalate, with potential repercussions on world political balances. The Ukraine crisis will not be the last aftershock from the sudden collapse of the Soviet Union. Talk of building a new security architecture in Europe is yesterday's issue.

Distance from Europe, Toward Asia

Today's "real" Russia keeps distancing herself from a "Europe liberating itself from the legacy of the past" as heralded in the 1990 Charter of Paris for a New Europe: one wonders whether the past has not surged back with a Russia moving ever closer to authoritarian Asia.

The evolution from Europe to Asia is the result of a long process that is explainable for historic, cultural and political reasons. The weaker the regime feels inside, the more rigidly it behaves inside as well as outside, towards its citizens and on the international scene. This reflex of self-defence has its origins in a Russian intellectual tradition (the Slavophil movement) that pushes the present "Masters of the Kremlin" towards authoritarian Asia more than democratic Europe.

To justify this evolution, Russia's leadership uses the emotional weapon of humiliation. "Beware we can move East as well as West. If you humiliate us, by not taking us seriously, we will definitely choose Asia." Dominique Moïsi still has in his ears this warning formulated to him more than twenty years ago by the then President of the Foreign Affairs commission of the Duma, Vladimir Lukin. Through her entire history, Russia has alternated between phases of rapprochement with Europe, and more globally, a West more in tune with the culture of its intellectual and artistic elites, and more "Asian" phases that were closer to her political culture. Describing the Soviet regime under Stalin, the philosopher of German origin Karl Wittfogel spoke of "Oriental Despotism."

This despotic temptation, which ignores any concern for the rule of law, has never been stronger than today, although it has been prevalent for the last two decades. Our older Russian friends evoke a return to the Brezhnev years. They are (and know it is a fact) listened to and controlled in ways that remind them of the communist era. Of course the freedom to travel abroad is an important conquest, but it is not accompanied with a corresponding freedom to think and express oneself freely. The treatment of NGO's that have representations on Russian soil, such as the German Adenauer or Ebert Foundations, not to mention local Russian ones - labelled "foreign agents, traitors to their motherland" - is totally unacceptable and constitutes one of the most frightening symbols of a regime that can only think of itself in a purely negative and repressive manner.

In spite of (or maybe because of) her energy wealth and the clout of her oligarchs, Russia exists as the country that says "No." It is as if Russia were afraid she would otherwise be forgotten. It is true that in international gatherings, China is mentioned far more often than Russia. But this is only fair. China is a re-emerging empire that creates wealth. Russia is a declining power that exploits wealth. While China was taking small steps in the right direction, Russia was doing just the reverse: big steps in the wrong direction.

The key explanation for this evolution is political: "Power corrupts, absolute power corrupts absolutely" Montesquieu used to say. All the more so when fear hides behind authoritarianism. Russian power is deeply aware of its weakness and of the fact that even beyond cities like Moscow and St. Petersburg, one can find a middle-class that is increasingly expressing democratic demands. The weapons of international humiliation and nationalist appeal may not always suffice.

In the mid-1990's, western diplomacy towards Russia could be summarized as follows: "let's engage her if we can, let's contain her if we must." Obviously engagement has failed, and so did containment. We need Russia, but Russia needs us (i.e. the West) even more so. From a strictly strategic viewpoint, the only threat for Russia comes from China, not the western world. Would Russia tolerate becoming the "little brother?" Hardly imaginable! And in the short term the only threat for Russia comes from herself. Russia seems incapable of accepting a simple fact: the greatness of a nation cannot be built at the expense of respect for its citizens, not to mention their happiness.

Vladimir Putin's Third Term

Since the end of the Cold War, for understandable reasons, the capacity within Europe and the Trilateral area for analysing and interpreting Russian actions has diminished. A synthetic analysis of Russia's current conditions and of its political and economical outlook must start from the presidential election of March 2012, when Vladimir Putin was elected to his third term of office after the constitutional interlude of Medvedev's presidency. In the months preceding and following the vote, significant events have occurred that still affect the Kremlin's policies and its relations with the West. An overview of these relevant facts may be of use:

- The electoral circumstances between November 2011 and March 2012 made blatantly clear how poorly the West had been assessing the role of Dmitri Medvedev. The outgoing President had been attributed an alleged autonomy and a reformist courage that he never actually had, conditioned as he was by a deal with Putin about the eventual handover of power. The misjudgement was particularly gross on the part of the United States, with Barack Obama who, before his visit to Moscow, referred to Vladimir Putin as a "man of the past";

- Mostly, but not only, in Moscow and Saint Petersburg, an urban middle class rose up and took to the street under the banner of the protest against electoral frauds (which certainly occurred, though they were not decisive). This is a well-educated class, versed in the use of modern electronic networks, which had never revealed itself so intensely and bravely before. The event excited western observers, but also misled them: the so-called "new opposition" was extremely varied in its political orientations, and had neither a leader nor an agenda besides dismissing Putin – in other words it did not constitute an alternative to the incumbent President;

- Nevertheless, the size of the protest marked a breach of the implicit "social pact" that Putin's previous two presidential terms rested on, when the Kremlin improved living conditions in exchange for social peace. As we will see, this seems to pose the most dangerous threat in the mid-long period to the President and his plans of getting re-elected in 2018.

In Spring-Autumn 2012, Vladimir Putin entered "phase two" of his new presidency – one mainly characterized by repression. We hardly need to mention the administrative measures and the laws passed by the Duma under indication of the Kremlin, ranging from increased penalties for demonstrators, to trials against less prominent protesters, to the well-known clamorous filing as "foreign agents" of NGOs relying on funds from abroad. The most significant aspect of this ongoing authoritarian turn is the mix of strength and weakness that, as in most of the similar cases, has been animating the man behind it. Putin's ascendency is apparently firm, but also potentially vulnerable – a concealed weakness that the street protests brought to light, although it is unlikely that these demonstrations will constitute the most vexing threat to the Kremlin.

Crisis in Ukraine

Underlying Factors

None of the parties involved has acted in full accordance with the rules of caution and realism that should underlie international strategy – especially when it comes to complicated, historically loaded geopolitical issues. It is no coincidence that Ukraine – the population of which is predominantly pro-Western in the West and pro-Russian in the East – did not follow the same pattern as other former members of the Soviet empire that joined NATO and/or the EU. The reason for this divergence was the awareness that Ukraine's "recruitment" would have sparked Russia's hostility, which considers the country not only a major economic partner, but also the centuries-old birthplace of its civilization and religion. Only one attempt was made, in 2008, promoted by President George W. Bush, to offer the NATO Membership Action Plan (MAP) to Ukraine and Georgia. Yet, Moscow's immediate opposition and, in particular, the doubts raised by European allies, resulted in an indefinite suspension of the project.

During recent events, the EU did not manage the situation well. It created excessive expectations on the side of Ukrainian people, and, at the same time, was not decisive enough to tell Ukrainian President Victor Yanukovych to stop his "cat and mouse game" just before turning Europe's proposals down in the autumn of 2013.

European governments have struggled to form a common view. To be effective, any European strategy needs to start with a shared understanding of the factors underlying the crisis. Why did Putin annex Crimea? Was this, as some have argued, part of a grand design by a resurgent Russia to restore the Soviet Union? Or was it an act of desperation triggered by weakness rather than strength?

Certainly Putin, like almost all Russians of his generation, laments the collapse of the Soviet Union, but not of Communism. That should surprise no one. He once remarked that anyone who had a heart should regret the USSR's collapse, but that anyone who had a head should know that it could not be put back together.

Significantly, in his Kremlin speech of 18 March 2014, Putin spoke of the "culture, civilization and values that unite the peoples of Russia, Ukraine and Belarus," picking out just these three of the 15 ex-Soviet states. The states of Central Asia, the Southern Caucasus, and even the Baltic, are recognizably "foreign." Russia will wish to exert a powerful influence over them and limit the influence of the West. Where there are significant numbers of ethnic Russians – in Moldova, Latvia, Estonia and Kazakhstan – it will use the minority communities as a means of leverage, asserting a right to protect. Ukraine and Belarus, however, are seen in a different light, not as "foreign" but as parts of the historical core of the Russian motherland, occupying large swathes of territory buffering Russia from the West. While their notional sovereignty can be tolerated, maintaining a hold over them and preventing them from becoming part of a Western "camp" is seen by Russian policy-makers, and especially by the national security establishment, as an existential question. This has been the consistent view, not just of Putin, but also of those who have held power since 1991.

Against this background, the first strategic miscalculation in the Ukraine crisis has to be pinned down on Vladimir Putin, and lies in his project of establishing a "Eurasian Union." The goal of this project is not, as some in the West fear, "to recreate the USSR," but rather, to expand Russia's sphere of influence to a number of allied or neutral countries. The Eurasian Union is designed to compensate, by some means, Moscow, for the EU and NATO's eastward advance in the wake of the USSR's collapse. Russia has apparently decided to regard NATO and the EU as organizations that stand in the way of a Eurasian Union. Clearly, without Ukraine, such a project would not make much sense; it is for this reason that the Kremlin responded to the EU's offer to Kiev of an Association Agreement with alternative economic schemes, but also with threats.

On the other hand, when the Association Agreement was ready for signature in November 2013, the EU assigned to it a negligible 600 million euro budget, demanding, in addition, reforms that were politically highly delicate (i.e. the reform of justice administration, a particularly sensitive issue in a country that suffers from endemic corruption). The highly predictable result of this approach was to push President Yanukovich towards Vladimir Putin, who in turn promised as much as 15 billion euro and a very special price for Russian gas.

The choice of Russia by Yanukovich ultimately triggered the Maidan Square revolt. The protest resulted in a large, shocking bloodshed. Western countries, at that point, supported the demonstrations so overtly that Vladimir Putin – probably based on his KGB agent mind-set – came to the conclusion that their intelligence agencies were involved. In these strained circumstances, Yanukovich manifested once again his ineptitude, while President Putin had to follow the events from Sochi "stranded" as he was by the Olympic Games.

At the height of the crisis, the "Weimar Triangle" countries – Germany, Poland, and France -- brokered an agreement between Yanukovich and the three leaders of the political opposition, witnessed by Russia, that the Parties signed on 21 February 2014: "The Foreign Ministers of France, Germany, Poland and the Special Representative of the President of the Russian Federation call for an immediate end to all violence and confrontation." The agreement has the names of Yanokovych and opposition leaders Vitaly Klitschko, Oleh Tiahnybok and Arseniy Yatsenyuk as signees, as well as Poland's Radoslaw Sikorski, Germany's Frank-Walter Steinmeier, France's Laurent Fabius and Russia's Vladimir Lukin as witnesses.

The three European foreign ministers of the "Weimar Triangle" informally accepted responsibility for its implementation, just to observe helplessly as the Maidan radicals broke the deal a few hours. President Yanukovich's bolt abroad to Rostov/Don in Russia brought it to a standstill. This gave Vladimir Putin a pretext for action he could only have dreamt about. We all underestimated how deeply Russia felt wounded and how determined it was to act.

President Putin kept quiet for a few days after the end of the Olympic Games, but when the short interlude was over, his reaction came about as could and should have been expected. Twenty-three years after it ceased being part of Russia/USSR, Crimea was seized by Russian armed forces under the guise of local self-defence forces. Over a few days, the Crimean population – for the most part ethnic Russian – voted in a mockery of a referendum in favour of the annexation to Russia.

Clearly this was a blatant violation of Ukraine's territorial integrity and of international law – not only the UN Charter, but also the NATO-Russia Founding Act, and the December 1994 Budapest Memorandum, which guaranteed the territorial integrity and political independence of Ukraine, Belarus, and Kazakhstan, in exchange for Kiev's decision to give up the world's third largest nuclear weapons stockpile, as well as other multilateral and bilateral obligations. Nor can it be condoned against the backdrop of western policy. In Ischinger's words:

> The claim that this is a justified Russian reaction to years of Western broken promises does not survive closer scrutiny. Assumed or perceived promises do not establish obligations under international law. Russia cannot present a single document demonstrating a NATO commitment or a U.S. commitment precluding membership in NATO of former Warsaw Pact countries. Of course, that does not mean the West has necessarily always done the right and prudent thing. But that's a completely different point.[37]

---

[37] *Ibid*

Yet international law has proved in many occasions, both in Russia and in the United States, to be flexible when faced with strong political will or strong interests perceived as "national interests." The consequences of the 2008 war in Georgia are today not recognised but de facto accepted by the West - to mention a close example - and nobody in western diplomacies believes that Crimea will come back to Ukraine, even if there is no public recognition of that.

Yanukovich's ouster and the Ukrainian decision to opt for an agreement with the EU rather than a Russia-led customs union was an ominous defeat for Putin, evoking memories of his humiliation during Ukraine's Orange Revolution in 2004/5. In this sense, the Ukrainian intervention is not an element of a strategic master plan, but a series of desperate, opportunistic, ad-hoc decisions by President Putin to shore up his own position. Putin didn't begin invading Ukraine to bring it back into the fold, but to compensate for the colossal failure to keep Ukraine close to Moscow by relying on Yanukovich. Putin established a patriarchal-oligarchic police state in Russia; the now universally despised Ukrainian president-in-exile was well on his way to establishing one in Ukraine. Putin's great fear is that the people of a future, better Ukraine might inspire an entirely different unification with their East Slav brethren on his side of the border – a common cause of popular revolt against him and other leaders like him. The revolution on Maidan is the closest yet to a script for his own downfall. The invasion of Ukraine is a counter-revolution by Putin and his government against Russians and Ukrainians alike – against East Slav resistance as a whole.

It must be noted that far-right activists (The "Right Sector") played a relevant role in the protest, and that the Europeans were slow in trying to salvage, even after

Yanukovich ran away, the deal they had helped strike. Western governments ultimately failed to seize the opportunity to play a peace-making role in Ukraine's power vacuum, and that helped Putin's strategy.

Since its independence, Ukraine has been unable to manage its country properly. Embarrassing as it is for honest and fair Ukrainian democrats, neither the "pro-Western" governments of Viktor Yushchenko and Yulia Tymoshenko, nor the "pro-Russian" ones of Viktor Yanukovych and others, were able to achieve that minimal level of stability and performance as had Russia. Corruption was rampant (far higher than in Russia!), the role of oligarchs extreme, and macroeconomic fundamentals developing from bad to worse. This also includes western Ukraine, where the posthumous children of nationalists, who collaborated with the Nazis and committed crimes against humanity during the Second World War and immediately thereafter, were part of the Maidan revolt from the beginning and were instrumental in militant events in the very last days before Yanukovych's fall and escape.

Still, what we have observed in Ukraine was a genuine revolt against a corrupted government, triggered by its decision to turn down the EU offer to conclude an Association Agreement. It was not a revolt by nationalists and fascists only, as Russian propaganda claims. On the contrary, it was an expression by a part of the Ukrainian people (but just one part) to see the future of their country converging towards Europe and the ideals it represents, encapsulated in the Rule of Law.

Today, after the annexation of Crimea, is it too late to ask whether Ukraine is honestly ready for an EU Association Agreement, not to mention future membership?

After 1989, the countries of Central and Eastern Europe had transformed their countries incomparably more.

Short-Term Success, Strategic Failure

Putin's reaction -- annexing Crimea and threating to invade the Eastern and Southern regions of Ukraine -- far from being a smart strategic move, looks more like a desperate and opportunistic attempt to even the score and shore up his own position. It is not a demonstration of strength, but rather, a power play designed to hide Russia's strategic weakness. Instead of building a prosperous future, Putin is trying to rebuild the past, thus missing opportunities and alienating neighbours.

In the short term, to be sure, it has been a success. Putin's ratings have soared. By December 2013, his poll ratings had fallen to their lowest level, and a large majority of Russians were opposed to his standing for another term in 2018. But Crimea boosted his popularity rate to over 80%! Those who were grumbling about corruption and mismanagement are waving the Russian flag. Aided by a ferocious and exceptionally mendacious propaganda onslaught in the state-controlled media, Putin has whipped up patriotic fervour and portrayed this as a great victory.

But it is a pyrrhic victory, if a victory at all. Domestically, he has chained his coterie's fortunes even more tightly to reactionary and revanchist policies. In strategic terms, Putin has won nothing, as Russia already had strategic control of Crimea through its naval base. He has alienated Ukrainians previously friendly to Russia, while taking over a million ethnic Russians in Crimea off the Ukrainian electoral roll. Russia has acquired an expensive burden in Crimea, including 300,000 potentially mutinous Tatars. Putin has created another precedent after

Abkhazia and South Ossetia, which will not be lost on dissident nationalities within Russia. Moscow is embarrassingly isolated in the world and has squandered an enormous amount of trust and goodwill.

The price Putin will pay for his aggressive stance on Ukraine is staggering. Given the capital flight from Russia and the investment plans of many foreign companies that are now being reviewed or cancelled altogether, the negatives may already outweigh the positives for Moscow.

Putin's Objectives

Putin can make a strong appeal to his countrymen, as he did on 18 March, rooted in the defence and restoration of Russia's historic "greatness." But given that he abandoned reform in 2004, his actions have never suggested that he is over-concerned about the long-term interests of the Russian people. His principal objective over the past decade has appeared to be to retain power and maximise the control that he and his associates wield over the government and economic resources of Russia, more to their own benefit than to the general well-being. His handling of Ukraine accords with that.

Russia's clear objective is to destabilise the fragile Ukrainian interim government by all available means – the threat of invasion, economic pressure, "active measures" of propaganda and agitation – while spelling out the terms of surrender: formation of a "legitimate" government (one better disposed towards Russia); Ukrainian "neutrality" (no EU or NATO membership); and revision of the constitution to create a federal state. Plus, of course, acceptance of Russia's annexation of Crimea and unilateral abrogation of both the 1994 Budapest Memorandum and the agreement on bases in Crimea.

While the possibility of a deeper invasion into Ukraine cannot be ruled out, the downside for Russia would be huge and the upside of dubious value. Logic (not always the best guide) suggests that a more attractive policy for Russia would be to sustain the threat and pressure until Kyiv capitulates and sues for peace on Moscow's terms. Given, from Moscow's view, that, "an unstable Ukraine, unable to reform, is preferable to one that moves towards the EU and the West," Ischinger assesses that, "even if the current crisis does not escalate much further, we may be looking at many months, possibly years, of political and societal crisis and violent unrest in Ukraine."[38]

A New Cold War?

In his first term, Putin worked energetically to rebuild relations with the West after the rupture of the later Yeltsin years, and Western leaders responded in kind. Since the Orange Revolution, however, he has taken an increasingly hostile line, portraying the United States and NATO as bent on the "encirclement" of Russia. Misguided attempts by some within NATO to promote Membership Action Plans for Ukraine and Georgia in 2007-08 played into Putin's paranoid narrative, which was given full voice in his speech of February 2007 to the Munich Security Conference. The 2008 Georgian conflict widened the breach.

The current Ukrainian crisis has not so much created a new situation as confirmed an existing trend. Any lingering hopes within the EU for a "strategic partnership" with Russia, or, in the United States, for a reset of "Reset," are now buried for as long as Russia pursues the course set

---

[38] *Ibid*

by Putin. Even the most rose-tinted spectacles are now cracked.

But this is not the "new Cold War" beloved of headline writers. Russia is not the Soviet Union, let alone the Warsaw Pact. It can meddle unhelpfully in Syria or Venezuela, and credibly threaten weaker neighbours; but it lacks both the will and the capacity to confront the West or to project long-range power. Its policy, of necessity, is essentially defensive rather than expansionist. Returning Russia to a Cold War footing would require the diversion of 80% of national resources away from consumer and citizen needs and into the military and defence industry. Short of a national emergency, the Russian people would not tolerate that. It is diplomatic self-isolation that Putin has imposed (against the wishes of the elite), not a renewed challenge to the West. In Ischinger's words, "Unless the Ukraine crisis is soon miraculously defused, we are probably looking at a long period of cold peace with Russia."[39]

After Putin

What lies ahead?

There is a fairly broad consensus among both Russian and external observers about the current state and direction of Russia. It is highly improbable that the present ruling group, often described as an assortment of competing clans associated with President Putin, will initiate a significant change of direction after 13 years in power: their interests point to continued defence of the status quo, and their strategic objectives do not appear to extend beyond retaining power, including over the commanding heights of the economy, for as long as they can.

---

[39] *Ibid*

Politically, Putin has boxed himself in. He has no succession plan. He cannot institute the structural reforms that might begin to turn the country around, because they would threaten his and his associates' grip on power.

There is no consensus on when a change of leadership can be expected; nor on the scenario that will bring it about. We might be looking at 2018, or 2024, or some other date within that approximate timespan. This all becomes highly speculative. We would therefore be wary of fixing our gaze on a particular date (2020 or whatever).

However, at some point the leadership will change. Most of the country's current power-brokers are in their fifties or sixties. Their careers were launched in the Soviet Union. Despite the present hiatus, a window will open for a future Russian leadership to create – if it so wishes – an entirely different set of relationships.

There would be real value in exploring what lies ahead for Russia under the successor generation and under the country's first post-Soviet leadership:

- What issues will confront the next leadership?
- What sort of a country will post-Soviet Russians want to live in?
- How will Russia's relations with her neighbours evolve?
- How will Russia fit into global politics and the world economy?

What may be useful is to look at some of the questions that will confront Russia in the post-Putin era, including those relating to issues where policy has effectively been frozen in the period of stagnation.

Economic Legacy

Vladimir Putin's future - as well as Russia's - depends on economics. No political-economic alternative to those who currently hold power is likely to emerge in the short term (aside from extreme and dreadful alternatives, like the nationalists, be they military or not). Aware of this situation, President Putin is trying to attract foreign investment (which he would rather not receive from China) by fostering a wide-ranging anti-corruption campaign. However, his efforts are ambiguous, and liable to raise suspicions in his own constituency, particularly among the "siloviki" -- ex military and KGB agents who, like Putin himself, now control huge fortunes.

Even so, Vladimir Putin's attempt reveals how unsettling Russian economic trends really are: without more investments in technology and modernization, the country's economy appears doomed, and the political repercussions might be extremely severe for the West, which strongly needs a stable Russia. The danger lies in the combination of a domestic economic crisis with a loss of status on the international stage, which might seriously destabilize Russia, all to the benefit of hyper-nationalists rather than pro-democracy protesters.

A new set of sanctions may endanger Putin's very position as leader. Consequently, he has every reason not to push his demands any further and just "retain" possession of Crimea, which Western governments have already quietly forgone. But he is a Russian and a nationalist, and the mixture is not at all a guarantee.

What would be needed for Russia to escape the oil curse and develop an advanced and competitive economy?

In 2009, Dmitri Medvedev asked whether Russia's future needed to be that of "a primitive economy based on raw materials and endemic corruption." Russia is no less dependent on hydrocarbons and other extractive industries now than it was a decade ago. Well over half of GDP is in the State sector. The number of small and medium enterprises – already low compared to other emerging economies – has been falling. Efforts by the State to promote and invest in innovation have produced only a few success stories. Research in science and technology has declined. Many highly educated and talented young Russians have left the country over the past two decades. Russia lags badly in the global competition for investment.

What social and economic legacy will the next leadership inherit? As President Putin has indicated, there are sectors in Russia needing heavy investment to bring them up to an acceptable level, including transport and power infrastructure, the public health services and education. On top of this, the State has to service huge bills for defence, the civilian bureaucracy, and pensions. If oil prices continue to fall as a result of shale oil and gas and other technological advances, how can the competition for shrinking resources be resolved?

Democracy in Russia?

To what extent do the Russian people want "democratisation" and "modernisation?" After a period of huge change, which brought hardship to many, they have enjoyed nearly a decade and a half of stability and rising prosperity, albeit unevenly spread. They will not wish to put this at risk.

There are those who argue that Russia has a centuries-old tradition of autocratic rule, and can only be governed in this way. Russia will not be able to balance its "otherness," the economic demands of both the whole country and of protracted vested interests groups, and its geopolitical ambitions, with the more general acceptance of basic democratic values that Europeans would like to see. The gap between smaller urban, middle aged and successful groups in society on the one side, and the much larger population group that accepted the authorities' adoption of conservative, Orthodox and nationalistic values on the other side, will continue to exist for decades ahead and, together with the geopolitical ambitions of present and future Russian governments, will remain a permanent source of tension between Russia and Europe. "Democracy," as we would like to see it, will not prevail in Russia. Wishes striving toward an ideal will not be fulfilled: Neither for Russians nor for us.

Others, however, argue that Russians are clearly dissatisfied with the way their country is governed – with the concentration of political and economic power in very few hands; with rampant corruption; with the highly uneven distribution of wealth; with the weak judicial system; and with the absence of separation of powers and independent institutions. There is a strong desire for better governance. It is particularly pronounced among the urban middle class, as demonstrated in the protests against electoral frauds and in the vote for Mayors and Governors. An increasing part of Russian society is asking for more freedom, less corruption, and the rule of law. What is more, the threat of an economic crisis impinges not only on the urban middle class, but also on the remote, rural parts of the country - the bedrock of President Putin's political support.

Some advocate a "Chinese model." Is there a "Chinese model" i.e. a model that can be exported, rather than one peculiar to the circumstances of China? The

Chinese system depends on a strong ruling Party, which is absent in Russia; and it is far too soon to say whether it will succeed in reconciling the tensions between a liberal market economy and an authoritarian monopoly of political power.

Which will prevail in the years ahead – the strive for the modernization of society, the ideology of conservatism, the visceral opposition of the Orthodox Church to liberalism, or the entrenched interests associated with the status quo -- is an open question. What sort of rules and institutions do the Russian people want? There is a strong desire for better governance. But what is not clear is how the Russian people wish to be governed. This is not something on which they have been consulted during the past two decades.

This leads to the question: Is the time approaching when it would be sensible to review the Russian Constitution? The existing Constitution, which gives sweeping powers to the Presidency, was adopted in haste during a national emergency. President Yeltsin's draft was debated for only one week by the Federation Council, and then rejected by the Supreme Soviet and the Congress of People's Deputies – leading to his forcible dissolution of the Supreme Soviet. It was then approved in a national referendum in April 1993. The experience of the succeeding twenty years suggests that the document Yeltsin forced through, which allows the Presidency to override all other institutions -- is a long way short of optimal. When a post-Putin, post-Soviet leadership comes to power, it might rationally explore whether the emergency Constitution of 1993 meets the needs of a more stable and prosperous Russia seeking to develop into one of the advanced nations of the 21st century. A properly elected, properly representative Constituent Assembly could be the focus for an inclusive national debate, which leads to the adoption, through referendum, of a system of governance and law that genuinely meets the needs and wishes of the Russian electorate, and provides the basis for a new national consensus.

External Policy Issues

In external policy, the future leadership will face choices, which will, in part, be influenced by the course it pursues internally. The geopolitical context will not be as it is now. Nevertheless, it is possible to delineate at least some of the issues that will continue to face Russia.

Europe

The Russian leadership seems to focus primarily on the United States and China as powers of reference, if only to preserve its global status: "Eye-to-eye" relations are restricted to these two big powers. Russia has little to no understanding, and a definite lack of positive attention, for smaller partners. Europe, in particular, appears to be of little interest and the EU's "soft power" profile is often ridiculed. The contemporary European concept of shared sovereignty finds no appeal in Russia. Classical security interests (including modern global threat perceptions) and the quest for rapid economic development take center stage. Hence Russia's playing of one EU member country against the others with a notable attention given to Germany as the single most important partner in Europe.

Do Europe and Russia have a common future?

Many dismiss this possibility outright (see paper by Dmitri Trenin: "Russia and Europe will have no common future"). This view has been dramatically supported by the Russian intervention in Ukraine and ensuing eruption of "patriotic" propaganda. The Russia that has emerged from these developments is not only a country that is pursuing a different economic and political course from the rest of Europe, but also a country that is actively working against European values and EU interests: neither a friend nor a fellow travel, but a challenger. It seeks to revise the current European order, and, more broadly, the global order. It strives to establish a Eurasian Union for which Ukraine would provide needed demographic, industrial and agricultural potential. Its domestic inspiration, a beacon, the new "Russian idea," is a mixture of nationalism based on Russian ethnicity and language, an imperial notion of "Eurasia," a socially conservative values agenda, and contempt for the western way of life. One only needs to read President Putin's March 18 Kremlin address to the Russian Parliament upon Crimea's "accession to the Russian Federation" to better understand motives and grievances. In the words of Norbert Röttgen, Chairman of the Bundestag Foreign Affairs Committee: "The foreign policy of President Vladimir Putin's Russia seems to be writing a new chapter in a book we thought we had closed a long time ago."

However, valid arguments can be put forward to the contrary. Trenin himself is at least ambiguous when he states that, "Europe's soft power remains its most effective tool vis-à-vis Russia." In order to take a more positive approach towards a common European-Russian future, it might be worthwhile to focus less on present Russian authorities, and more on the Russian people and their aspirations for the future. No government, in the long run, will be capable of resisting deeply felt popular sentiment. Every government is expected to deliver tangible results rather than stale hostile rhetoric.

Russians might not wish to become Europeans – fair enough. However, there is a considerably deeper understanding and appreciation for the "Russian soul" among Europeans than among the Chinese, Americans or Indians. There is a closer sense of cultural affinity between Europeans and Russians than with the other tribes of the global village. Russian singers, dancers, musicians, poets, writers, composers, scientists and researchers are respected and valued parts of European identity and vice-versa. Similar problems – maybe even fears - arise in both regions with regard to the integration of those perceived as culturally "different." Today, the European Union, not unlike the historical Habsburg Empire, manages to combine respect for diverse cultural and religious identities with a political technology to advance joint interests in a regional and global context. To the benefit of both Russia and the EU, the subjects of demography, migration, immigration and social integration could thus be interesting new agenda items.

Post-imperial Europe is an unequalled champion in transforming former foes into partners and friends. In the 21st century, this is a precious political expertise. Resolving disputes of all kinds through negotiation, rather than violence in political relations, are at the core of this European soft power expertise. This includes a particular regard and specific protective mechanisms for minorities. A positive attitude towards smaller states and their need for self-assertion, identity and independence are part and parcel of this new political technology. A quarter of a century after the fall of the Berlin Wall, countries in the East and South of our continent have all reasonably established or confirmed their respective national identities. For some, like Serbia, EU-membership is taking precedence over NATO-membership. This new development should reassure Russia and could provide a new perspective for others. It should, in particular, facilitate advanced economic cooperation such as a common free trade zone encompassing Russia, the Ukraine and eventually even Belarus. The Russian-Serbian free trade agreement proves to be no obstacle for a closer European integration policy of the Balkans or Serbia, in particular.

Ukraine and Belarus each have a distinctive geographical location. Both will realistically not become members of NATO in the foreseeable future. Demographically and culturally they constitute a natural bridge between Russia and the EU. Russia and the EU could and should contribute to the positive long-term social, economic, and political development of Ukraine and Belarus, without any open or hidden claim to exclusive influence. Competitive bargaining for influence only leads to stalemate and increases internal political tensions and rivalries. Infrastructure, health, agriculture, education, energy, market access, institution building and strengthening, science and technology – Ukraine and Belarus will need all the support it can get from its big neighbours acting jointly.

Ukrainians and Belarusians might in due time decide about closer forms of integration. Clearly, a broad domestic political consensus based on full freedom of choice still has to emerge. However, a free trade zone should not be considered a "political favour / award" but rather, a rational building block in the interest of all concerned. It would certainly not prevent Europeans from openly speaking their minds on issues such as human rights, freedom or democracy. Free trade has never been a "certificate" of maturity for a democracy or a satisfactory human rights record. As an example, Switzerland and China have recently concluded a free trade agreement. Nobody would interpret this as sign of Swiss "approval" of Chinese human rights standards. Nor would the EU's explicit goal of establishing a free trade zone with the Gulf Cooperation Council mean accepting Saudi Arabia or other partners in the region as flawless democracies.

The case of Moldova is different, its medium-term future similar to the Balkan states seeking EU-membership. Once Moldova has been re-united, neutral Austria might serve as a valid model for its future military security status. Moldova might thus join the "Balkan track" and exclude NATO-membership of its free will. Time has also come to address seriously the frozen or protracted conflicts in the vicinity of Russia and Europe. Turkey has already made some effort to contribute its share and should re-engage in the Armenian question.

At a time when a new balance of power is in the making in the South-East of the continent (100 years after the outbreak of WWI) and the Arab revolutions are shaking predominantly Muslim societies around the Mediterranean, the European Union and Russia should jointly renew efforts to support these transitions in a forward-looking manner. The common OSCE experience might provide a useful and uncontroversial toolbox in that regard. The current crisis serves as a reminder that the OSCE can monitor elections, send observers, and, under the Vienna Document, deploy military observer missions. Regional border management could benefit from the expertise of the OSCE Border Management Staff College in Dushanbe, Tajikistan, which trains border officers and promotes cross-border co-operation. The OSCE Office for Democratic Institutions and Human Rights (OIDHR) in Warsaw is active in the fields of election observation, democratic development, human rights, tolerance and non-discrimination, and rule of law. Over the years, ODIHR has developed what is currently considered the "gold standard" of election monitoring. The OSCE also provides a universally recognized code of conduct for the democratic control of armed forces, which some Arab partners might find helpful in their current situation. Furthermore, the political beauty of putting to use OSCE tools lies in the fact that these tools have been agreed upon by the United States, Russia and the EU. They thus flag the potential of trilateral cooperative instruments. Maximizing the use of available OSCE instruments is critical, from the current observer mission to supervising and monitoring the electoral process.

Russia will grow stronger once it gradually sheds its underlying fears and suspicions. The EU experience might, in turn, become a source of inspiration for Russia's urgently needed economic and social development. As a best practice example for the rule of law, the EU provides reliable rules for its citizens, economic actors and investors planning their respective future activities. Inevitably, rising living standards in Russia will increase the inner demand for a truly rule-based social and political system. The new Russian middle classes will push for the European way of life, including a growing commitment to ecology, sustainability and accountability. No economy can be successful in the long run without encouraging and fostering small and medium sized companies. Here again, Russian authorities might benefit from the EU experience in creating space for a dynamic productive "Mittelstand."

Today, Russia is at best a semi-democracy. Tomorrow, Russia might yet not be a perfect democracy. But as its authorities become less suspicious and distrustful, the space of individual and collective freedom will expand. Centralization and authoritarianism might then be substituted by a smart balance of power on several levels, eventually leading to more efficient governance. Russia will also learn to understand and respect the EU's institutional set-up, thus abandoning its craving for special relationships with single EU members such as Germany. The EU, in turn, will learn that its interest is not rivalry with Russia, but constructive offers for joint support of free and independent partners in the neighbourhood.

Despite the present hiatus, there is huge potential for business and interaction of every kind between Russia and Western Europe, to mutual benefit. Nothing offers more opportunities to Russia than a stable and close relationship with the EU. Just as Presidents Yeltsin and Putin reached out to Western Europe in the early years of their Presidencies, and were made welcome, a window will open for a future Russian leadership to create – if it so wishes – an entirely different set of relationships.

A fresh start could be made. The Russian leadership could consider, for example, that NATO is not only a great instrument of conflict prevention, but also, as Ischinger put it, "the most successful instrument of nuclear non-proliferation policy ever invented."[40] European countries ranging from Turkey to Germany to Poland might as yet be tempted to go nuclear in the absence of the NATO umbrella.

At the same time, we have to be careful not to pursue policies that might backfire if no agreement is possible. Unresolved tensions regarding NATO's missile defence project continue to worry the Russian government. Given the lack of trust on both sides, the risk is that – the lingering hope of turning ballistic missile defence (BMD) into a game-changer notwithstanding – the BMD project might turn out be a game-breaker. In this situation, further unilateral steps by NATO need careful calibration. This

---

[40] *Ibid*

includes steps in the direction of further NATO enlargement, which would surely provoke Russian reactions.

In Central and Eastern Europe, attitudes towards Russia are complex and often ambiguous: understandable caution prevails. There are political forces that perceive Russia as a principle danger that should be contained by any and all means. This is exacerbated by the fear that the mutual interests of both German and Russian business circles will win through at the expense of Central European interests. On the other hand, ever-larger parts of the population are disappointed by the political and economic transformation after the collapse of communism. Citizens are disillusioned by the deficiencies of democracy and everyday politics, by the European crisis and its indebtedness, and the ensuing impact on the region's economic performance. Europe did not deliver as much as was expected of her, and parts of society are turning their attention to Russia as well as other political and economic models. Consequently, Central and Eastern European society is divided on Russia.

It is important to distinguish who exactly wishes to see "his Russia in the future." Central European Czechs have a particular historical experience with Russia, as well as extensive trade and economic relations with the country, both strengthened and damaged by forty years of close cooperation within the Communist bloc. Czechs, Slovaks and Poles are Slavic people, as Russians are. There is a larger language, cultural and habitual closeness, compared to the rest of Europe.

Central Europe has a difficult experience with another mighty neighbour in the West as well: Germany.

Nobody regrets recent trends in Russia as much as Germany. As Ischinger explained:

> [W]e have been grateful to Moscow for over 20 years now, for participating in the decision to allow Germany to be united country again. And no European country has spent more political energy and, frankly, capital, and no country has been more engaged than Germany to create a lasting and constructive partnership with the Russian Federation. We have not forgotten the devastation, the horror and terror caused by the Nazi invasion in western Russia, and in all parts of Ukraine. Politically, historically, and morally, Germany owes it to Russia, to Ukraine, and to Eastern Europe in general, to be generous, to be open, and to help overcome past and present East-West divides in Europe.[41]

Nevertheless, there is one segment that is extremely pragmatic: the business community. Those who have either already penetrated into Russia, or see a chance to redirect their business toward the country because of Europe's economic malaise, are exerting increasing political leverage.

In the Ukraine crisis, the only available route to us beyond sanctions is negotiation, led by the United States. Here, we must be clear. If Russia were to claim political and military control beyond the west of Crimea, then bad times are ahead. We would have no other option than to "stand up and fight," quickly bolstering NATO military presence in Eastern Europe. The Baltic nations will be at stake, and the Baltics, "that's us!"

---

[41] *Ibid*

The United States

Mutually Assured Destruction, which underwrote nuclear stability during the Cold War, seems in recent years to have been replaced by Mutually Assured Paranoia. Just as the Kremlin has turned up the volume knob of anti-American invective, so echoes rebound from across the Atlantic. Republican Presidential candidate Mitt Romney went so far as to describe Russia, in September 2012, as "our number one geopolitical foe"; and numerous commentators have since defended his remark, citing issues from the Magnitsky Act to Syria to Edward Snowden. On both sides, the invective is more convincingly explained by domestic politics than by geopolitics. In the United States, President Obama is going to have to deal with severe political constraints, despite his public statements, manifesting a sort of new "Syrian syndrome." While there are real differences over Syria, it is hard to see objective reasons why the United States and Russia should now treat each other as foes. The relatively small amount of attention that the Obama Administration has paid to Russia testifies to a lack of real concern: Other issues have been of far greater importance.

Russia's foreign policy is flawed and makes mistakes like any other country, but it also endeavours to pay due attention to a series of "permanent" aspects that guides its action: national interests (also in the economic field); ambition to achieve great power status beyond the UN Security Council; the importance of the military; and the threat posed by nationalists (only partially overlapping with the military). Given this assumption, it becomes clear how mistaken it was to look for a solution in Syria while excluding Russia due to its differing views, only to beg for the Kremlin's diplomatic support shortly thereafter. As long as we do not understand how important it is to Russia to "get involved" (and the United States is the only one that can successfully do that), a risky dialogue of the deaf will continue.

Expert commissions like Carnegie's "Euro-Atlantic Security Initiative" or the Nuclear Threat Initiative's report on "Building Mutual Security" have proposed pragmatic steps, which could be taken immediately in the interest of both sides. There is no shortage of forward-looking ideas on how to enhance and solidify European security. We do not have to be best friends to continue joint work to overcome dysfunctional and costly Cold War doctrines and postures. Who would lose if Washington and Moscow reduced the number of missiles on ready alert, or dismantled at least parts of the nuclear arsenal, as President Obama suggested in his 19 June 2013 speech in Berlin?

During the Medvedev presidency, the Russian government presented proposals on a European security treaty. A future leadership in Moscow, less steeped in the Cold War, might well try a more constructive approach; and would probably meet a willing response.

The Neighbours

Outside the doorsteps of the EU, we have seen force used as an instrument of choice many times in the pursuit of national and nationalist interests. Since the 1990s, think of Bosnia-Herzegovina, Nagorno-Karabakh, Transnistria, Georgia, Kosovo, and now Crimea. Fear of military intervention is back with a vengeance, particularly in Eastern, Southeastern Europe, and adjacent regions, raising the question of whether existing borders are safe and will be recognized.

The 2006 Report observed that Russians saw the "post-Soviet space" as "their backyard, buffer zone, and zone of influence. To the extent possible, they wish to keep it within their orbit and oppose the gravitational pull of other powers."[42] Russia's relations with the 14 independent countries that were under Moscow's rule until 1991 are still far from a state of equilibrium. To a greater or lesser extent, they are ready to cooperate with Russia, but not to surrender sovereignty. A series of initiatives to build collective organisations has thus far produced little of substance. As the histories of other dissolved empires have shown, rebalancing relations between a former metropolitan power and its former territories takes time and needs generational change.

Can a strategy be developed to diminish conflict and instability in the North Caucasus? The region is a simmering cauldron. The present leadership has had some success in keeping the lid on the pot and containing spill-over, but appears to have no strategy for resolving the issues within it. At some point, the deep-seated problems of the region will need to be addressed.

China

Russia is not alone in having to adjust to the rise of China, but doing so will continue to raise very difficult issues. China is an increasingly important market for Russia's raw materials, and has the potential to be a much-needed investor in Russia, especially in upstream resource extraction. But China is also a neighbour with growing military clout, and historic claims to parts of the Russian Far East. This makes for an uneasy partnership -- one in

---

[42] "Engaging with Russia," 159

which no Russian government will wish to play the role of junior partner.

Key Points for a Common Strategy

It is quite easy to define the Russia of our wishes: This would be a country living at peace both with its neighbours and with itself. It would be a nation with a stable democracy, in which everyone would be free to pursue their own happiness. It would be a country that defined itself as a European country. It would be a power working to build sustainable relationships based on mutual trust, acting constructively in the UN Security Council, and carrying its fair share of the burden in securing international peace. And it would engage in stable economic partnerships, contributing to the welfare of all our people.

The "Russia of our wishes" is a close relative of the "European Union of our wishes": modern, diverse, innovative, pluralistic, economically successful, with vibrant and challenging civil societies and competitive private sectors, an anchor of stability and social justice, at peace with its neighbours, a post-imperial power of the future, linked in friendship to its partners small and big in the global village.

The hope is to see a future Russia – disregarding many internal tensions and problems – stable and predictable, with acceptable economic growth. We should wish to face Russian leaders who understand the need for balance between their domestic and foreign policies, and the policies and interests of both the United States and Europe. We must hope that Russia's economic decision-makers will pursue long-term policies that diminish the country's dependence on natural resources -- namely on oil and gas -- and increase the share of manufacturing and value-added production in general. This would enhance economic stability in the longer run. Proper policies to address unfavorable demographic trends will be crucial, especially pension system reform. And as Russia is a conglomerate of nations, its stability depends on how successful the Russian Federal government will be in maintaining the country's internal peace and integrity.

It is far more difficult, however, to explain how we can make this dream a reality. Is "engagement" called for, or "estrangement"? Only a few months ago, calls were made to treat Russia as a partner, not a threat. While it sounded minimalistic, it remains a historic achievement of the last two decades since the time when the Soviet Union was a mortal threat to Europe and the West at large.

Neither the United States, nor especially Europe, given their own domestic problems, will be able to influence internal Russian developments. The United States is exhausted from two unsuccessful wars in Afghanistan and Iraq, faces the challenge of China's rising global role, and suffers from domestic political stalemate. The West is considerably weaker than it was in 1991. It is especially the European crisis and the expected reluctance of some EU members to take a hard stand that convinces Vladimir Putin that he can act decisively and unscrupulously in Crimea. Mutual solidarity and unity are not Europe's strongest virtues, be it during the Euro crisis or under external pressure.

Even if Russia were to remain satisfied with Crimea, the West is not in an easy position. It has taken responsibility to provide massive financial injections (true, mainly via the IMF) into Ukraine, but where are the assurances that the country will be able to govern itself properly? And again, is it not too late to ask whether the idea of Ukraine's neutrality is subversive? The German Russian Forum, a highly representative body of mainly German industrialists, asked the same question. Ukraine is clearly not prepared for EU membership and there is immense homework to do beforehand. Shouldn't we have agreed with Vladimir Putin earlier to have a neutral Ukraine? Now we have to guarantee Ukrainian reforms and prosperity improvement by any means, as it is and will become difficult to make any concessions to Russia in the light of Crimea. The genie is out of the bottle.

Understanding our past mistakes and accepting Russian "otherness" should be a starting point for forming our views on Russia's future. The West must establish clear red lines when Russian transgressions occur, but should be careful to avoid unnecessary escalation. The EU has to resolve its internal crisis before it can look outward. The EU and their partners need to embed their actions in a clear and reasoned strategy towards Russia and her neighbours, seeking the widest possible international support. They should also develop better mechanisms for handling threats to the security and stability of Europe.

Thus, after years of neglect, crafting a Russia strategy must become Europe's highest priority. **What is needed is a strategy that would not begin with lofty aspirations, but would be based on a *realistic assessment of common interests and goals* -- a strategy that describes a place for Russia in the European architecture that is satisfactory for Moscow and useful for Europe.** Without a concept of such a place, Europe has little to offer to Russians, who in turn are unable to conceive of a role for their country other than that of a separate power without allies. It is not at all certain that Russia would react to such a strategy the way we want. However, there is now much for Russians to reflect upon. And much will depend on the younger, well-educated generation, which wants to live in a modern, democratic European Russia. A European Union principled, strategic and open for partnership with Russia will help this important country choose cooperation over confrontation.

The International Agenda

It is vital that the "West" works to maintain the widest international support, and refrains from any actions that might polarise the Ukraine dispute or allow Russia to turn it into an argument between Russia and the West. What is at issue here goes much wider than Russia's relations with Ukraine, or with "the West," however defined. In Crimea, Russia committed an open territorial aggression against a sovereign neighbouring state. Despite some simplistic sentiments flourishing around the world ("Crimea was always Russian, so what is all the fuss about?"), aggression it was and violations of international order must be opposed.

Russia has manifestly violated the UN Charter, in particular, Article 2.3 on the peaceful settlement of disputes, and Article 2.4, which prohibits the "threat or use of force against the territorial integrity or political independence of any state." This was recognised in the UN Security Council, where no member supported Russia's position; and in the UN General Assembly, where only 10 client and maverick states, some of which are themselves under UN sanctions, voted with Russia. If the principles at stake here are not defended and enforced, the risk of new conflicts breaking out around the globe are self-evident.

Over time, the pressure of diplomatic isolation within the international community will have an effect on Russia. Russia's rulers have always sought to be respected in the world as leaders of a "great" power, and to play a role in the resolution of global problems. Since the end of the Cold War, they have sought, with considerable success, to join the international status quo. President Putin's actions have now placed the Russian Federation's status in jeopardy. In an increasingly globalised world, to be isolated in the company of the likes of North Korea, Syria and Zimbabwe is not where Russia wishes to be.

Support for Ukraine

With Crimea lost, the most immediate task is to help Ukrainians recover from the collapse of their political and economic governance and prevent a further destabilization of Ukraine.

The West does not seek to "capture" Ukraine, nor does it have strategic designs on the country: it wants to ensure that the sovereign right of Ukraine is upheld and that Ukrainians are in a position to determine their own future. The challenges facing Ukraine are huge: electing credible political leaders, writing up a new constitution, and overhauling fundamentally its economic and social system, among others. For that task, Ukraine will require all the help from its neighbours. EU assistance should be comprehensive and generous in particular in the areas of finance, market access and integrating Ukraine into the European energy market. EU institutions should also learn the lessons of the flawed and ultimately failed "Eastern Partnership," exemplified in Vilnius last November.

Bolstering Ukraine's independence and right of self-determination should be at the centre of Western policy. This should not be done in a way that is anti-Russian or designed to exclude Russia: indeed, once Ukraine has been stabilised, her Western partners should encourage the

Ukrainians to work towards the gradual restoration of normal relations with Russia. Since independence in 1991, the majority of Ukrainians have wanted both to maintain their sovereignty -- and therefore their right to develop relations with other countries -- and to sustain their historically close ties with Russia. It is very hard to envisage a stable and prosperous future for Ukraine without harmonious relations with Russia.

The immediate issue, however, is to stabilise the situation and prevent Ukraine from collapsing or capitulating under Russian pressure. Initial steps to provide financial support have been taken. "Every carrot to Kyiv is a stick to Moscow," as Swedish Foreign Minister Carl Bildt recently said, but writing cheques is not enough. After two wasted decades, Ukraine needs a fresh start, and the "to do" list is daunting. A broad political consensus needs to be established beyond the 25 May Presidential election; presumably requiring new parliamentary elections, the formation of a national unity government, and possibly a review of the Constitution, on Ukrainian, not Russian, terms. The country must be weaned off corruption, split loyalties of civil servants, and oligarchic power, and onto independent institutions and the rule of law. It needs a functioning economy. The success of Poland next door shows that this is not an impossible dream.

If Ukraine is to have a viable future as a genuinely independent country, rather than an impoverished satrapy of an under-performing Russia, it will need a high level of proactive support – not just in money, but in the input of expert advice at all levels for a decade. Are the EU, the United States and the relevant international institutions ready to gear up a *"Friends of Ukraine" Task Force*? If a major commitment is not forthcoming, we shall face the prospect of deepening instability in a country that occupies a large area of Eastern Europe, and of continuing tension in the West's relations with Russia.

Dealing with Russia on Ukraine

The West must maintain a firm and united approach; and make clear that it will not entertain the Kremlin's ambition of a "Yalta 2" acquiescence of a Russian zone of influence, which limits the sovereignty of other post-Soviet states. It is not acceptable for Moscow to dictate terms to Kyiv; and the West cannot negotiate the future of Ukraine over the heads of the Ukrainians.

Crimea has to be treated as an outlaw territory. Not only because Russia violated basic international principles of law and security, but also because such a debilitating situation in a large European country constitutes a substantial risk to European security. Unpunished, Crimea risks becoming an inspiration for all those who think, "Why should I be a minority in your country if you could be a minority in mine?" As Ischinger explained:

> If we started to accept that borders are redrawn based on "well, this province used to belong to us," and so on "We have a duty to defend the interests of those who speak our language but happen to live in a different country," we would be in a world of deep and permanent trouble. Imagine for a moment where we would be if everyone in Europe applied that principle: The Germans, for example, would still argue that Alsace-Lorraine used to belong to Germany, and that Silesia is really not part of Poland, but of Kaiser Wilhelm's German Reich..., and so on, and so forth. And Austria might present a historic claim to much of the Balkans, and to parts of Italy, and so on, and so forth. A recipe for peace?

A recipe for disaster!

Nationalists and extremists in EU member countries to the north and west are already referring to the "Crimean option" in their statements. We must stand firm on the current position, for as long as it takes, until such time as Ukraine is able to normalize relations with Russia on an equal basis.

Persistent efforts, using both persuasion and sanctions, should be made to make Russia join assistance efforts for Ukraine. Its refusal to help, and its continuation of pressure and blackmail, will bring additional suffering and losses to millions of people, many of them of Russian origin. Russia must be made fully aware that its political and economic relations with Europe will remain impaired and that it will not be able to draw benefits from European integration and globalization so long as it doesn't normalize relations with Ukraine.

The purpose of the measures taken or signalled thus far has been to register strong opposition to the annexation of Crimea and, to the extent possible through non-military actions, deter the Russian leadership from intruding further on Ukraine's sovereignty. The West should keep channels of diplomatic contact open with Russia, to make clear that:

- Pending an agreement freely reached with the Government of Ukraine and the people of Crimea, a change in Crimea's status will never be recognised.
- Destabilisation of Ukraine would deepen the existing breach and trigger further measures.
- Our objective is *not* to wrest Ukraine away from Russia or to "own" Ukraine. We would like the Ukrainians, of their own free will, to develop good relations with all of their neighbours.

- While we shall never deal over the heads of the countries concerned, we are concerned about the risks to European security from instability and conflict in countries neighbouring Russia and the EU, and would like to develop more effective mechanisms to address this, with the full participation of all relevant parties and with full respect for the UN Charter and international law.

"Geneva I" in April 2014 defined useful principles but did not determine an adequate framework for talks with all sides. There was no consensus on a follow-up process, and the agreed points have not been implemented. As German Foreign Minister Steinmeier has proposed, the Geneva meeting should be turned into a "Contact Group" on Ukraine -- an ongoing process, based on the Geneva declaration, which could create a practical and comprehensive crisis management structure. Ischinger envisions the contact group on Ukraine providing "a basis for longer-term ideas about revisiting the grand vision of a more comprehensive European security architecture."[43]

We must recognise, however, that Putin is most unlikely to back down from his present course. This would leave us with little alternative but to stand firm on the current position, for as long as it takes, until such time as Ukraine is sufficiently stable to begin a process of normalising relations with Russia on an equal basis. It is up to President Putin to make the next move, and it is up to western diplomats to verify if the Russian proposal of a "Ukrainian Federation," with Kiev's consensus, can become the basis at least for a provisional compromise.

---

[43] *Ibid*

Pragmatic Compromise

Russian behaviour rules out business as usual. It is hard to imagine the Russian government offering concessions on those pressing issues today in which cooperation between the West and Russia is essential: whether it is Ukraine, Syria, or tactical nuclear weapons in Europe. Views on Russia have become more critical all over Europe. Europeans expect their leaders to stand up for their values and not close their eyes when their values are violated. EU relations with Russia have to rest on greater distance, discipline and caution.

We can't however ignore the fact that the EU and Russia straddle the same continent: both must cope with many common issues. A permanently divided continent is too depressing a prospect to resign to it. We should not seek to deepen Russia's isolation, unless forced to do so. This would be counter-productive.

As a result, a pragmatic compromise is probably the best way forward: While European leaders should criticize Moscow when necessary, they should also continue to pursue pragmatic cooperation with the Russian government and avoid any reaction that might be used to depict the West as the eternal enemy. Western governments should deal with the Russian government on a selective and transactional basis where it is in their interests to do so. We cannot afford not to keep trying, not to keep the door open, in simple terms.

A "Keeping the door open" policy is a second best, perhaps the only realistic choice, but certainly unable to address Europe's long-term needs and interests. At a more opportune time, Ischinger has suggested that a "Doppelstrategie" should be applied – a "twin strategy of denying Putin opportunities in Europe while pursuing a dialogue with him about cooperation in the interests of all." Discussions on "grand structuring initiatives concerning an all-encompassing Euro-Atlantic security community" should entail proposals on how to create "a more sustainable, more resilient, more crisis-resistant and more comprehensive European security architecture." The Treaty on Conventional Armed Forces in Europe and other arms control projects such as the elimination of short range nuclear forces should be revived. Ischinger also envisions the convening of another OSCE summit within the next three years. Building on the 1990 Summit – which produced the Charter of Paris on the basis of the Helsinki Final Act – the OSCE summit, with Russia's participation, would explain strategic objectives and lay "the groundwork for a credible and sustainable reaffirmation of principles of European and global security."[44]

Economic Cooperation

Russia is neither a friend nor a fellow traveller. It is a challenger that has two principle points of leverages over Europe: energy supplies and substantial European economic and business interests in Russia. But we the West might play a certain role in shaping Russia's future. This is especially true in terms of economic cooperation. In business, many Russian companies are well managed today, with a dynamic and very skilful leadership.

We must find our own balance in dealing with Russia in the future as well: balance between defending our own interests and allowing for Russian economic presence in Europe. This will be a tall task, but a necessary one. EU authorities should monitor the behaviour of Russian

---

[44] *Ibid*

enterprises on our markets and European investors should be warned about the risks of excessive engagement in Russia. Russia's implementation of WTO rules should be scrutinized far more closely. But if we demonize Russia and exclude Russian companies on political grounds, we will only deteriorate Russia's internal development. Europe should stand strong and self-confident in relation to Russia and accept its mighty neighbour as it is, allowing for as much economic cooperation as possible.

The very concept of sanctions should be revisited, as it restricts rather than increases the EU's scope of action. Sanctions, as Ischinger put it, "are usually the instrument you use in international diplomacy if you have no idea how to move forward. It is what you do if you lack better instruments."[45] Russian companies that help to support, or are owned or controlled by the current leadership, are obvious targets, as are those that are used as instruments of economic pressure. But it is neither in the Western interest, nor in the interest of the long-term development of a more cooperative Russian state, to cut off non-defence-related trade with Russia. Sanctions are unlikely to change Russian behaviour. However, there is a large array of business links, which give Russia an incentive to conform to international norms. Putin's policy of "fortress Russia" is not popular with the business class. Sanctions can be part of a comprehensive strategy, but not a substitute for defining strategic priorities.

However, assuming that President Putin were to shoot himself in the foot by launching new military interventions in Eastern Ukraine, or simply by encouraging social disorder in that region, the united West would most certainly adopt much heavier economic and financial

---

[45] *Ibid*

sanctions against Moscow. With two consequences: the acceleration of Russia's already visible economic difficulties, and, on the opposite front, highly divisive domestic debates in countries like Germany and Italy, which would be severely damaged by the stricter sanctions imposed on Russia. The ball is in Putin's court. Most of the "old Europe," including France and Great Britain, hope that the third level of sanctions won't be necessary. Domestic concerns are surely present in Obama's policy as well considering that the White House has been accused repeatedly of "weakness" during and after the Syrian crisis of 2013.

Doubts, however, about U.S.-German unity on Russia policy are overstated. It is true that stiffer sanctions would harm German companies more so than their U.S. counterparts given that investment in, and trade with, Russia is more significant for Germany than for the United States. But overall, the risk is manageable. Russia ranks only 11th in terms of market size for German exports. While Russia is Germany's largest gas supplier -- supplying 38.8% of imports in 2012 -- gas accounts for only 22% of the German energy mix, a figure lower than a number of Eastern European EU partners. The number of Germans that consider Russia a "trustworthy partner" has taken a significant hit. And even if the German public remains opposed to economic sanctions, Merkel is willing to spend political capital if necessary. Merkel and Steinmeier have already pushed back against export industry representatives and influential German business groups that are arguing against sanctions. Particularly in light of past previous divides within the EU, Merkel and Steinmeier are fully aware that another EU split would be tantamount to handing Putin a gift on a silver platter.

Some of the consequences of the crisis are here to stay regardless. Europe will have to recognise that recent events have major implications in terms of its energy security – even more so because the alternative of importing shale gas from the United States will still take several years before becoming viable and, in any case, would be more expensive.

Democracy and Human Rights

Can we in Europe and the West at large accept, with passive, cynical resignation, Russia's utter disregard for the rule of law? Doing so, would not only be for us a sheer violation of our values, it would be very bad for the future of Russia itself, a country that under Putin's guidance is clearly moving in the wrong direction.

We the West need a clear and consistent strategy on such themes as repression and the protection of rights. We need to start from our identity, that is, from our values, since Russians understand and respect those who stand by their principles. Ignoring the increasing pressure Russia is exerting on the opposition and on minorities would be morally indefensible, and at odds with the emerging majority view in the West on Putin's Russia.

One strategy would be to support categorically those "modern" elements of Russian society, hoping that they will succeed in changing Russia for the better, while at the same time limiting cooperation with the Russian government to a minimum. But alas, this would not help those who we would like to help. Putting pressure on the Russian government would probably tend to make things worse, not better. As the 2006 Report emphasised, "the Russian people will need to decide for themselves what sort of future they want for their country."[46] As elsewhere in the world, attempts by outsiders, however well-intentioned, to prescribe Russia's future tend to be resented, and therefore, are counter-productive.

This insight does not entail giving up our sympathies for the liberal Opposition. Open and consistent constructive criticism will doubtlessly remain part and parcel of our relationship. But it does call for an understanding that Russia's domestic conflicts will have to be settled internally and that we should be prepared to accept the results, as they come about and whatever they may be. It should also prompt one inward-looking European question. Why, almost twenty-five years after the collapse of Communism, are our own European values so little compelling for the Russians (and others)? Is our European way of life, our welfare state mentality, our over-regulation, and our political super-correctness indeed a model for the people living in our closer or more distanced orbit? Food for thought, perhaps.

The West – particularly the United States – should avoid over-idealist awakenings followed by extremely pragmatic attitudes. A proper line of conduct is the one followed by Germany: despite being Russia's main trading partner, Merkel is highly explicit in affirming German ethical-political values without suffering negative consequences.

Although it is increasingly difficult to penetrate the Russian media -- the regime is exercising tighter control over the Internet and social media -- determined efforts should be made to counteract the false narrative of

---

[46] "Engaging with Russia," 159

victimisation and Western hostility that the Kremlin is feeding to the population.

The recognition of a common destiny will pave the way to less suspicion and more openness on all sides. "People to people" contacts should be increased by engaging the young. The EU should urgently develop a special scholarship program similar to ERASMUS specifically for students from Russia, Ukraine and Belarus, and perhaps name it "CHEKOV," "TCHAIKOVSKY," or "DOSTOEVSY."

For similar reasons, personal travel by ordinary Russians and educational, cultural and professional links should be sustained and developed. Bridges to ordinary Russians, civic society, and the next generation of policy makers must be multiplied. Phasing out visa restrictions is the most effective way for the EU to use its soft power to the benefit of the whole continent.

Strengthening Europe

Putin has given Europe a great opportunity to foster cohesion and revitalize NATO. The longer term for Europe looks clearer, but is as difficult. If we have a challenger who happens to be our big neighbour and main energy supplier as well, we have only one option: to become economically and militarily stronger. We have to overcome the present European crisis.

We need to increase defence spending to match, to some extent, the United States. In Europe, we debate ad nauseam between pan-European and national powers, the Community method versus inter-governmentalism, while one area strikes out as obvious: the urgent need for a common defence policy and a coherent and united EU foreign policy.

Our future strength would also render economic sanctions obsolete, as a strong Europe will not have to resort to them to gain respect from a challenger. Energy supplies, which need to be diversified, are an exception. Europe's energy market must be rapidly integrated, perhaps through a European energy union as proposed by Polish Prime Minister Donald Tusk. But the present crisis will hopefully provide the much-needed wake-up call to Europe, especially regarding the absurd attitude toward nuclear power that is prevalent in some countries.

Recent events are nevertheless a reminder that, when it comes to security, the United States is still Europe's indispensable power. A reduction of the U.S. presence in Europe may force Europeans to take their defense efforts more seriously, but Europe is still not ready to take full responsibility for its own defense. We need the U.S. presence.

Conclusion

Above all, the West needs to exercise patience. The aura of Putin's quick win in Crimea will not last. Putin, like Brezhnev before him, has locked himself onto a track leading towards stagnation and failure. The realities of a mismanaged economy, further damaged by the consequences of Ukraine; flat-lining living standards; poor public services; and regional hardship; will return to the fore.

The West will be constrained in its dealings with the present leadership, with which its differences appear irreconcilable. Even if Western countries could all recommit themselves to a strategy of keeping the door open, Russian leaders will always be tempted – especially given the protracted European crisis – to push their policies to achieve the maximum possible, at our expense. Substantial structural changes in the Russian economy away from oil and gas are unlikely, unless triggered by a dramatic and prolonged fall of commodity prices. Demographic trends are dangerous, but not much has been done to cope with this dramatic issue so far. And despite a relatively calm period nowadays, it remains to be seen how much the Russian Federal government controls the situation in ethnically sensitive regions.

Yet, these are issues that only the Russians themselves can legitimately answer. It is our job to keep our eyes open and call a spade a spade if their fundamental rights are encroached upon, but it is also our responsibility to avoid making their situation worse: we would only help those whose "Russia of their dreams" still looks like a modernized Soviet Union. At some point the generations will change, and the opportunity to explore a more beneficial relationship will re-emerge.

AN ASIAN PERSPECTIVE

Yukio Satoh

Since assuming the presidency in 2012, President Vladimir Putin has taken a series of steps to underscore Russia's new overtures to Asia. In 2012, he visited China and India and hosted a summit meeting of the Asia-Pacific Economic Cooperation (APEC) process in Vladivostok. In 2013, he received Chinese and Japanese leaders in Moscow, visited Vietnam and South Korea and attended the APEC summit held in Indonesia. And this year he visited China in May on the occasion of the Conference on Interaction and Confidence Building Measures in Asia (CICA) summit meeting, and plans to visit Japan later in the year. He is also expected to attend meetings of the APEC, East Asia and G20 Summit to be hosted respectively by China, Myanmar and Australia.

Domestically, he created in 2012 the Ministry for the Development of Russian Far East to develop Eastern Siberia and the Far East and expand Russia's presence in the Asia-Pacific region. And, in his annual Presidential address to the Federal Assembly on December 12, 2013, he stated that developing Siberia and the Far East was Russia's "national priority for the entire 21st century."

President Putin's foreign policy focus on Asia seems to reflect Russia's growing need to engage in the thriving Asian economy and develop the country's long neglected eastern regions. Europe's weakening economy and Russia's confrontation with the West over Ukraine, particularly the annexation of Crimea, has added political momentum to Moscow's shift toward Asia.

It remains to be seen, however, if Moscow's new overtures are conducive to Russia's "broader participation in regional integration" in the Asia-Pacific region -- the policy objective emphasized in the Executive Order On Measures To Implement Foreign Policy, which President Putin signed in May 2012 at the beginning of his renewed presidency.[47]

As this paper argues later, the socio-economic development of Russia's eastern regions is a very difficult venture. Geopolitically, Russia has diminished its presence in the region due to Moscow's post-Cold War policy focus on Euro-Atlantic and Eurasian diplomacy. More conspicuously, Russia's low profile in Asia-Pacific diplomacy is overshadowed by the rise of China. Moscow's dependence on Beijing in its overtures to Asia would only make Russia's profile pale further in comparison with an already strong and growing China.

More fundamentally, although Russian territory covers the northern part of Asia and reaches the Pacific Ocean, Russia is a remote country to the Asians. Even those in Northeast Asian countries bordering Russia regard their neighbors as foreigners of European stock. Asians are generally not well informed on Russia's domestic situation. Nor are they interested in Russia's political evolution unless it affects their countries.

Russia's annexation of Crimea has made many Asians openly critical of Moscow's policy stance. At the UN Security Council, South Korea voted in favor of a resolution to deny the validity of the referendum on the status of Crimea. While Russia vetoed the resolution, China abstained, seemingly out of concern that Crimea's

---

[47] Official site of the President of Russia, 7 May 2012

separation by referendum might encourage separatist movements in Tibet, Xinjiang and Taiwan. Japan joined the G7 condemnation of Russia's violation of international law. Major ASEAN countries voted, together with Japan and South Korea, for a UN General Assembly resolution calling upon states, international organizations, and agencies not to recognize any alteration in the status of Crimea and Sevastopol. China and India abstained.

Yet, unlike the Americans and Europeans, who see the Ukrainian crisis in the context of their relations with Russia, many Asians are concerned about the geopolitical implications that the Ukrainian crisis could have for their region. They are worried about the possibility that Russia's annexation of Crimea might embolden China in its already aggressive pursuit of territorial claims. They are concerned about the prospect that Russia's confrontation with the West drives Moscow into a closer anti-Western alliance with Beijing, particularly against the United States. And some pundits are anxious that the Ukrainian crisis might further diversify U.S. strategic focus, weakening Washington's commitment to its announced policy of rebalancing to Asia.

From a long-term perspective, Russia's increased presence in the Asia-Pacific region, should it be realized, would affect the dynamics of the region's geopolitics. But it is too early to predict Russia's future in the region based on the country's current low profile.

Russia's Standing in the Asia-Pacific Region

—*Diverse Relations*

Relations between Russia and the Asia-Pacific countries are diverse. President Putin's Executive Order elaborates Moscow's country-wise foreign policy priorities in the region according to the following order: "deepening equal, trust-based partnership and strategic cooperation with China", "deepening strategic partnership with India and Vietnam" and "developing mutually beneficial cooperation with Japan, South Korea, Australia, New Zealand and other key countries in the Asia-Pacific region."

It is notable that the presidential executive order did not mention North Korea, although the more diplomatic Foreign Ministry's concept announced in March 2013, treated North and South Korea equally and stressed that Russia was "in favor of the non-nuclear status of the Korean Peninsula."[48]

Asia-Pacific countries' relations with Russia, too, are different from each other, particularly in the political agendas they pursue. **Japan**, for example, is pursuing the goal of recovering the four islands that are called "the Northern Territories" by Japan and the "South Kuril Islands" by Russia, and concluding a peace treaty with Russia, which has not been signed since the end of World War II. The islands have been under Russian control ever since Soviet forces occupied them in 1945 after "Emperor Hirohito's 15 August broadcast announcing the end of the war."[49] It is significant in this context that Prime Minister Shinzo Abe's visit to Moscow in 2013 has catalyzed progress in bilateral relations.

China, on the other hand, seems to be attempting to strengthen its partnership with Russia as part of a broader strategy to replace what Beijing sees as a unipolar world dominated by the United States with a multipolar world order . But, as this paper argues later, the two countries'

---

[48] *Concept of the Foreign Policy of the Russian Federation*, Official Site, MFA of Russia,2013/3/14

[49] John J. Stephen, *The Russia Far East* (P.241-2), Stanford University Press, 1994

relations are complex, and their future remains unpredictable.

South Korea needs Russia's cooperation to denuclearize North Korea and achieve the country's long-term goal of peaceful reunification. But Seoul, like Washington and Tokyo, counts more on Beijing than Moscow for political influence on Pyongyang. Russia's proposed plans to connect the Russian Far East with South Korea by rail, grid and gas pipelines through North Korea seem to be far-fetched as yet, but, if realized, would add to Moscow's influence on the Korean Peninsula.

It needs to be noted, in this context, that Russia, as the Soviet Union's successor, is not a party to the 1953 armistice in Korea.[50] Russia had also been "completely left out"[51] of the diplomatic process that resulted in the U.S.-North Korea Framework Agreement of 1994 to dismantle North Korea's nuclear facilities, as well as the subsequent agreement signed in 1995 by the United States, South Korea and Japan to establish the Korean Peninsula Energy Development Organization (KEDO). That the KEDO was to provide South Korean nuclear reactors to the North was a sharp reminder to Moscow of its loss of influence. During the Cold War, the Soviet Union dominated North Korean nuclear-related activities.

This history notwithstanding, President Putin's 2013 meeting with President Park Guen-Hye in Seoul produced many agreements aimed at "a quality increase"[52] of

---

[50] *Agreement between the Commander-in-Chief, United Nations Command, on the one hand, and the Supreme Commander of the Korean People's Army and the Commander of the Chinese People's Volunteers, on the other hand, concerning a Military Armistice in Korea*, July 27, 1953

[51] Chikahito Harada, *Russia and North-east Asia* (P.63), Adelphi Paper 310, IISS

[52] *Press statement following Russian-Korean talks*, Official site of the President of Russia, November 13, Seoul

economic ties between the two countries. The agreements underscored the congruence of the two countries' interests in many areas, ranging from trade, investment and finance to fishery and agriculture, from nuclear energy and space to youth exchange and tourism, from aviation, automobile and shipbuilding industries to security consultations and military technology cooperation.

Preoccupied with the rise of China in their immediate vicinity, the member countries of the **Association of Southeast Asian Nations (ASEAN)**, with the exception of Vietnam, do not seem to have any near-term political agendas in their relations with Russia. Leading ASEAN countries are engaged in military build-ups, often buying Russian arms. But the purchase of Russian weapon systems does not seem to have significant political implications. These countries buy arms from various sources, including the United States and some European countries.

Vietnam has increased in recent years its purchases of Russian weapon systems. It has also deepened energy cooperation with Russia and agreed to provide logistic support for Russian naval vessels at the Cold War-time Soviet naval base of Cam Ranh Bay. The country is expected to conclude a free trade agreement (FTA) with the Russia-Belarus-Kazakhstan Customs Union. Yet, these steps seem to reflect Vietnam's growing security concern about China rather than a strategic leaning towards Russia. Hanoi is balancing its relations with Moscow by establishing closer relations with Washington. President Truong Tan Sang's visit to the United States in July 2013 produced an agreement to "form a U.S.-Vietnam Comprehensive Partnership" aimed at promoting cooperation in broad areas, including defense and security.

India, with its non-aligned foreign policy and long friendly relations with Russia, participates in the groupings for dialogue and cooperation to which Russia attaches importance, such as the Russia-China-India "trilateral" consultations, BRICS, the Shanghai Cooperation Organization, G20 and the East Asian Summit. But this obviously does not imply India's strategic leaning toward Russia. New Delhi is also strengthening its partnership with Washington, as symbolized by the agreement on nuclear energy cooperation.

Further south, **New Zealand** is negotiating a FTA with the Russia-Belarus-Kazakhstan Customs Union, although, "following the events in Ukraine/Crimea", Wellington announced [53] that it would suspend the negotiations "in the mean time." **Australia**, on the other hand, enthusiastic about the export of natural resources to China, seems to pay little attention to Russia, the country's competitor in the export of energy resources. It remains to be seen, however, how Canberra's foreign policy towards Russia will be affected by the recent slow-down of the Chinese economy (and the consequent reduction of Australia's export to China), and the change of government from Labour to Liberal-National coalition in September 2013.

Given all these factors, cooperation between Russia and countries in the Asia-Pacific region would be better pursued bilaterally rather than multilaterally, at least in the near future.

It needs to be noted further that Russia's proclaimed vision of forming a "polycentric system of international

---

[53] New Zealand Ministry of Foreign Affairs and Trade

relations"[54] has little political appeal to countries in the region other than China and North Korea, as it seemingly reflects Moscow's anti-West stance and rivalry with Washington. At the same time, Asian countries, except for Japan and South Korea, do not associate themselves with the geopolitical concept of the "West." ASEAN, for example, has been aimed at checking big powers' influence regardless of whether they are in the "West" or not. Among ASEAN countries, Indonesia has been particularly open to multi-polarity in East Asia, but it is from the perspective of the country's traditional non-aligned foreign policy rather than an anti-West policy stance.

The United States, the mainstay of cooperation for peace and prosperity in the Asia-Pacific region, has paid little attention to Russia in its post-Cold War regional diplomacy. This has been due largely to Moscow's low profile in the region's diplomacy, to be described below.

From a long-term perspective, however, it would be most desirable, for the sake of peace and prosperity in the Asia-Pacific region, for the United States and Russia to develop a cooperative partnership in the region. Now that Russia seeks to expand its presence in the region, it is advisable for Washington and Moscow to start exploring possible cooperation in the region. Given that geopolitical conditions vary broadly between the Asia-Pacific and Euro-Atlantic regions, it is particularly important for Washington and Moscow to develop cooperative relations in the context of regional geopolitics, rather than as an extension of the Euro-Atlantic dimension of their diplomacy.

---

[54] Executive Order on measures to implement foreign policy, President of Russia, May 7, 2012

—*Russia's Low Profile*

What has been most notable in Asia-Pacific diplomacy for the last two decades is the absence of dynamism in Asia-Pacific countries' relations with Russia. Beijing's growing partnership with Moscow is an exception. This is the consequence of two trends: Russia's low profile in Asia-Pacific diplomacy and Asia-Pacific countries' generally limited and diverse interests in Russia.

Russia's low profile is Moscow's own making. Moscow's diminished interests and investments in Eastern Siberia and the Far East, and the consequent economic decay and depopulation of the regions, have deprived Russia of the means and opportunities (except for energy and arms exports) to expand its presence in the Asia-Pacific region, where economic interdependence through trade, investment and assistance is the primary focus of international relations. Diplomatically, too, Moscow, in focusing on Euro-Atlantic and Eurasian diplomacy, has paid little attention to relations with Asian countries except for China and India and, to a lesser extent, Vietnam. It was only with President Putin's new overtures to Asia, announced in 2012, which began to change Moscow's approach to Asia.

In the meantime, Russia has been overshadowed by China. The rapid growth of China's economy, coinciding with Japan's two decades-long economic stagnation and frequent changes of government (ten prime ministers during the past two decades), has drastically transformed geopolitical dynamics in the region, giving Beijing increased weight in regional diplomacy.

In terms of security, the rapid growth of Chinese military power has made the U.S.-China strategic balance the central focus of Asia-Pacific geopolitics. By contrast,

U.S.-Russia strategic relations are almost irrelevant to the regional situation, at least so far.

Against this backdrop, President Xi Jinping proposed, at his first meeting with President Barack Obama in California in June 2013, a "new model of major country relationship"[55] with the United States. And at the CICA meeting in Shanghai in May this year, he advocated a "new Asian security concept."[56] If the former proposal was seemingly aimed at assuring the United States that China, as a rising power, does not intend to counter the United States, the latter stressed that it was "for the people of Asia to run the affairs of Asia, solve the problems of Asia and uphold the security of Asia," pointedly excluding the United States. These statements together seem to suggest that China aspires to stand on an equal footing with Washington in the Asia-Pacific region, apparently with the ultimate goal of excluding the United States from exerting influence in areas of vital interest to China.

On the other hand, the expansion of Chinese military power, together with Beijing's aggressive attempts to enforce territorial claims in the East and South China Sea, adds to the security concerns of many countries in the region. Russia's annexation of Crimea has alarmed many Asians, who worry that it might embolden China in its attempts to change international borders by threat or use of force.

These countries have long regarded the U.S. force presence and the Japan-U.S. Security Treaty as essential stabilizing elements for regional diplomacy and security.

---

[55] Remarks by President Xi Jinping at the joint press conference with President Barack Obama at Sunnylands Retreat on June 8, 2013.

[56] *New Asian Security Concept For New Progress in Security Cooperation*, the Ministry of Foreign Affairs of the People's Republic of China, uttp://www.fmprc.gov.cn

The Japan-U.S. Security Treaty is the mainstay of allies' support for the deployment of U.S. forces in the Asian-Pacific region and the Indian Ocean. Their reaction to the announced "pivot" or "rebalancing" of U.S. strategic focus to Asia is favorable. If their support is generally tacit, Australia's agreement to facilitate the rotational deployment of U.S. Marines, and Singapore's decision to accept the rotational deployment of U.S. Littoral Combat Ships (LSC) offer clear testimony to these countries' support for U.S. rebalancing to Asia, as does the Philippines' agreement[57] to accept the rotational presence of U.S. forces in the country, announced during President Obama's visit to Manila this year.

Russia and China

—Strategic Partnership

In retrospect, the reversal of the Russia-China relationship from confrontation to strategic partnership has been a singular development. During the Cold War, Beijing broke with the Kremlin over ideological polemics, distanced itself from the Soviet strategy against the West, militarily confronted the Soviet Union over territorial disputes, and normalized relations with Washington through a dramatic rapprochement in 1972. It is therefore all the more striking that Russia now gives top foreign policy priority to the strategic partnership with China.

Yet, put in perspective, China is a natural partner for Russia. Sharing long borders, both need stable and cooperative relations with each other. Beijing shares with Moscow the strategic goal of creating a multipolar world

---

[57] The Enhanced Defense Cooperation Agreement between the United States and the Philippines

order, which is seemingly aimed at undercutting what they consider to be U.S. predominance in world politics. Like Russia, China abhors the West's interference in the country's domestic affairs.

Economically, China has been a valuable importer of Russian oil and advanced weapon systems, and will become an important customer of Russian natural gas exports through the Russia-China 30-year, $400 billion deal worth signed during President Putin's visit to Shanghai in May this year. A "strategic energy alliance,"[58] which President Putin plans to establish with China, would provide Russia with the means to counter the prospective reductions of natural gas exports to Europe following the Ukrainian crisis.

At the same time, China has the upper hand in bilateral energy relations. For Russia now needs Chinese markets for its gas exports more than China needs Russian gas -- the reason why the two countries' state-owned companies agreed on a deal at this time after more than ten years of negotiations.

To attain the gas deal, Russia seems to have made some conciliatory gestures. In addition to the rumored concessionary gas price, the deal is reportedly "coupled with a relaxation of informal restrictions on Chinese investment in the Russian economy across a variety of sectors."[59] Moscow is also said to be indicating that it might change its hitherto cautious approach to military sales to China in favor of selling the most advanced weapon systems such as the Su-35 fighters and the S-400 air defense missiles.

---

[58] President Putin's "Interview to China's leading media companies" on May 19, 2014. Website of President of Russia.
[59] Andrew Small, *UKRAINE, RUSSIA, AND THE CHINA OPTION*, EUROPE POLICY PAPER 2/2014, The German Marshall Fund of the United States, P. 9

It is also noteworthy that President Putin accommodated Chinese political interests in the wording of a joint statement with President Xi. For example, he publicly agreed this time to join his Chinese counterpart in opposing the falsification of World War II history.

Although the announced position was similar to the one issued by President Dmitri Medvedev and President Hu Jintao in their 2010 joint statement, the same common position was not reiterated in a joint statement issued on the occasion of President Xi's first visit to Moscow in 2013. The difference between the 2010 and 2013 statements was notable in light of the Chinese Foreign Ministry's unilateral statement, issued after the 2013 meeting, to the effect that President Xi told President Putin that the two countries should protect the results of World War II and the world order thereafter. This episode made it clear that China was more interested in the subject than Russia.

—Possible Conflict of Interests

The Russia-China partnership is not without potential causes of conflict. For example, Central Asia, which Russia seems to regard as part of its sphere of influence, is becoming ground for a tug-of-war between the two countries. China is increasingly active in trying to acquire energy supplies from the region without Russian involvement, as seen in its imports of oil from Kazakhstan and gas from Turkmenistan. China's trade with the five Central Asian countries has already exceeded Russia's trade with them. President Xi's visit to four Central Asian countries in 2013, when he proposed the concept of a "Silk Road economic belt" for cooperation between China and the Central Asian countries,[60] demonstrated anew Beijing's pull

---

[60] President Xi's speech at the Nazarbayev University in Astana, Kazakhstan, September 7, 2013

in the region. It must be noted also that the Central Asian countries are wary, albeit to different degrees, of Russia's influence. This is most tellingly demonstrated by Uzbekistan's decision to suspend participation in the activities of the Russia-led Collective Security Treaty Organization (CSTO).

China's growing interests and increasing activities in the resource-rich Arctic Ocean are yet another cause for Russian concern. The expedition of a Chinese survey vessel, Xuelong (Snow Dragon), to the Arctic Ocean, particularly its repeated passage through the Sea of Okhotsk since 1999, is said to have alarmed the Russian military, which regards the Sea of Okhotsk as its inland waters, reserved solely for Russian naval operations. According to National Institute for Defense Studies fellow Shinji Hyodo, some Russian naval exercises conducted in the Far East since 2011 appear to be planned to demonstrate Russia's preparedness to counter Chinese vessels' access to the Arctic Ocean through the sea of Okhotsk.[61]

It is also reasonable to assume that Russia is increasingly concerned about China's military capability. Russia's reliance on nuclear weapons, with a declaratory policy of possible "first use," as indicated in its military doctrine announced in February 2010,[62] seems to indicate Moscow's growing concerns about the growth and modernization of Chinese military power, including nuclear forces. That well-informed Russian non-governmental experts pointed out conceivable discrepancies between the widely-accepted estimate of China's nuclear stockpile, and the country's declaratory policy of "no-first-use," seems to

---

[61] Shinji Hyodo, *Foreign and Security Policy of the Second Putin Government*, Chapter 8, *Changes in Russia's Political System and Their Impact on Foreign Policy*, The Japan Institute of International Affairs (JIIA), March, 2013, published in Japanese

[62] Decree No 146, February 5, 2010

reflect the same line of thought.⁶³ Russia should also be worried about China's possession of intermediate-range ballistic missiles, the category of missiles Russia eliminated with the United States under the Intermediate-Range Nuclear Forces (INF) Treaty of 1987. It is reportedly alleged that Russia has tested a new ground-launched cruise missile in violation of the INF treaty.

It needs to be pointed out, too, that Russia's export of arms to China decreased sharply since 2010, although it recovered a little in 2013.⁶⁴ This could reflect Moscow's concerns about China's increased arms production capability obtained through reverse engineering. Or, this could be a consequence of China's increased confidence in its own capability to produce advanced weapon systems.

On the other hand, if Moscow decided to export advanced weapon systems (including those mentioned earlier) to China, it would signify an important shift in Moscow' policy priority from a long-term strategic anxiety about China to a short-term need for strengthened partnership with the neighboring power. President Putin's expected visit to Beijing for the APEC summit meeting in November could be an important opportunity to see how Moscow addresses the issue.

—Differences between the Two Countries

Russia and China are different from each other in many aspects, even leaving aside their civilizational and historical backgrounds and religious practices, let alone the ethnicities of the majority of their peoples.

---

⁶³ Alexei Arbatov and Vladimir Dvorkin, *The Great Strategic Triangle*, Carnegie Moscow Center, April 2013,
⁶⁴ SIPRI Arms Transfers Database

Economically, Russia, seemingly because of the readily attainable lucrative export of natural resources and arms, has so far failed to create the conditions for sustained economic growth, promoted by a broad range of modern industries. China, by contrast, is already a leading powerhouse for the growth of the global economy, although its economy is slowing down in recent years.

Politically, Russia has embarked upon democratization, even though its practice is rife with cronyism, autocratic trends, repression of the opposition, and human rights abuses. In comparison, China gives priority to the Communist Party's continued dominance over democratic politics. Unlike the Russian military forces, the People's Liberation Army (PLA) is the military arm of the Chinese Communist Party.

Diplomatically, Moscow's policy generally seems to be defensive. Russia is trying to retain the status of a global superpower, buttressed by its Permanent Membership on the UN Security Council and nuclear weapons, while solidifying its sphere of influence through the Commonwealth of Independent States (CIS) and the Eurasian Economic Union (EEU), starting with the aforementioned Customs Union with Belarus and Kazakhstan. The EEU is now agreed to take effect next January.

Beijing, on the other hand, pursues more ambitious goals, such as "the Chinese dream of the great national renewal,"[65] advocated by President Xi Jinping. China seems to be aiming at recovering its great power status and that which the country has lost to colonial powers ever since the nineteenth century, including the territories that China

---

[65] Remarks by President Xi Jinping at the joint press conference with President Barack Obama, June 8, 2013

regards as its own since "ancient times."⁶⁶ The escalating Chinese arguments to recover lost territories have begun to worry some Russians. Through the 1860 Beijing Treaty, Czarist Russia acquired the major part of the present Russian Far East, which includes Vladivostok and Khabarovsk, from the Qing dynasty.

In security policy areas, Russia is far more transparent than China thanks to the U.S.-Soviet/Russia arms control negotiations. By contrast, China's lack of transparency about its strategic goals and military capability, particularly nuclear, space and cyber forces, is increasingly a major cause of global security concern.

More fundamentally, given the prospect that China's political influence and military power will continue to grow, and that Washington and Beijing will eventually move to make their bilateral relations strategically stable and economically interdependent, it is not certain how long Moscow and Beijing will continue to see eye-to-eye with each other in their policy stance with regard to the United States. Nor is it clear how closely Russia and China share a vision of what they regard as a polycentric, or multipolar, world order and their respective positions therein.

As argued by Aoyama Gakuin University professor Shigeki Hakamada, it seems that Moscow's participation since 2012 in the U.S.-led multilateral naval exercises Rim of the Pacific Exercise (RIMPAC), are motivated by Russia's wish to safeguard its long-term security interests against China while prioritizing security cooperation over

---

⁶⁶ Statement by Chinese Foreign Minister Yang Jiechi at the UN General Assembly, September 27, 2012

economic relations in their recent talks with Japan.[67] Russia's absence in this year's RIMPAC exercises, which included twenty-three countries and, for the first time, China, is therefore puzzling, particularly since the reasons behind Russia's absence are not known at the time of this writing.

一Russia's Optimal Option

The most important challenge Moscow faces in its overtures towards the Asia-Pacific region is distinguishing Russia's identity from China's. Without such an identity, Russia will continue to be overshadowed by China in regional if not global diplomacy.

Yet, perhaps in contrast to the perceptions and expectations of the Russian government and people, it is already widely believed in the region that China is a growing power, while Russia is a declining one, even in global terms. Should Russia embrace political and economic partnership with China as a consequence of its strained relations with the West, it would be perceived as a tilt in the bilateral power balance toward China.

From an Asian perspective, Russia's European heritage and its geographical position connecting Europe and Asia are the two unique assets that Russia could cultivate for the sake of establishing its own identity, particularly in contrast to China. Indeed, the aforementioned Russian Foreign Ministry's policy concept asserts that Russia is "an integral and inseparable part of European civilization" and that "to promote creating a common economic and humanitarian space from the Atlantic to the

---

[67] Shigeki Hakamada, *the Putin Government's Stability and External Relations*, Chapter 5, *International Political Circumstances of the 2010s and Japanese Security*, The National Institute of Defense Studies, Tokyo, August, 2013

Pacific is the main task for Russia in its relations with the European Union (EU).[68] Accordingly, Russia's efforts to expand its presence in Asia would be better pursued on the basis of Russia's already deep and wide connections with Europe, even though their relations are now strained over Ukraine and Russian political trends.

Asia is indeed an uncultivated frontier for Russia's progress, but it is not in Russia's long-term interest to regard the region as an alternative to Europe.

All in all, it would be optimal for Russia to deepen relations with the West -- Europe in particular -- while reaching out to Asia. Plans to develop Russia's eastern regions would provide all concerned with opportunities to cooperate.

Development of Eastern Siberia and the Far East

—New Opportunities for Russia

The socio-economic development of Eastern Siberia and the Far East is emerging as an opportunity for cooperation between Russia and Asian countries, particularly those in Northeast Asia: China, Japan and South Korea.

For Russia, the development of these regions would provide important opportunities for progress, domestically as well as externally. Domestically, revitalizing the economy of the resource-rich Eastern Siberia and the Far East is essential for modernizing Russian economy as a whole. The potential for these regions to support Russia's

---

[68] *Concept of the Foreign Policy of the Russian Federation*, item 56

economy was demonstrated during the Soviet era, albeit under centrally controlled planning with coercive power to provide labor. Now that energy production in Western Siberia is reaching its peak, resources in Eastern Siberia and the Far East are more important than before.

The economic potential of these regions, should it be cultivated, could help reverse population declines and mitigate what is perceived to be Russia's potential strategic vulnerability in its relations with China.

Needless to say, the socio-economic development of Eastern Siberia and the Far East would have to include a broad range of industries, from mining, agriculture and forestry to manufacturing and service as well as high-tech industries. It would be logical, as a first step, to develop a range of "water-intensive industries" such as agriculture, timber processing, pulp and paper – a plan endorsed by the Valdai Discussion Club's analytical report of 2012.[69] Given the potential for the shale gas revolution to increase global oil and gas supply over the long-term, Russia cannot rely solely on the export of energy (and arms) to sustain the growth of the country's economy as a whole, let alone for the socio-economic development of the long-neglected eastern regions.

Externally, the development of Eastern Siberia and the Far East, should it be realized, would help solidify Russia's position in the Asia-Pacific region and connect the Russian economy with the thriving Asia-Pacific economy. Without this development, it would be difficult for Russia to enhance its profile in Asia-Pacific diplomacy, where economic interdependence is the primary focus of international relations.

---

[69] *Toward The Great Ocean, or The New Globalization of Russia*, July, 2012 <valdaiclub.com>

— Values for Asia

The socio-economic development of Russia's eastern regions would be productive from the perspective of Asian countries as well. It would increase opportunities for investment and business and, consequently, expand the space of Asia-Pacific economy.

To integrate the regions with the Asia-Pacific economy, at least three aspects of Eastern Siberia and the Far East could be cultivated. First, these regions could become steady providers of energy resources. Despite the prospect for shale gas to increase the energy supply in global markets, there is no doubt that Russia's export of energy will continue to be important for the further growth of Asia-Pacific economy as well as for the diversification of energy sources for importing countries like China, Japan and South Korea.

Second, these regions could provide land and sea (the Northern Sea Route) lines of communication between Europe and Asia. This would no doubt add to Russia's economic value for Asia and Europe. This would also, at least theoretically, provide the regions with opportunities to develop business and industries as well as municipalities along the lines of communication in both inland and coastal areas.

Third, these regions could expand contacts with Asia-Pacific countries through trade and business cooperation, cultural, academic and student exchanges, tourism and people-to-people contacts. Such exchanges and contacts would help expand grounds for mutual understanding and cooperation between Russia and Asia-Pacific countries, as well as for attracting foreign investment to these regions. After all, Eastern Siberia and the Far East are much closer to the Asia-Pacific region than to the European part of Russia and have a history of contacts with neighboring countries. Communities in the Far East have, despite the predominance of Russian population, multi-ethnic and multi-cultural traditions.

—Problems and Difficulties

These promising features notwithstanding, there is little room for optimism with regard to the prospects for the socio-economic development of Eastern Siberia and the Far East.

First of all, there are prohibitive natural conditions. They include the geographical and natural impediments to development, namely "Russia's size" or "distance" within the country, and "the extraordinary cold of Siberia," which Fiona Hill and Clifford Gaddy identified in their succinctly titled book, *The Siberian Curse*.[70] Natural conditions are harsher in Eastern Siberia than Western Siberia, so that the socio-economic development of Eastern Siberia would be more difficult and costly in the case of Western Siberia.

In addition, the infrastructural improvement required for the regions' future development would be greater than before. It would have to include transportation, communication and other facilities for industrial and agricultural production, as well as improved living conditions to attract people, such as health care, education and other amenities.

Second, the Russian Federation's policy towards the eastern regions, historically, has not been encouraging. A

---

[70] Brookings Institution Press, 2003

strong and lasting commitment by Moscow would be essential in order to promote the development of Eastern Siberia and the Far East. But the "disparity between rhetoric and reality," seen repeatedly in Moscow's attitude toward plans to develop the regions, darkens the prospect for implementing the programs advocated by President Putin. As Professor Hiroshi Kimura points out, "since 1996, we have been hearing pronouncements of such grandiose schemes and their revised and re-revised versions" -- pronouncements unrealized because of Moscow's failure to implement what it had promised.[71] Indeed, Moscow's political attention might move on yet again from the Vladivostok APEC Summit to other "projects" such as the World Cup in 2018 or the construction of New Moscow.[72]

Thirdly, doubts persist about Moscow's political preparedness to address issues of critical importance for the sustained development of the eastern regions. They include, among many others, the "redistribution of a considerable part of natural resource revenue from the federal to regional budgets"[73] as well as the rectification of the so-called "rent-sharing" system wherein, according to Kimura, those close to power benefit from rents obtained by the increased prices of natural resources at the expense of resource-producing regions such as Siberia and the Far East.

Another more fundamental issue is the long overdue need for structural reform of the Russian economy. The socio-economic development of the eastern regions would not be successful without the modernization of the Russian economy as a whole.

---

[71] Hiroshi Kimura, *Nesootvetstvie mezhdu retorikoi i real' nosti' iu: chto dolzhna sdelat' Moskva dlia rasvitiia Dal' nego Vostoka Rossii?*, Rossia: ATR (Russia and the Pacific), Vladivosok, No. 2, 2013. P. 15

[72] Dmitri Trenin, *Russia Can Pivot to the Pacific, Too. The Globalist*, September 7, 2012

[73] Vladimir Ryzhkov, Vladislav Inozemtsev, Ilya Ponomarev, *From a Colony to a Global Player*, Continent Siberia, December 27, 2012

—Russia's Own Responsibilities

While Russia would need cooperation from foreign countries and businesses in order to develop the eastern regions, Russia will need to undertake intensive efforts to make the country's business environment attractive for foreign investment.

Russia is still placed 92nd in the World Bank's rankings on the ease of doing business for 2014,[74] although the ranking rose from 112th in 2013. According to a survey conducted annually by the Japan-Russia Economic Committee of Keidanren (Japan Business Federation), Japanese companies engaged or planning to be engaged in business with Russia have a long list of requests for improved business environment, ranging from administrative and legal practices concerning trade and investment to custom procedures and tariffs, accounting systems to visa and working permits.

Russian authorities bear the primary responsibility for improving the country's business environment. Moscow's firm commitment and sustained effort are essential for ensuring the growth of foreign investment and trade. Coherent and coordinated efforts on the part of regional and local authorities are also indispensable. Hopefully, Russia's membership in the WTO could lead relevant authorities to embrace the internationally accepted norms for trade and investment that are necessary to make Russia's economic and financial systems transparent and predictable.

---

[74] *Doing Business 2014*, the World Bank and the International Finance Corporation

Political and social conditions cannot be totally separated from business. Democratization, the practice of rule of law, and the protection of human rights in Russia are important to attract foreign investors and prevent the flight of capital and talent. Moscow's efforts to address the social problems hindering Russia's modernization are also important to these ends.

How Russia's annexation of Crimea and strained relations with the West affect the socio-economic development of the country's eastern regions remains to be seen. But capital flight and diminished foreign investment, and the consequent stagnation of the Russian economy, are casting a shadow over the already difficult venture.

—Japan as Another Partner

Geographically, China is a natural partner for the development of Eastern Siberia and the Far East. Moscow and Beijing agreed in 2009 to a ten-year program of cooperation between Russia's Eastern Siberia and Far East and China's northeastern regions. Local economies in Russia's eastern regions are already heavily dependent upon Chinese commodities and immigrants, legal and illegal. But, as the Valdai report warns, cooperation with China entails "a threat that Russia will develop a one-sided dependence on China in important sectors of the economy, and later in politics".

Japan, equipped with advanced technology, finance and business expertise, would be an ideal partner for the socio-economic development of Eastern Siberia and the Far East. So would South Korea, as demonstrated by the agreements of cooperation announced by Presidents Putin and Park.

Japan agreed at the meeting between Prime Minister Abe and President Putin in April 2013 to work together in vitalizing trade and economic cooperation with Russia's Eastern Siberia and Far East, with a particular focus on "energy, agriculture, infrastructure and transportation." Equally significant is Japan's agreement to cooperate in modernizing Russia's transportation, urban environment, food industries, medical technology and pharmaceutical production -- areas in which Japanese technologies and practices are advanced. Cooperation in these areas would no doubt help to promote Japanese and other foreign investments in the eastern regions.

Since Prime Minister Abe's visit to Moscow, Japanese businesses and industries have more than ever, given serious attention to opportunities in Russia. Although they have become more cautious in the aftermath of the Crimea annexation, cooperation in agriculture and medical care is progressing and investment in energy-related projects is increasing. It is also noteworthy that voices were raised stressing "the need to consider" Russian ideas such as making Vladivostok the economic capital of Russia and constructing "smart cities" around it, and expanding academic cooperation with the Federal Far Eastern University on Russky Island.[75]

Nevertheless, as President Putin knows quite well, the Japanese government's willingness to cooperate with Russia is motivated, politically at least, by a desire to create a political atmosphere favorable to solving the long pending territorial issue. Although there is little direct linkage between negotiations on the territorial issue and the Japanese private sectors' business activities, progress on

---

[75] *Road Map for Japan-Russia Cooperation*, a policy recommendation made by a group of academics and experts led by Nobuo Shimotomai, : translation from a paper published in Japanese

these negotiations inevitably affects Japanese companies' enthusiasm for engaging in business with Russia.

The history of negotiations to date does not allow for any optimism on the prospects for a mutually acceptable solution to the issue. But Russia, like the Soviet Union before it, accepts that wartime military occupation cannot justify its territorial claim over the Northern Territories. It is commendable that Russia has agreed to find "the solution of this issue on the basis of historical and legal facts and based on the documents produced with the two countries' agreement as well as on the principles of law and justice."[76] Nevertheless, Moscow and Tokyo would have to make difficult decisions to make a breakthrough in the negotiations on the long pending territorial issue.

Need to Recover the Country's Credibility

Even before the Ukrainian crisis, misgivings have persisted, if only latently, in many Asians' perceptions of Russia. Asian observers were troubled by Moscow's coercive conduct in the post-Soviet space (Estonia, Georgia and Ukraine, to name a few) and the Kremlin's increasingly autocratic tendencies. The annexation of Crimea is alarming to many Asians, who were taken aback by the blatant violation of international law and are concerned that the Russian annexation of Crimea will embolden China in its attempts to enforce its territorial claims.

In Japan, Russia's continued occupation of the Northern Territories reinforces the country's negative image in public opinion polls – an image exacerbated by Medvedev's trips to Kunashiri, one of the four islands, as

---

[76] Tokyo Declaration on Japan-Russian Relations between the Prime Minister of Japan and the President of the Russian Federation in 1993 : provisional translation

President in 2010, and as Prime Minister in 2012. The visits -- demonstrations at the highest level ever of Russian control over the disputed islands -- have deepened Japanese doubts about Moscow's commitment to resolving the long pending question. Even after President Putin agreed with Prime Minister Abe in 2013 to accelerate negotiations for a peace treaty, Japanese public opinion remains skeptical about Moscow's commitment. The annexation of Crimea through the use of force, which demonstrated the Russians' unbridled nationalistic attachment to territory, only reaffirmed this skepticism.

Against this backdrop, it is essential for Russia to recover the credibility of its stated commitment to uphold international law if Moscow wishes to enhance its profile in the Asia-Pacific region, let alone globally. The propagation of international law and the norm of rules-based international relations are matters of global importance. Their need is acutely felt in the Asia-Pacific region, where China's irredentism is a growing cause of security concern.

Some Points of Advice

It would be advisable for Russia to do the following if Moscow wishes to engage productively in Asia-Pacific diplomacy and establish Russia's identity in the eyes of the Asians.

> ➤ *First, make every effort to improve prospects for the sustained growth of its own economy, including the socio-economic development of Eastern Siberia and the Far East.*

Structural reform of the country's economy and improvements in the business environment are critically important to attract foreign investment and facilitate economic cooperation. These measures are particularly urgent now given that economic growth is expected to dim in the coming years as a consequence of capital flight, diminished foreign investment, and strained relations with the West.

Geopolitically, improving prospects for sustained economic growth is essential for Russia to establish the country's identity, particularly in contrast to China.

> ➢ ***Second, beyond its on-going partnerships with China and Vietnam, strengthen political cooperation with democracies in the region, notably Japan, South Korea, Australia and New Zealand.***

Such efforts would testify to Russia's departure from Cold War-era logic. Moscow's recent agreement to hold security dialogues with Japan and South Korea is significant in this context.

Particularly important are the Japan-Russia "Two Plus Two" security consultations involving both foreign and defense ministers, the first meeting of which took place in Tokyo in November 2013. Russia is the third country after the United States and Australia (and before France) with which Japan holds the "Two Plus Two" meetings. For Russia, Japan is the first Asian counterpart (and the fifth in global terms after the United States, Britain, France and Italy, and before Egypt) for security meetings of the same format.

Cooperation between the two countries' forces on terrorism, piracy and cyber security, as well as exercises between the Japanese Maritime Self Defense Forces (MSDF) and Russian navy in both bilateral and multilateral formats such as RIMPAC, would help enhance the level of political cooperation between Japan and Russia. Defense cooperation, however, would produce only limited security cooperation between the two countries' pending a solution to the territorial dispute.

> *Third, participate in existing mechanisms for regional cooperation more earnestly and effectively before proposing alternatives.*

Moscow has been floating, since the Soviet era, the idea of creating a new security architecture in the Asia-Pacific region. A complex of multilateral mechanisms for regional cooperation – the result of an evolutionary process of consensus building, for different purposes, among countries -- is already in place in the Asia-Pacific region. These mechanisms promote, albeit in a step-by-step manner, economic, political and security cooperation in the region. They include the ASEAN-led dialogue forums, such as the ASEAN Post-Ministerial Conference (ASEAN-PMC), ASEAN Regional Forum (ARF) for foreign ministers, and the ASEAN Defense Ministers Meetings Plus (ADMM Plus), as well as the APEC Summit meetings and the EAS.

Given that all of these institutions include Russia as a member, and that they are all related to each other, it is important for Russia to participate in all of their activities in order to make them useful to Moscow. It is also important for Moscow to adapt itself to the evolutionary nature of Asia-Pacific diplomacy if wishes to be effective in it.

The Six Party Talks on the Korean Peninsula, in which Russia is a participant, might eventually become the core for yet another sub-regional mechanism for security and stability in Northeast Asia. But this is a remote possibility. Given the involvement of major powers in sub-regional geopolitics, cooperation in Northeast Asia will not develop in the same way as it has in Southeast Asia, where ASEAN has been a catalyst for increased sub-regional "connectivity" (in ASEAN's jargon) and closer integration among Southeast Asian countries.

> ➤ ***Fourth, cooperate with countries in the region in pursuing the broadly-shared goal of economic interdependence as well as human, or non-traditional, security against a wide range of threats and problems of common concern.***

To promote economic interdependence with Asia-Pacific countries, Russia can readily offer cooperation on energy supply and development, including in the peaceful use of nuclear energy.

Issues of common concern, moreover, could be wide-ranging, including, among many others: terrorism, piracy, natural disaster, global warming and drug and human trafficking as well as problems in the new dimensions of security, such as space and cyber. This would no doubt provide Russia with many opportunities to promote cooperation with countries in the region.

> ➤ ***Fifth, promote universal values, such as democracy, the rule of law and human rights.***

Unlike their North American and European counterparts, Asian countries are reluctant to put these issues on the agenda of official discourse with Russia. In addition to Asians' general disinclination to meddle in other countries' domestic affairs, the so-called "universal values" are still politically delicate issues for some Asian countries.

Nevertheless, Moscow's autocratic politics, often pursued at the expense of basic human rights, have put doubts in the minds of Asians, increasingly democratized, about whether Russia has changed from its Soviet past. Moscow's efforts to protect universal values within the country would be critically important in improving Russia's image in the Asia-Pacific region. Progress on this issue would also be constructive in attracting foreign investment.

> ***Last but not least, take initiative on global issues that would have significant implications for the peace and stability of the Asia-Pacific region.***

Given Russia's position as a nuclear superpower and Permanent Member of the UN Security Council, it is particularly important for Moscow to take initiative on two issues of global importance: UN Security Council reform and reducing nuclear weapons.

UN Security Council reform is long overdue. The Council's composition of five Permanent Members and ten non-permanent seats has been kept unchanged since 1963 in spite of the more than 50% increase in the number of UN member states during the last fifty years. That the Permanent Membership is monopolized by the five victorious powers of World War II, and includes only China from Asia, is simply anachronistic. Permanent members' veto often prevents the Security Council from discharging its responsibilities. These realities are undercutting the legitimacy of the Security Council and, in the end, the UN itself.

Twenty years have passed since the UN General Assembly began debates on the subject of UN Security Council reform in January 1994. As Russia attaches special importance to the UN, it would be appropriate for Moscow to exercise leadership in promoting the long-required reform. The 70th anniversary of the UN's creation in 2015 presents the most appropriate, albeit belated, opportunity to realize Security Council reform.

Equally important is for Russia to join the United States in efforts to reduce the threat of nuclear weapons. Beyond the cause of global nuclear disarmament, nuclear security is more important than ever for Asia-Pacific security. By reducing their stockpiles, the two nuclear superpowers would not only encourage China to join multilateral nuclear disarmament efforts, they would also increase political pressure on North Korea and Iran. Persuading China to make its nuclear strategy and force posture more transparent should also be a matter of common interest, not only for the United States and Russia, but for all those concerned about the threat of nuclear weapons.

Conclusion

As the Ukrainian crisis demonstrated, a global perspective is required for any engagement involving Russia, particularly since the gravity of the global economy is shifting to Asia. The Euro-Atlantic political cliché "from Vancouver to Vladivostok," defining the space for cooperation with Russia, is already too narrow for the global approach that is required to engage Russia, positively or negatively.

The geopolitical conditions surrounding relations with Russia vary distinctly between the Euro-Atlantic and Asia-Pacific regions. It is important, therefore, for all concerned, including the Russians, to understand contextual differences between Asia-Pacific and Euro-Atlantic geopolitics. Engagement with Russia, which belongs to both regions, could provide all of them with opportunities to do so.

A Retired Chinese Diplomat's View of the Ukraine Crisis

Yang Wenchang
President of the Chinese People's Institute of Foreign Affairs

■ **The Ukraine crisis is the product of residual Cold War mentalities.**

With the disintegration of the Soviet Union and later the Warsaw Treaty Organization in the early 1990s, the U.S. and Western Europe rejoiced at the realization, earlier than expected, of former U.S. President Richard Nixon's prediction in *1999: Victory Without War*. Whereas Central and South European countries embraced, one after another, Western Europe, Ukraine wavered between Russia and the EU. For over twenty years now, the EU has never abandoned efforts to lure Ukraine, through economic aid and EU membership, into breaking, once and for all, with Russia and embracing Europe.

■ **For Russia's own geopolitical security, President Putin will never tolerate Ukraine becoming a member of NATO.**

Russia today is no longer what it was in the early 1990s. Putin the Strong is neither Gorbachev nor Yeltsin. Russia is a country several times bigger than the EU's 29 member states combined. Although Russia's economy is not as developed as Western Europe's, it boasts unique growth potential. Russia's military strength is second only to the U.S. What is more, Russia has an oil weapon that scares

Central and Western Europe more than anything else. More importantly, President Putin's military actions to protect Russians in Crimea have won the support of most political parties in Russia. It can be said for sure that Putin will not back down in the face of sanctions imposed by the West. Neither coordinated U.S./EU sanctions nor U.S. warship exercises will coerce Putin into stepping back.

- **A new *Cold War* triggered by the Ukraine crisis is in no one's interests.**

First, Ukraine, located in the middle of Eastern Europe, is not only a link among East European countries, but also a region of immense importance for Russia's security in the south. Russia and Ukraine share a long border and, for a long period of history, were united as one country. If Ukraine breaks with the CIS and joins Europe, Russia's southern border will no longer be protected. This is something Russia cannot bear. President Putin's strong intervention in the Ukraine crisis and his push for a swift referendum to return Crimea to Russia were motivated by his interest in securing Crimea, a strategic military stronghold, since he could not hold Ukraine. If Ukraine at this point is forced to choose between the U.S./Europe and Russia, the situation will be destabilized further and Ukraine will risk another round of disintegration losing Crimea. Ukraine's economy will also be drawn into greater difficulties. A turbulent and unstable Ukraine will be extremely dangerous for the U.S./Europe, Russia and for its neighbors alike.

Second, for geopolitical reasons, EU member states have major economic stakes in Russia. If the EU breaks with Russia over Ukraine and the two sides end up in what western media are calling a "new Cold War," both of their interests would be jeopardized, with the costs far outweighing the gains.

■ What is the way out for Ukraine?

U.S./EU-Russia relations are at crossroads. Russia is not in a position to overturn the existing international order. The recovery of Crimea should not be viewed as a signal that Russia is taking the offensive against the U.S./EU. Rather, it should be seen as the breakdown of Russia's forbearance in reacting to the incessant push over the past two decades for EU and NATO enlargement to the very doorstep of Russia. Likewise, the U.S. and EU do not seem to be ready to fight a new Cold War with Russia. In this sense, he who "tied the bell on the tiger" should take it off. The U.S. and EU, being the ones tying the bell, should perhaps refrain from over-reacting, despite their strong rhetoric against Russia's countermove. Mutual compromise through sober-minded dialogue is an option with minimal costs to both sides.

The top priority for the moment is to find options for resolving the Ukraine crisis and avoiding further escalation. The solution should strike a balance between the interests of all sides. Both the U.S./EU and Russia should give the other side an out. The international community should urge Ukraine to set up a new government acceptable to all parties, i.e., one that may be a friend of Western Europe but not an enemy of Russia. The people of Ukraine should be allowed to decide by themselves whether or not to join the EU. To balance the interests of the U.S./EU and Russia, however, Ukraine's membership in NATO should be a red line. It is worth noting that an ultra-nationalist government in Ukraine will not be in the interest of peace and stability in the country. If the U.S./EU and Russia can reach agreement on this, it is possible to open a door to compromise by both sides.

It is my sincere hope that the leaders of the major countries in question will realize that Cold War thinking has become something of the past, and that military confrontation and sanctions are outdated. Those who can turn a crisis into opportunity after exhausting military deterrence are the wise men.

Russia and the Eurasian Balance: An Indian Perspective[77]

C. Raja Mohan[78]

Introduction

India's apparent tilt towards Russia in the crisis unfolding in Ukraine has once again underlined Delhi's enduring political ties with Moscow despite the significant improvement in India's relations with the United States and Western Europe. It has also reinforced sceptics in Washington who never believed India could be a credible partner for America on the global stage. A closer look, however, reveals a more complex dynamic emerging in India's relations with Russia. This paper reviews the evolution of India-Russia relations from the perspective of balance of power politics in Asia. It suggests that *the principal driver in India's policy towards Russia will be the rise of China rather than the nature of the relations between Washington and Moscow*.

The first part lays out the factors that facilitated the construction of a strong alliance-like relationship between Delhi and Moscow during the Cold War. The second looks at the more limited bilateral partnership that has emerged over the last two and a half decades. The third explores the prospects for India's collaboration with Russia in structuring a stable balance of power in Asia. The paper concludes with the proposition that *enduring tensions*

---

[77] Prepared for the Trilateral Commission's Task Force on Russia, April 2014.

[78] C. Raja Mohan is a Distinguished Fellow at the Observer Research Foundation in Delhi and heads its strategic studies programme. He is an adjunct professor of South Asian Studies at the S. Rajaratnam School of International Studies (RSIS), Nanyang Technological University, Singapore and a non-resident senior associate at the Carnegie Endowment for International Peace, Washington DC.

between Russia and the West in Europe will work to the advantage of China and the disadvantage of India. It suggests that the strategic priorities of the West and Asia may have begun to diverge and that the gap is reflected in the way they look at Russia. If Europe and America see Russia's assertiveness as a major threat, Asia worries about Moscow's lack of strategic ambition in the East.

Improbable Allies

India was the only democracy during the Cold War that built a strong security partnership with Soviet Russia. Delhi was also alone among the major Asian nations to nurture sustained political warmth towards Moscow. This might not look so strange if seen in the context of the regional alignments in the Cold War that saw the U.S. drawing close to the military dictators in Pakistan and the Chinese Communists. The partition of the Subcontinent and the Cold War engineered a profound inversion of the geopolitical equation between Delhi and Moscow. For nearly a century and a half before India's independence, the British Raj was in an extended rivalry with Tsarist Russia in what was widely known as the 'Great Game.' For the Raj, the principal security threat to the Subcontinent was the prospect of a Russian invasion through the North West. Calcutta (and later Delhi) was also concerned about the danger of a Russian incitement of the Subcontinent's Muslims, especially the frontier tribes, against the Raj. The emergence of the Soviet Union saw the deep division of the Indian elite's attitudes towards the Soviet Union. An important section of the national movement was deeply inspired by the experiment to build socialism in Russia. Others were deeply concerned by the dangers of communism and saw Soviet Russia as a potential destabilising influence on India. These political divisions were overcome by the consequences of Cold War politics on the Subcontinent.

Five factors helped bind India and Russia in a tight embrace: *First,* Nehru and his successors saw the special relationship with Soviet Russia as useful in containing the threat from the Indian Communist movement. *Second,* India was deeply discomfited by the Western anti-Communist alliance with Pakistan, with which the U.S. had a security pact in 1954, on the Kashmir dispute. The Soviet Union, by exercising its veto in the UNSC on Western resolutions on Kashmir, won much warmth in Delhi as a champion of India's territorial integrity. *Third,* India's inward economic orientation and the emphasis on building heavy industry saw the emergence of the Soviet Union as a significant partner. *Fourth,* the Sino-Soviet split coincided with the Sino-Indian conflict in the early 1960s and moved Russia and India closer in the geopolitical domain. The U.S. rapprochement with China a decade later made Russia central to India's calculus on regional balance. *Fifth,* the inability of Delhi and Washington to develop a military partnership, which appeared possible after the provision of U.S. support to India against China in 1962, made the Soviet Union the main source of India's military hardware and advanced strategic technologies.

Limited Partnership

Despite the confluence of these factors, India's non-aligned tradition meant that Delhi kept some political distance from Moscow. It refused to back Soviet proposals for collective security in Asia, was critical (behind closed doors) of the Soviet intervention in Afghanistan, and refused to turn the military relationship into a broader security partnership. By the 1980s, India was also conscious of the costs of too cosy a relationship with Soviet Russia in different parts of Asia, especially the Muslim world and South East Asia. Both Indira Gandhi and Rajiv Gandhi sought to bring greater balance to India's great power relations by reaching out to the West and other traditional partners in Asia in the 1980s. Above all, the last quarter century saw the slow but certain negation of many factors that compelled the Indo-Russian embrace.

If the Clinton Administration's diplomatic activism on Kashmir reinforced Indian concerns about U.S. regional policy in the 1990s, the Bush Administration's warmth towards India, its de-hyphenation of relations with India and Pakistan, its neutrality on Kashmir, and, above all, its vision of India as a partner in shaping Asia's balance of power, significantly reduced the salience of the Pakistan factor in India's relations with the West. India's economic liberalization and globalization from the early 1990s rapidly reduced the weight of Russia in India's developmental strategy. Despite the best political efforts on both sides, trade and investment ties have remained anaemic. The growing economic, political and military ties between Russia and China have turned on its head India's regional security calculus. In the past, Delhi saw Russia as a bulwark against China; today it is deeply concerned about the dangers of Russia beefing up Chinese strategic capabilities as part of its effort to acquire greater leverage with the United States. On the defence front, India began to access more and more weapons systems from the United States and the West, generating some concerns in Moscow at the possible loss of its primacy. While Russia is likely to retain its role as an important supplier of weapons to India, its special relevance to India lies in its willingness to supply advanced strategic technologies that are not accessible in the West, such as military nuclear propulsion and missile technologies.

As its own relative weight in the world grows and its relations with the West acquire greater depth, Russia is no longer central to India's existential concerns in the manner that it was during the Cold War. India does not view U.S.-Russian relations through the prism of democracy or human rights. Having seen the U.S. back dictatorships in its own neighbourhood, India has reasons to be sceptical. Even more important, realists in Delhi are acutely conscious, thanks to their own regional experience, of the great difficulties in maintaining any measure of consistency in the pursuit of 'universal values' in foreign policy. India cannot ignore the fact that Communist China gets a lot of slack from Washington on democracy issues relative to authoritarian Russia. For India, Russia's central relevance is its potential role in shaping the Asian balance of power.

Asian Balance of Power

Strong political ties with Russia are an integral part of India's hedge against the current uncertainties in U.S. policy towards Asia, especially the unintended outcomes of American engagement with Pakistan and the potential negative consequences of a political accommodation between a rising China and a weakening America. This simple objective, however, is complicated by shades of grey in Russia's own regional policy. The end to the U.S. combat role in Afghanistan and the uncertainties in U.S. policy towards Afghanistan and Pakistan after 2014 underline the urgency of India developing a regional strategy. During the Taliban rule of 1996-2001, India actively collaborated with Russia and others to counter Pakistan's growing influence in Afghanistan. While the situation is unlikely to be exactly similar, Russian collaboration becomes an important element of any Indian strategy towards Afghanistan.

In Central Asia, partnership with Russia has been crucial for raising India's strategic profile in the region, for example, through a potentially significant military presence in Tajikistan. Russia has been supportive of India's full membership in the Shanghai Cooperation Organization, but has been constrained by China's insistence on bringing in Pakistan. If riding piggyback on Russia has had its advantages, India also finds itself limited by the quest of the Central Asian governments for greater distance from Moscow. As in Central Asia, so in the Middle East and North Africa, India has often found itself on the side of Russia, for example on Libya, Syria and Iran. These convergences are tactical rather than strategic. Delhi's stakes in the Gulf and the Middle East are very high and its policy towards the region is historically rooted and has a cultural, political and economic dynamic all of its own. As India develops its engagement with Iran, Saudi Arabia and Israel, Delhi's aim will be to develop an independent foreign policy towards the region rather than to tail either Washington or Moscow.

India's interests in East Asia run parallel and there is no direct conflict of interest between the two in the region. In South East Asia, India collaborated with Russia in the past in limiting Chinese influence, for example, in Indo-China. Their current military cooperation with Hanoi underlines their shared interest in having a strong Vietnam that can emerge as an independent actor in the region. India's willingness to explore oil in Vietnam's waters claimed by China is based in part on Moscow's deepening naval cooperation with Hanoi. In North East Asia, India would like to see a more active Russia and has been enthused by the prospect of a long overdue rapprochement between Moscow and Tokyo. The Russian imperatives in East Asia, however, seem to be overwhelmed most of the time by Moscow's logic of aligning with China to counter Europe and America.

In the end, India's partnership with Russia will be significantly influenced by Moscow's approach towards two important bilateral relations—with Pakistan and China. Since the end of the Cold War, Delhi has worried about possible normalisation of relations between Moscow and Islamabad. It has managed so far to prevent Moscow from selling arms to Pakistan and establish an "even-handed" policy towards Delhi and Islamabad. Despite relentless pressure from Pakistan, no president of post-Soviet Russia has visited Islamabad. Preserving India's exclusive and special relationship with Russia vis-à-vis China is proving to be lot more challenging amidst the deepening strategic partnership between Moscow and Beijing. India is aware of the hidden tensions in the Russia-China relationship, but they seem relatively dormant as both of them seek to leverage collaboration with the other in their efforts to limit American power.

India, Russia and the West

The end of the Cold War liberated India from the constricting impact of the rivalry between the United States and Russia and allowed for a prolonged period in which India could rework its relations with all the major powers and focus on its economic development. As it comes to terms with the re-emergence of great power rivalries in the world, India is acutely conscious of one important and enduring geopolitical feature in its neighbourhood. The confrontation between Russia and the West has worked to the advantage of China and the disadvantage of India. Through the Great Game, when the full resources of India were being mobilised against Russia, Britain was willing to cede space for Beijing on India's northern frontiers because of its focus on containing the Russian threat. Much the same happened in the Cold War as the West facilitated the rise of China in order to isolate and contain Russia. Renewed tensions between Russia and the West in Europe might end up doing the same, and complicate the efforts to structure a stable Asian balance of power.

India would like to believe that it is in the interests of the United States, Europe and Russia to construct a stable equilibrium in Central Europe that would allow all three of them to focus on the emerging challenges in Asia and the Indo-Pacific. India shares the concern in many parts of Asia that strategic inertia and entrenched domestic interests will continue to distract Washington's attention away from East Asia to the Middle East and Europe and undermine the much heralded rebalance to Asia. Delhi, like the other Asian capitals, wonders about the depth of the Russian commitment to Asia. The ASEAN was eager to bring Russia, along with America, into the discussions on a regional security architecture.

Much of the region, however, is disappointed with Russia's lacklustre participation in the Asian security dialogue and its preoccupation with asserting itself in Europe and standing up against America. *Europe, which has never ceased to lecture Asia on the virtues of regionalism, seems unable to cope with the security challenges that have arisen in its own backyard. Europe, it seems, has neither the power to enforce the ambitious norms it professes nor the pragmatism to pursue more modest regional goals in collaboration with Russia.*

A failure to find mutual accommodation in the Western part of the Eurasian landmass would weaken America, Europe and Russia in the Eastern part of the great continent. For all three, the logic of economic collaboration and political partnership with China is gaining greater traction and the conflicts among them will only increase Beijing's leverage with Russia and the West. This in turn amplifies Asia's problems in coping with China's growing power. For China's Asian neighbours, the problem is not Russian assertiveness but Moscow's seeming reluctance to play an effective role in Asian security. A prolonged confrontation between Russia and the West in Europe will have profound geopolitical consequences for Asia by accelerating the regional power shift in China's favour.

India will find it increasingly hard to rely on Russia, as in the past, to limit China's power in its neighbourhood. The hopes, raised in the middle of the last decade, for a tighter strategic partnership with the United States to balance China have been dampened by uncertainties in American policy and India's perennial ideological confusion at home about the meaning and content of "non-alignment." India has also sought to deepen its engagement with China, but a political breakthrough on territorial issues has been elusive.

In the end, Asia's major powers, including India, might have to find their own solutions to the changing regional power play. Hopes for a cooperative security system in Asia, led by the ASEAN, are diminishing amidst China's muscular regional policies and America's strategic incoherence. Many smaller Asian nations may have no option but to accept Chinese primacy. Some of the larger ones, especially those with unresolved territorial disputes with China, will have to focus on building strong regional coalitions that might provide some hedge against Beijing's strength, Russia's European preoccupations, and America's apparent lack of a Eurasian strategy.

A RUSSIAN PERSPECTIVE

The first report of the Trilateral Commission on "East-West relations" appeared in 1986, when the initial steps taken by Mikhail Gorbachev as Secretary General of the Central Committee of the Communist Party inspired a sense of change on the horizon. The report's authors were convinced that this thaw in relations was temporary, driven by domestic political factors in the US and USSR. Two superpowers had reached a strategic stalemate and were forced to take steps of a conciliatory nature.

In this report, Gorbachev was no favorite of the West, but rather, a cunning politician seeking to drive a wedge between the countries of the Trilateral Commission. The authors predicted that East and West would remain rivals, albeit less intense ones. The USSR was still perceived as the enemy, whose strength at that point the authors clearly overestimated (or were cautious about underestimating).

From this position, the authors formulated their proposals for action. They were convinced of both the opportunity and the need for further arms reductions, but also insisted on a very rigorous approach. They welcomed the idiosyncratic "ceasefire" that had emerged between the East and the West in third-world countries, but were wary of Soviet influence in Southern Africa, which they feared would disrupt the fragile stability in the region. The authors saw a short-term thaw in relations between the USSR and the countries of the Trilateral Commission, but cautioned that this was only a tactical trick by the USSR to provide the socialist superpower with a reprieve in anticipation of renewed confrontation. Hence the key recommendations: negotiate the most advantageous conditions on nuclear arms reductions and achieve parity in conventional armed forces.

Security was priority number one. Issues like economic cooperation were not considered separately, but rather, were considered in the context of the socialist bloc's economic difficulties.

Certain observations in the first report were accurate and remain relevant to this day. They spoke about the interdependence of international processes and changes in the foreign policy priorities of both the USSR and the US. They viewed transformations in Soviet strategy simply as functions of tactical Soviet successes in foreign policy and US reactions to Soviet moves. In other words, they implied, albeit indirectly, shared responsibility of the East and the West in the logic of the Cold War. The West, in their view, should behave more proactively in this window of opportunity to contain the USSR as a potential adversary, and support it as a possible partner. Furthermore, the authors suggested that there was a need to exceed expectations in foreign policy due to the lack of trust in East-West relations and the high degree of uncertainty in predicting events -- not only for the Soviet Union, but also for the US.

Caution and apprehension predominated in the second report of the Trilateral Commission, published in 1989. Here, the authors exuded a slightly more trusting attitude toward the USSR, but they suggested that Soviet reforms would be long and complicated.

The authors had a clearer sense of Soviet weaknesses and believed that these weaknesses could be put to good use. They proposed further armament reductions and a policy of prying Eastern Europe away from the Eastern Bloc. The authors even asserted that the USSR extended too far in the Asian direction to be considered a European power. It seems that such a stance, which sought to isolate the Soviet Union as a regional Asian power, would have been highly unproductive and potentially conflict inducing, comparable, in a certain sense, to the isolation of Germany following the Treaty of Versailles. The authors of the report even seemed to accept the option of allowing events to develop toward a conflict situation.

The authors proposed five areas of work with the USSR. Three were related to military and political interaction, one concerned human rights, and the last one was devoted to economic cooperation. On the one hand, the authors declared the need for supporting Soviet market reforms. On the other hand, they openly proposed that the governments of their countries assist the USSR in overcoming its economic crisis in exchange for political concessions. The latter policy was adopted.

Rules of decency, the report insisted, should guide the provision of economic aid to the Soviet Union and Eastern European countries, including financial discipline and avoidance of exorbitant debt burdens for the recipients. This recommendation was not fully accomplished.

The authors of the two reports operated from the logic of a bipolar world: aiming, in the short term, to lower their own military and security risks, while minimizing the opportunities of its likely adversary in the medium- to long-term. This was both a strength and weakness of these reports. They failed to perceive the contours of a new world in which confrontation would cease to be the defining feature of international relations. If, by the late 1980s, the countries of the Trilateral Commission were more focused on partnership with the USSR, perhaps history could have turned out differently.

In the 1995 report "Engaging Russia," the authors for the first time began to speak of cooperation between Russia and countries of the Trilateral Commission, all the while noting that "cooperation" was perhaps not the most correct or appropriate term. Arms control remained the top priority on the agenda, but for a very different reason. Before, arms reductions were seen as a necessary means of limiting the military capabilities of a likely adversary; in the mid-1990s, the necessity of keeping WMD out of the hands of extremists (nuclear arms in particular) emerged as a key priority. The issue of a new European security architecture became more important for Moscow: the aspirations of Central and Eastern Europe and the Baltic countries to join NATO evoked a painful reaction. Bringing these countries into the sphere of influence of the Trilateral countries was accompanied by another aim – to explain to Russia that the engagement of these countries was not directed against it. In this the West failed, undermining trust between Russian society and the countries of Europe, America and Japan.

Importantly, in contrast to the multitude of political declarations during those years, the Trilateral Commission report bore no illusions about the democratization of Russia. To the contrary, having analyzed both the historical preconditions and emergence of Russian statehood, along with the events of the early-1990s, its authors came to the conclusion that if Russia did become a democracy, it would only happen years down the road. This did not mean, however, that the West should not support democracy in Russia. The report's pragmatic and well-supported position made it possible to avoid issues of values in relations between Russia and countries of the Trilateral Commission. To a certain extent, this position was more constructive in terms of the emergence of Russian democracy, as it entailed the endorsement of values, while actual negotiations were based on interests and economic benefits.

An important aspect of the third report is the fact that it was prepared during a difficult period for the Trilateral Commission. Europe, the US and Japan were searching for new common causes in the absence of a common enemy that had reinforced relations between these countries. The notion that the states represented at the Trilateral Commission could achieve success only when acting in unison was a very important idea. In the end, it could be applied in a broader sense: relations between the countries of the Trilateral Commission and Russia would be quite successful and effective if there was recognition of common interests and the need for collective efforts in achieving common goals. At the same time, successful interaction would be possible when the involved parties clearly recognize and respect differences in interests.

The fourth report of the Trilateral Commission, published in 2006, was more systemic than previous reports. For the authors, Russia was not some black box, but rather, a fresh discovery, every detail of which seemed a curiosity. Russia was considered, if not a partner, then something similar. The authors recognized the problem of rejecting Russia as a non-player in international affairs in the 1990s, and, in a narrower sense, in relations with the countries of the Trilateral Commission. In this regard, what was incorrect was the paradigm of insisting that Russia ought to choose democracy.

The authors admitted that the Trilateral Commission was subject to flip- flopping from one approach to another: periods of acute interest in Russia were followed by periods of disappointment and neglect; various guidelines and conclusions were formulated either out of bitter experience or in hopes of a better future. This unbalanced approach was one of the reasons for the lack of success in engaging

Russia; thus the authors suggested "not to engage Russia but to engage with Russia." They recognized Russia as a competent counterparty and partner for whom a long-term strategy should be developed with a corresponding, specific, action plan. Important were not only the proposals and areas of cooperation themselves, but also how they were formulated and presented.

At the same time, the authors realistically pointed out that Russia and the countries of the Trilateral Commission could not be called strategic partners. The focus should be on active engagement for the sake of mutually beneficial, cooperative processes. Any talk of closer partnership would be premature. Nonetheless, there were areas where interaction could be developed more actively. These included tourism and education, cooperation between business communities and NGOs, etc.

Furthermore, the authors of the fourth report identified a number of areas where the West should support and even defer to Russia. This primarily concerned the situation in the post-Soviet space and Russia's accession to international organizations (first and foremost, WTO membership). Such concessions, in part, reflected a new balance of power in which Russia claimed the role of an energy superpower. However, this was largely a reflection of the Trilateral Commission's new position that had matured over the course of 20 years: in the long term, there was no alternative to the rapprochement of the countries of the Trilateral Commission and Russia. Pragmatic, mutually beneficial and positive cooperation in areas of common interest, over time, could produce a bona fide strategic partnership.

The logical evolution from perceiving Russia as an enemy to recognizing the mutually advantageous nature of relations between the former East and West; Russia's status as an equal partner; the broad range of issues for a common agenda; and Russia's special interests development trajectory — all of this gave reason to hope for closer interaction between Russia and the countries of the Trilateral Commission. This interaction should make it possible to create, based on experience in negotiations and joint efforts, common values for mutual understanding and cooperation. Today this scenario may seem unrealistic, but to the same degree the situation today would have seemed unachievable to analysts only 30 years ago.

To conclude this part of the historical excursus, it should be noted that the Trilateral Commission provided more or less correct analysis on the prospects for developing relations with Russia and the conditions in which mutually beneficial cooperation could develop. One striking fact is that the Commission's many desires with regard to Russia's behavior on the international arena have been met, albeit with predictable complications. During a meeting between a Trilateral Commission delegation and Secretary General Mikhail Gorbachev on January 18, 1989, these wishes were clearly stated by Valéry Giscard d'Estaing, Yasuhiro Nakasone and Henry Kissinger: "The West is willing to cooperate if the following conditions are met: joining the international governance systems – GATT, IMF, IBRD, OECD; the convertibility of the ruble; and a defensive doctrine for the development of armed forces." All of these conditions are reality nowadays, with the exception of joining OECD.

2. Modernization's False Start. Politics, the Economy and Society

Social tensions in Russia eased in the period after the last report was published, mainly due to favorable trends on the energy market. The public mood was improved by uplifting rhetoric, demonstration of influence in international affairs, and the start of large-scale and symbolic projects (like the planning, as early as 2007, for the Sochi Olympic Games). But in politics and economics, the absence of needed and effective reforms pointed toward a regression in the overall situation.

In the process of getting up from its knees, the country has continued to stagger backwards. Dependence on raw materials exports is growing. Russia manufactures very few of the products it consumes. Its high-tech sector produces virtually nothing. When measured by the level of technology used, Russia appears to be a modernized country, but this is an imported modernity. According to some of our spending habits, Russia is a modernized country, but according to the sources of income, it is not.

At first glance, the fabric of political life in the second half of the 2000s did not appear to be problematic for Russia. A sense of high-level political stability remained in Russian society even at the lowest point of the economic crisis. The level of trust in the country's leadership remained at high levels for many years.

The concentration of power and limitation of political pluralism is not unusual for societies that are in transition and facing comprehensive modernization. In the first decade of the 21st century, these processes took place simultaneously as a chosen course to improve the state's effectiveness, stimulate economic recovery, fight poverty, and restore the country's position on the international arena. The question of how all these issues are interconnected is a complicated one. However, two manifestations of this connection are self-evident.

First, the success in state building and social-economic development legitimized such a political course in the eyes of Russia's majority. The unwritten social contract between the state and society, in which society would not pay particular attention to the limitation of political competition in exchange for better living conditions, worked without fail. It would be difficult to expect anything else given Russia's poorly developed civil society and lack of institutions of political competition. The achievements of the young proto-democracy – preserving civil peace in the period of acute social tension during the early-1990s, and creating institutional foundations for democracy and a market economy – were considered things of the past, which had lost their relevance in the years of abundance.

The flip side of this social contract is that a tangible downturn in living standards automatically delegitimizes the political course and its actors. Russia's democratic institutions, now deformed and imitational, are not capable of making up for this deficit of legitimacy.

Second, with the extended period of increasing state revenues, driven by a rise in the price of energy resources, the political regime of Russia in essence turned into an ever-expanding reallocation coalition that was attractive to the paternalistically-inclined portion of the population -- the middle class and the elite. With a constantly expanding resource portfolio, joining the reallocation coalition in exchange for loyalty to authorities was, in many cases, a preferred strategy.

Russian authorities continued to indicate that the current political system was a temporary construct — "our transitional economy is being served by a transitional political system," Vladimir Putin said in 2010. However, the years of abundance, which were notable for a high level of public trust in authorities, were not used for structural modernization of either the economy or the social sphere.

To the contrary, the oil-driven economy gave rise to oil-driven politics: government resources became highly concentrated and vertically organized. By the end of the first decade of this century, the political system of Russia became fully monocentric and vertical in nature. Today, as a result, the role of players independent of this vertical construct is highly limited and strictly controlled.

Regional and local authorities have become inclined to redirect key risks to the federal level. The central government is forced to assume hands-on administration. However, the federal authorities are not capable of providing systemic and responsible local governance.

Attempts to reform the judiciary during President Medvedev's term did not break the decline in judicial authorities' real independence. Russian judges act with reverence to the bureaucracy, the prosecutors and investigators, and judicial power vertical, which determines the fates of their careers. Rulings against the state and in favor of defendants remain exotically rare.

Attempts to fight corruption have also been met with strong resistance. The adoption of anticorruption laws has been too slow, and their application in practice has been very limited. Russia is still not fulfilling obligations it assumed upon signing the European convention against corruption. A slight uptick in the number of corruption cases cannot provide qualitative changes in this area, which, according to all public polling, ranks consistently as the government's number one problem in the eyes of the Russian populace. Russia was ranked 126th in the world corruption rating of Transparency International when the last Trilateral Commission report was written. In 2014, it dropped even lower.

The rigid power vertical, expanding hands-on administration, and the bureaucracy's immunity from opposition and mass media pressure, have all eroded the effectiveness of public administration.

The current government model has impacted the political awareness of Russian society. Russia's top figures, along with a few institutions of power, enjoy a rather high level of trust. However, there is a profound lack of trust in the rest of the power vertical. The political elite is alienated, and social apathy is pervasive. With such a development model in place, we see, in the public at large, further growth of paternalistic attitudes, suppression of grassroots social initiatives, and an insatiable demand for social benefits from the state. The emerging middle class defined by successful careers and productive creative endeavors, is forced to choose between openly opposing state authorities and cynically and pragmatically isolating oneself from any type of political engagement.

In 2011, the authors of "Attaining the Future. Strategy 2012" [79] (INSOR's report for a new election cycle) insisted that the Russian state

> has only one recipe to avoid this civilizational dead end: to use its authority and concentration of power

---

[79] Attaining the Future: Strategy 2012. Synopsis. Moscow, 2011 http://www.insor-russia.ru/files/INSOR_Attaining_the_Future_final.pdf

for profound structural reforms, optimization of the government apparatus, encouragement of the active and enterprising portion of the population and the easing of the social impacts of difficult transitions.

In the preceding years, Russia missed many opportunities. "Substantial and real successes were used not for solving long-term problems but only to contain actual and potential problems and social imbalances, to shield the coalition of the allocation vertical from criticism and competition."

However, just as the price of oil becomes the main benchmark for an oil-driven economy, in oil-driven politics, the popularity rating of authorities becomes the critical number. Fear of a decline in this rating undermines the political will to carry out structural reform, hence the indecisiveness in advancing questions and searching for long-term solutions to painful problems in the residential housing sector, the pension system, medical insurance, etc. It is not even considered appropriate to admit that there are such political problems, although the allocation of resources and burden of obligations is the No. 1 question for any state. The Russian political system simply strives to contain decision-making on sensitive issues within the bureaucratic vertical, while opposition politicians, civil society and expert groups are excluded from serious discussions.

The likely outcomes of this scenario range from torpid degeneration -- the speed of which will much depend on energy prices – to, in the worst case, a threat to stability, further social-economic deterioration and a return to rule by iron fist.

3. Sacrificing the Future for the Sake of Stability.

Russian society survived the economic crisis of the late 2000s with minimal damage to its well-being. However, public optimism, both political and consumer, has been visibly declining. Correspondingly, a critical attitude toward authorities has taken hold, even in loyal segments of society.

The switch of presidential places between Putin and Medvedev in September 2011 was perceived as a final decision by the Kremlin to avoid other scenarios of succession for the sake of "stability", and as a clear signal of imitation democracy. As a result, the portion of society that found this choice to be unacceptable was dramatically and substantially radicalized. This segment of society succeeded in making itself heard in the disputes surrounding the State Duma elections of December 2011.

The massive efforts to exercise public control over the Duma elections not only limited the ruling party's results, they also presented a challenge in ensuring absolute victory for Vladimir Putin in the March 2012 presidential elections.

In response to an unexpected wave of protests, the authorities launched several new legislative measures limiting the rights and freedoms of Russian citizens. Numerous legislative initiatives, already adopted or in the process of development and adoption, rode the peak of this wave – stiffening punishments for laws regulating public gathering and offenses against religious believers, restoring criminal liability for libel, banning the "propaganda of homosexuality," and forbidding US citizens from adopting Russian orphans. This trend has also been reflected in greater judicial harassment of leaders, activists and even ordinary members of the opposition movement, along with massive inspections of insufficiently 'trustworthy' NGOs, often labeled "foreign agents" due to funding from abroad. Increasing tensions in domestic politics have contributed to the substantial strengthening of the so-called *siloviki*, the position in the government structure representing the Ministry of Internal Affairs, Prosecutor's Office, and Investigative Committee since 2012.

In addition to the executive branch, United Russia, which dominates in the parliament, and the Russian Popular Front, initiated by Vladimir Putin in 2011, have been coalescing around a conservative agenda. The systemic opposition -- other parties with representation in the State Duma -- is also joining in this effort.

The few concessions made by authorities in late 2011 and early 2012 – permitting the election of governors and liberalizing the law on political parties -- have been changed through new legislative amendments. They include the so called "municipal filter" -- which closes off the path for candidates unacceptable to the Kremlin -- the cancellation of elections by local legislatures in a number of regions, and the radical lowering of the barriers for registering parties and lack of control over their applications. As a result, the Russian political realm is now dominated by the Kremlin's political projects; the same people use practically the same documents to register several parties while the real opposition forces continue to be denied access.

Society's disassociation from the political elite and its institutions -- the representative system, parties and local authorities -- is becoming ever more significant. The main political and administrative challenge for modern Russia is the problem of trust between society and authorities, as well as between specific groups of the elite and various social strata. The massive demonstrations at the turn of 2011-2012 represented a sort of initiation for new social forces, which reached such a scale for the first time since the period of 1989-1993.

More so than the political opposition's mass public demonstrations, however, the budget, poses a problem for Russian authorities. Exhausting the budget system's resources (a rather real one) would strip the authorities of their most important instrument for generating political support.

The budget has been stretched thin even at current world energy prices. The practice of transferring budget obligations from the federal center to the regional and local levels is exacerbating tensions between Moscow and the regions, which could weaken the center's capacity to exercise political control over local elites.

4. Domestic Policy

The Kremlin has three kinds of political opponents. The first is economic liberals and human rights advocates. The second is nationalists, who, lacking a developed political party structure, do not pose a serious threat for the moment. The third type is left-wing movements, including their radical branches.

Since the early 2000s, the idea of a big distribution state has prevailed in left-wing movements alongside nostalgia for the Soviet Union, anti-oligarchy sentiment, and aggressive anti-Western rhetoric. Russian authorities in turn have tried to implement the big state model by constantly increasing or promising to increase social spending.

Dmitry Medvedev's presidency represented a period of thaw. The Kremlin started toying with the liberal electorate. Privatizations plans for government property were introduced, and a reset was declared in relations with the West. This thaw is giving way to a "frost."

Vladimir Putin's third presidential term is focused on serving the interests of the political left, with all government institutions focused on satisfying social needs. The ruling elite stays a step ahead of the liberals by denying them media access and restraining their political maneuverability through stringent legislative and other measures. It has also gained the upper hand on the left wing by assimilating many of its main slogans without embracing their desire for full nationalization. The government competes mainly for left, nationalist voters. They are the force underpinning Putin's electoral majority.

Vladimir Putin has managed to consolidate this majority after the events of late 2011. The political shocks allowed him to attract supporters through slogans calling for order and stability in the country. This was essentially the foundation of his presidential election campaign.

Vladimir Putin needed an impressive victory, not only in the first round, but with a two-thirds supermajority to secure wider room for diverse maneuvers through the next term.

Anti-Western rhetoric, primarily anti-American, was chosen as one of the focuses of the media campaign. In simple terms, it was formulated in the following manner: the aim of the West is to provoke unrest in the country and only the present government can withstand such attempts.

It is important to mention that before the Ukrainian crisis, the anti-Western propaganda focused more on the United States than on Europe and the European Union. It almost totally bypassed Japan. This reflected the traditionally more constructive relations and mutual dependence with the European Union and the preferences for the "European choice" prevailing among elites and the general public.

The Ukrainian crisis raised the intensity of criticism towards Brussels.

The escalation of the conflict with Ukraine and the annexation of Crimea enabled the government to make several former opposition groups -- predominantly leftwing -- its allies. The simplified Soviet identity proved to be stronger than the traditional animosity between the opposition and the government.

The stability of Putin's majority is linked to economic successes or failures. The official forecasts are unnerving, as the country has already fallen into stagnation. If the situation significantly deteriorates, the majority could dissipate and switch to various camps of the discontented.

Consolidated media resources provide the authorities with a powerful tool. They played an important role in attracting some opposition groups to Putin's majority. However, they have also helped to create a high-tension environment in the country that will be almost impossible to maintain at such a level in the coming years.

The main challenge for Russia -- conceded even in official circles -- is that a well-articulated program of Russia's own making cannot offer the world an attractive alternative model, let alone one that could be proven in practice.

That is why, in opposing the West, official Russia uses a short list of "traditional values" that do not constitute an articulate ideology.

The role of Vladimir Putin as a symbol is dramatically increasing. The future of the country's development has strongly become attributed to this one person. Some blame him for all problems, while others give him credit for all things positive.

5. Foreign Policy in the New Environment

Since the Trilateral Commission's last report on Russia was published in 2006, the majority of Russian society has had conflicting opinions about Moscow's behavior outside the country. Nevertheless, there is still consensus on some basic approaches.

Russia's rapid loss of its foreign policy position, and its exclusion from decision-making on key problems of global politics and security in the 1990s, gave rise to a strong internal demand for raising the country's military and political status in the world. These aspirations have been stimulated, in part, by a wide-scale information campaign emphasizing external trends unfavorable for Russia. We have experienced a kind of "Weimar syndrome."

At the same time, the will to support the excessive mobilization efforts and economic costs associated with this status remains limited. This stems from a sustained demand for a stable and peaceful environment – both domestic and external. However, a substantial portion of the population sees the use of force in resolving isolated problems within and at Russia's borders as acceptable in principle.

The demonstrative effect of economically developed countries (primarily the United States and EU members) has influenced the aspirations of Russia's middle class with regard to income level, social comforts and international mobility. New generations that only briefly encountered Soviet realities have become accustomed to a new standard of living and express a high level of willingness to "follow the norms of the global community." These norms are particularly associated with legal and social standards no longer perceived as something purely foreign in nature. Such attitudes somewhat contradict the recent conservative trends in Russia's foreign policy behavior.

What unites different groups is a desire for an independent foreign policy, though with different understandings of what "independence" entails. They are convinced that, at least since the mid-2000s, Russia has attained a sovereign position in the world and can make independent foreign policy decisions.

However, public perceptions of Russia's foreign policy independence may turn a new page. Sooner or later this perception will come to grips with the Chinese factor. The historical image in the Russian minds of their country as a "big brother" in this tandem has been growing dim, if it has not disappeared altogether. Simultaneously, more groups are becoming concerned by the consequences of Russia's rapid turn to the East, i.e. to China. This discomfort is not reflected in the mass media, where one finds rather few critical remarks about Beijing. This does not mean that further moves for the sake of a "friendship" would influence perceptions about Russia's independent position vis-à-vis China. Outside steps perceived as negative or hostile to Russia might assuage the traditionally apprehensive view of China among Russian citizens.

The interconnection of Russia's foreign policy initiatives with its tasks and priorities for domestic development is a key factor informing Russian concerns on the turn to China. If the public is inclined to pursue a comprehensive modernization agenda, then it should be more aware of what specific global players could contribute to implement such an agenda. If not, the choices could be rather limited. There is growing awareness of the fact that the East is more interested in rechanneling energy resources from the Western direction, than it is in supporting Russia's industrial and technological renaissance.

China's resource scarcity is manifested in Peking's active Central Asia policy. China is circumventing Russia as part of an ambitious effort to strengthen long-terms relations with the former Soviet republics, sustain energy supplies from the region, and widen its share in domestic markets. In September 2013, Chairman Xi, in his speech in the Kazakhstan capital, called on Central Asian countries to join China in creating an "Economic belt of the New Silk Way." This project is aimed at increasing China's zone of influence. Russia so far has ignored this challenge, as it has China's growing ambitions in the resource-rich Arctic area. In Moscow's view, the emphasis on "strategic partnership" with Peking is timely in light of Western pressure.

Nevertheless, Chinese activities in Central Asia are fraught with substantial challenges in the political and economic landscape of the region, all of which could further concern Moscow in the coming years. This refers not only to Russian bilateral relations, with Kazakhstan in particular, but also to the possible impact on multilateral tracks, including the Customs Union and the newly created Euro-

Asian Economic Union. Russia is facing difficulties in finding acceptable compromises with Peking. The present U-turn to China might limit Russia's ability to achieve them in the region -- a new "headache" for the Kremlin.

The Ukrainian crisis reshuffled regional priorities in China's favor. Nonetheless, the impact of this turn on prospects for the country's comprehensive modernization remains unclear.

Today, Russian foreign policy lacks a clear understanding of long-term guideposts and prospects for domestic development. The declared turn from Europe to Asia, in practice, has manifested itself in a refusal to select a modernization model, and hence, appropriate partners.

Still, the essence of Russia's foreign policy course, in the near term, will be determined by the fact that, regardless of which global scenario plays out – the rebirth of the West, the consolidation and surge of Asian powers, or a balanced confrontation between these two poles – its actors will be more powerful than Russia.

Without a clearer strategic domestic plan, Russian foreign policy can only react tactically to international and regional events.

The tactical objectives of Russia's foreign policy can be generalized as the pursuit of world power status without a strategic understanding of how this status should be underpinned. Developments around the Syrian and Ukrainian conflicts have shown the gap between Russia's tactical endeavors and its understanding of longer terms tasks and interests. Apart from the positive response Moscow has received from a certain part of Russian society for its handling of these conflicts so far, no other substantial dividends seem forthcoming – both in terms of foreign policy and economics.

The state of the Russian economy and its likely dynamic through 2020 will not allow Moscow to play a major international role. Russia's ruling elite will continue to focus on its own parochial interests, from assuring domestic control to protecting and expanding the assets it owns.

Benefiting from its UN Security Council permanent membership, Moscow will still be able to punch above its weight. Russia will persist as a fairly significant and strategically independent player on the world stage. It will continue to oppose US global dominance and enhance cooperation with China and other BRICS countries. Moscow will, with obvious difficulties, try to restore relations with the EU as a traditional and close economic partner.

Russia's foreign policy will continue to be more reactive than proactive, with one notable exception. Moscow will seek to speed up its Eurasian integration project with some of its CIS neighbors. Since 2009, this process has acquired a dynamic, which makes it, in principle, viable and sustainable.

The ultimate success of the Eurasian Economic Union (EAEU), entering into force in 2015, will depend on a number of conditions. It will have to remain economic par excellence, stopping well short of pooling national sovereignties. Neither Kazakhstan nor Belarus is ready to give up their sovereignty to a supranational body dominated by Moscow.

Of the larger CIS countries, Ukraine will continue its integration with the EU. At the same time, while decreasing its dependence on them, Kiev will try to sustain economic ties with Russia and the EAEU members.

Russia's strategic interest requires the development of stable partnerships with the West. Prolonged confrontation with the West will make prospects for Russia's evolution as a modern society more remote. The withdrawal from modernization in 2012, combined with the launching of a political war against Russia's creative class and "mobilization economy" programs, is designed to shift resources to inefficient parts of the economy, including defense industries. The Ukrainian conflict simply intensifies these domestic trends, moving the country further away from modernization.

The government's inclination toward import substitution of technologies and equipment was apparent before the Ukrainian crisis. Painful Western sanctions would push Russia further in this direction. Moreover, they would weaken Russian integration with its global counterparts.

Here lies the crux of the current situation, which may persist for years to come. Russia is squeezed between two poles of power. The West is planning an economic war. The other, in the East, is ready to smother Russia in its friendly embrace.

Conclusion

Russia and the countries of the Trilateral Commission share more security concerns today than at any point since the end of the Cold War. Even without identical interests, their cooperation can benefit from meeting important overlapping policy objectives. Separately, they do not have adequate resources for robust defense and security. They share a sense of uncertainty and even vulnerability in the transformations of the global balance of power.

While Russian history is replete with outstanding foreign policy victories, achieved with clearly insufficient resources, it also gives examples of many missed opportunities, unrealized chances, unfortunate mistakes, and miscalculations. There are reasons to doubt that these opportunities have been lost forever.

THE WEST AND RUSSIA: AN OUTLOOK TO 2020 AND BEYOND

Discussion paper by Dmitri Trenin
Director of the Carnegie Moscow Center

Written in June 2013

What Kind of Russia Is Emerging?

In 2011-12, Russia entered a new period in its post-Soviet evolution. Its key features are a new social environment; new methods of governance and control; new challenges in the economic sphere; more intense ideological debate; and a changed pattern of foreign policy and foreign relations. These changes had been gestating for some time during the two decades after the end of the Soviet system. What brought them into the open was Vladimir Putin's September 2011 decision to return to the formal leadership role, and the mass protests against the State Duma election results, widely believed to have been rigged.

The new Russian middle class of urban professionals, mostly concentrated in Moscow, St. Petersburg, and to a much smaller extent, in a handful of big cities across the country, has broken the unwritten mutual non-aggression pact with the authorities, when a degree of personal freedom granted to these sections of the population guaranteed their political quiescence. Having achieved many of their personal goals, the urban groups are now stepping out of their private and often comfortable niches into the uncertainties of the public square. The socially active group is numerically small, embracing 20-25% of the population at most, but it is well-educated, connected to the world outside Russia, and increasingly vocal. It is the principal driving force behind what can be termed the Russian Awakening.

Faced with the challenge of this small but vocal minority, the authorities employed a new mix of policies. They made token concessions to the public demands, i.e. easing the registration of political parties and allowing direct elections of governors, although both were laden with constraints. They engaged in targeted repression of the protestors accused of using violence, and of the protest leaders, accused of various crimes. They branded those non-governmental organizations that accepted donations from abroad as "foreign agents." And they sought to discipline their own ranks, making loyalty an indispensable but no longer sufficient condition for enjoying the perks of office.

Having barely recovered from the global downturn, the Russian economy began to stagnate despite the relatively high and stable price of oil. The model of growth based on the ever-increasing oil price, which led to the boom of the 2000s, cannot be revived. With little investment, massive capital outflow and rampant corruption, the state of the Russian economy not only belied the earlier Kremlin ambition to elevate the country's global status, but put in doubt the fulfillment of the government's social obligations, a necessary pre-requisite for social peace and continued political acquiescence.

The Russian Awakening covers the entire waterfront, from libertarians to fundamentalists. Various groups have begun to air their views publicly, producing cacophony. The authorities, who, for a long time, had been publicly neutral on ideological or value issues, abandoned that aloof stance. They have openly embraced an ideology of conservatism and are busy creating an official version of

Russian patriotism, based on a government-sanctioned view of Russian history, special role for Orthodox Christianity as the spiritual guide of the Russian people, and skeptical and suspicious attitude toward the West.

In foreign policy terms, Russia has emphasized post-Soviet integration with Belarus and Kazakhstan, under the rubric of a Eurasian Union. Moscow's relations with the European Union have palpably cooled. The EU, in crisis, has ceased to be either a mentor or a model for Russia. The Kremlin has rebalanced its foreign policy toward the Asia-Pacific region. And relations with the United States, having gone through an election-period crisis in 2012, remain highly ambivalent. Globally, Russia has made a stand on Syria. For the first time since the break-up of the Soviet Union, Moscow is not only voicing its opposition to Western policies, but is undercutting those policies through its own actions.

The next five to seven years are likely to be decisive for Russia's future. Will Russian society be deterred by the authorities' policies and keep its heads down, or will it find the resources to mature and start building a political nation? Will the ruling elite continue as a monolith, or will it fracture and fragment, creating political openings? Once the leadership becomes convinced that its economic goals cannot be reached with existing policies, will they choose reform or mobilization? Will there continue to be relative freedom as far as values and ideologies are concerned, or will the state succeed in imposing a Russian national ideology of sorts? All these questions imply sharp conflicts of interests and ideas. The outcome of these conflicts will impact Russia's position and role in the world, and its international standing.

As of this writing, there is a lot of uncertainty about all of these issues. We will base our narrative on several key assumptions. The Russian Federation is unlikely to break up. Its population will stagnate, or even demonstrate slight growth rather than decline rapidly, as recently predicted. Russia's economy will continue to be based on raw materials. Everything else is up for grabs.

What Kind of Russian Foreign Policy through 2020?

The state of the Russian economy and its likely dynamic through 2020 will not allow Moscow to play a very large international role. Moreover, the Russian ruling elite will continue to focus on its own parochial interests, from assuring domestic control to protecting and expanding the assets it owns. Foreign policy will be important largely due to the exigencies of prestige; facilitating trade and travel (in part, as a safety valve for the opponents of the system); and providing a measure of national security, particularly along the country's southern border. Yet, benefiting from its UN Security Council permanent membership, and exploiting the Soviet and tsarist legacy, Moscow will still be able to punch above its weight. Thus, through the current decade Russia will continue as a fairly significant and strategically independent player on the world stage. It will continue to oppose U.S. global dominance, enter into situational or partial alignments with other major players such as China, and seek to maintain peace and expand trade and economic links with its two biggest neighbors on the continent, Europe to the west and China to the east.

Northern Eurasia

With Russia still self-absorbed, its foreign policy will continue to be more reactive than proactive, with one notable exception. Moscow will seek to create a system of economic, security and humanitarian arrangements with its post-Soviet neighbors in Eurasia. Since 2009, the Eurasian economic integration process has acquired a dynamic that makes it, in principle, viable and sustainable. However, the ultimate success of the Eurasian Union (EAU), the launch of which is now set for 2015, will depend on a number of conditions. It will have to stay economic par excellence, stopping well short of significantly pooling national sovereignties. Neither Astana nor even Minsk is ready to give up their sovereignty to a supranational body dominated by Moscow. For its part, Moscow, would not agree to genuine equality with its much smaller partners.

The EAU essentially will have to remain limited to Belarus, Kazakhstan, and Russia. Of the larger CIS countries, Ukraine will be a highly ambivalent and unreliable partner, and Uzbekistan, which sees itself as the regional power in Central Asia, will continue to be very independent-minded, even under a changed leadership. Of the smaller countries, Kyrgyzstan and Tajikistan are economically too backward, and politically too unstable to be ready for full-blown integration. Largely for geopolitical reasons - creating a barrier to China's deeper penetration into Central Asia - they are being drawn into the integration process, but they will remain on the periphery. Of the rest, Moldova will probably continue to look to the EU, notwithstanding its uncertain prospects for accession and the implications for the country's nominal unity. Georgia's relations with Russia will be burdened with the issue of Abkhazia and South Ossetia. Oil-rich Azerbaijan will just be happy to stay away from any integration, whether with Russia or the EU. Across the Caspian, gas-rich Turkmenistan, ruled for a quarter-century in a despotic manner, will keep its vaunted "neutrality." This only leaves land-locked Armenia, which is traditionally allied with Russia but does not have a border with any of the EAU member states, plus the former Georgian territories Abkhazia and South Ossetia as potential new participants in Eurasian economic integration. That said, the EAU is likely to be a common market with some supranational institutions like the Eurasian Economic Commission, which has existed since 2012. There is virtually no chance that the process will lead to a revival a single politico-economic and military entity in northern Eurasia reminiscent of the Soviet Union.

Apart from the EAU, Russia will seek to bolster security cooperation with its CIS partners, primarily bilaterally or through the Collective Security Treaty Organization (CSTO). This cooperation is more relevant and urgent in light of the withdrawal of U.S./NATO combat troops from Afghanistan. Its allies being very weak and insufficiently reliable, Russia will emphasize the enhancement of its own military strength. The military modernization program may be stretched out a bit, given Russia's financial situation, but as long as Putin remains in office, it will remain of high priority. As Russia rebuilds its military forces and defense industry, it will continue to see the United States as its main potential adversary. Moscow will follow closely, with eyes and ears wide open, but mouth shut, China's strategic evolution. And it will look intensely toward the south, along the Afghanistan-Central Asia axis, as its most vulnerable direction. Europe, the traditional principal theater of war, will be seen as essentially as a zone of peace – unless disturbed by some new U.S. system deployment or a revived prospect of NATO's enlargement toward Ukraine or Georgia.

Europe

Along with the Arab world and Turkey, Russia is a significant part of Europe's geopolitical environment that is going through a serious internal upheaval – very different, of course, in substance and style from the developments in the Arab world, though somewhat closer to the dynamics of Turkey. At the same time, Russian-European relations will be fundamentally reshaped in the next few years.

In the foreseeable future, Russia and Europe will continue to drift apart. Europe's dependence on Russian gas will decrease even more, leading to a drop in the revenues that Russia receives from Gazprom's gas business in Europe. As Europe proceeds to diversify its sources of gas imports, Russia will seek to diversify the geography of its exports, mainly to China, Japan and South Korea, even though it will have to accept losses. The EU will continue to be Russia's biggest trading partner, though its share may drop below 50%, due to faster growing trade with Asia (particularly, China, Japan and South Korea) as well as Russia's EAU partners. European investments in Russia will be greater than anyone's, but they will not experience a boom, as Russia's investment climate is unlikely to improve qualitatively through 2020.

Political relations will be increasingly tense as Russian domestic politics become more conflict-ridden. With the Kremlin and its supporters applying harsher tactics against their more numerous and vociferous opponents, Europe's media, public, and politicians will take a progressively more critical approach to their actions. European governments and EU institutions will need to take a more critical approach to the Russian government's policies, inviting Moscow's backlash. Relations with Germany in particular, long a model of Russo-European entente and cooperation, are likely to become more contentious. These changes will begin incrementally, but eventually, will add up to a new state of relations characterized by growing disinterest, reduced expectations, and even mutual alienation.

This situation may be exacerbated by disagreements over Ukraine. President Putin is pushing strongly for Ukraine to join the process of Eurasian integration, which, he calculates, will give the process much-needed critical mass. The Ukrainian elite realizes that integration is likely to lead to Ukraine losing its independence and accepting again Moscow's hegemony. Whatever their differences, Ukrainian elites are all united behind their country's independence vis-à-vis Russia. Ukraine, however, will not be able to back up its declared choice in favor of integration with the EU. For some time, Ukrainians will be engaged in a balancing act between Brussels and Moscow, seeking to get the most from each side with minimal concessions to either. Such gaming may incite EU-Russian competition over Ukraine, leading even to a real conflict between Russia and the EU.

Other conflicts may arise between Moscow and Brussels/Berlin over Moldova and Georgia. As the EU seeks to unify elements of its foreign policy, Russia may feel itself among the first objects of such unification. In the past, a more assertive EU stance on Russia was prevented by the special relationship between Moscow and Berlin. With Germany's more sober policy toward Russia, a conflictual relationship may be in the offing.

In terms of values, the gap to which European critics of Russian authoritarianism have always pointed has finally become recognized – with pride! - by Russian authorities. Moscow no longer accepts Europe as a mentor or a model. Russia's leaders see it as living beyond its means, downgrading the very factors, such as its sense of mission that, in earlier times, were crucial for Europe's rise and mastery of the globe. European-Russian differences are apparent on such issues as religious faith and the role of the church; the definition of the family; the balance of citizens' rights and responsibilities; immigration, tolerance and multiculturalism; and state sovereignty. As Europe is accepting ever more liberal values, Russian leaders are stressing conservatism and adherence to tradition. This gap will widen, straining Russia's relations with its western neighbors in the Council of Europe and the Organization for Security and Cooperation in Europe. Russia's expulsion from either body, however, is unlikely for fear of provoking a major crisis and Russia's complete alienation from Europe.

Stagnation in economic ties and mounting difficulties in government-to-government relations will coincide with a boost in human exchanges between Europe and Russia. In all likelihood, the visa requirement will be relaxed but not abolished in the next few years. But whatever happens with regard to the visa regime, more Russians will come to Europe. A few will take refuge from conflicts at home, and a portion of these émigrés will use their stay to sensitize European publics and governments to developments in Russia.

Asia Pacific

Asia's importance to Russian foreign policy will grow for three principal reasons. Moscow sees its resource-rich, but underdeveloped and under-populated eastern provinces as vulnerable, and will continue to seek new resources for their development. To spur growth, Russia will seek to hitch its wagon to dynamic Asia rather than stagnant Europe. Moscow also has to pay more attention to the continuing rise of China, a neighbor and partner across a 2,700-mile long common border. Finally, Moscow closely follows "pivots" in U.S. foreign policy.

Russia will pursue the following primary goals in the Asia-Pacific: (1) maintaining stable good-neighborly relations with China to assure the security of its eastern flank; (2) expanding trade and economic relations with China to capitalize on its growth and market; (3) complementing relations with China through productive links with other Asian countries: a strategic and military-technical partnership with India; an economic and arms-trade relationship with Vietnam; a political and technological relationship with South Korea; and a normalized relationship with Asia's technological leader, Japan; (4) contributing to Asia-Pacific strategic, political and economic matters in the frameworks of the East Asia Summit, APEC, and ASEAN Regional Forum.

Relations with Japan are particularly important. Moscow will seek to expand trade with Japan, and attract Japanese investment and technology. Putin realizes that the full potential of Russo-Japanese cooperation can only be realized with full normalization of bilateral political relations, i.e., a resolution of the territorial issue over the South Kuril Islands, which the Japanese refer to as the Northern Territories. Putin has already indicated his willingness to reach a compromise deal with Japan over the islands on the basis of the 1956 Moscow declaration. He remains open to serious dialogue, but will not simply accept all Japanese claims. In the foreseeable future, Putin, due to his strong nationalist credentials, remains the only Russian leader capable of reaching a territorial settlement with Japan, and delivering on it.

The United States

Since 2011, Russian-American relations have acquired a new dimension: Russian domestic politics. Putin repeatedly accuses the United States of interfering in

Russia's internal affairs, including in parliamentary and presidential elections. Russia's new anti-Americanism is largely a domestic political tool, but it clearly impacts U.S.-Russian relations, no longer a preserve for the top leaders and their trusted diplomats. As Russia's domestic politics will inevitably lead to occasional showdowns and even crises, Russian authorities will use the United States as a bogeyman by Russian authorities, and will be pressed to "do something" by the Kremlin's opponents at home and abroad.

Massive anti-American propaganda is largely responsible for the fact that Russians view the United States as their country's main foreign enemy. What is striking is that most Russians are prepared to live with that. Only a very small minority voice supports an improved relationship with the U.S. Public sentiments will vacillate, but Russia's nascent nationalism has already been imbued with the strong virus of anti-Americanism, which cannot be easily expunged. Russian authorities will use the notion of an external threat by a powerful adversary not only to keep control of the domestic situation, but also to stimulate a competitive spirit in Russia where the State can make use of it: in science and technology, the defense industry, and its military forces.

Russia has lowered expectations of a missile defense agreement with the United States, believing that while the pace and configuration of missile defenses may vary, Washington will continue to build such defenses. If possible, Moscow believes that the U.S. will construct robust defenses well beyond what might be needed to intercept a rogue state's missiles. At the same time, Russians fear that decapitating strikes could make their own nuclear arsenal unusable. In response to these developments, the Kremlin will prioritize the enhancement of Russian strategic missiles' penetration capacity, which should strengthen nuclear deterrence.

This environment has important implications for arms control. Russia will not be interested in phasing out nuclear weapons. On the contrary, it will rely more on nuclear deterrence for its security. Russia will agree to further nuclear arms cuts with the United States only if missile defense and non-nuclear strategic systems are part of the deal. Increasingly, Russia will be paying attention to other military powers, particularly in Asia, which are expanding their nuclear and missile arsenals. In principle, Moscow is likely to support a trilateral strategic stability dialogue with the United States and China.

Moscow will continue to avoid full-blown Cold War-style confrontation with Washington, but it will not shy away from actively opposing U.S. policies that affect Russia's most important interests. From this perspective, Moscow's stance on Syria has marked a new stage in the evolution of Russia's foreign policy. From the Balkans to Libya, various U.S. actions have made Russia unhappy many times before. On Syria, however, Russia has not only disagreed with the United States, it has acted. Beyond its votes at the UN Security Council, Russia is forestalling the use of force against Damascus and regime change under outside pressure by providing arms deliveries to the Assad government. Russia's calculus regarding Assad's staying power and the nature of the armed opposition to his régime has proven more accurate than the U.S. government's. The agreement between Moscow and Washington to hold a peace conference on Syria looked like one of co-equals -- a stunning success for Russian diplomacy.

It was soon revealed, however, that an ad hoc diplomatic alliance between Russia and the United States on

Syria was unlikely. For Washington, outreach to Moscow was a means of removing the Assad regime from power in Damascus and ending the alliance between Syria and Iran without committing U.S. military forces. The United States and its allies rejected Moscow's insistence on a compromise political settlement between the government in Damascus and the non-extremist part of the opposition, undermining the U.S.-Russian initiative. As long as it continues, the Syrian civil war will negatively impact Russian-Western relations.

Syria, Iran, and other Middle Eastern issues will be at the center of U.S.-Russian relations. Back in the Middle East after a 20-year-long break, and steeled by the Syrian experience, Russia is likely to take a more active position on these issues. Preventing the use of force by the United States without the authority of the UN Security Council, where Russia has a veto, and scuttling attempts at regime change from the outside have become the key elements of the Russian position. With the election of a more moderate president in Iran in 2013, Russia may become more sympathetic toward Tehran in its protracted stand-off with the United States and Israel.

After the withdrawal of coalition combat troops from Afghanistan in 2014, Russia will have to take a more active role in security-building around Afghanistan. Cooperation between Moscow and Washington is possible, based on their reciprocal interests, but Russia will not see eye to eye with the U.S. on many Afghanistan-related issues. One additional problem is posed by U.S. intentions to park some of their military hardware in the region, creating "quasi-bases" in Central Asia. Central Asian leaders, privately, may welcome such diversification of their security alignments, but Russia will see it as an encroachment on its leading security role in the region.

However, to buttress its leadership role, Russia will need to do a lot to make the alliance it leads, the Collective Security Treaty Organization, an effective security provider.

Pakistan, challenged by extremists, will feel the changes in Afghanistan most intimately. Sensing Pakistan's new importance, Moscow will quietly expand its ties with Islamabad, even as it seeks to strengthen the traditional strategic relationship with India. Given Delhi's prickliness, Moscow will desist from steps that might irritate India, but it will expect its partner to continue to buy large quantities of Russian military hardware – an area where competition from the United States and European Union countries has been growing.

On North Korea, Russia will remain committed to resolving the nuclear issue through negotiations. It will condemn Pyongyang's provocative behavior, should it resort to nuclear and/or missile saber-rattling, but it will also oppose tough sanctions against North Korea, not to mention the use of force against it. Russia will be in broad agreement with the United States regarding the general goal of nuclear non-proliferation, but it will often take the same stance as China on the counter-productiveness of tougher sanctions. Moscow will essentially seek an understanding with South Korea, which it sees as the leader of the Korean reunification process. In cooperation with Seoul, Russia will continue to promote its project of building a gas pipeline and railroad across North Korea.

In general terms, Russia probably will see the U.S. presence in Asia and the Pacific as part of a new power balance in the region. The United States and its allies, such as Canada, have much in principle to contribute to the economic development of the Russian Far East and Siberia. The Russians will aim to steer clear of Sino-American differences, making sure not to get sucked into a potential conflict between Beijing and Washington. At the same time, Russia will insist on maintaining its strategic independence vis-à-vis the two biggest powers of the 21st century.

For Russia, expanding economic relations with the United States became a priority at the start of Putin's third term. Russia needs U.S. investment and technology, and seeks to enter the U.S. market in several fields. U.S.-Russian economic relations will depend, above all, on the business climate in Russia. The Russian government understands that and seeks to improve the country's standing in the World Bank's *Doing Business* Index. More challenging for Moscow is reassuring potential investors on the protection of property rights and the rule of law in the country. Russia will continue to suffer from its extremely negative public image in the West.

Of particular importance to Russia will be its cooperation with the United States on a range of non-political issues, such as science and technology, education, health, immigration and integration. Cooperation in many of these areas, however, will be less of a priority to the United States, given the U.S. lead in many areas. A lot will depend on the ability of Russian stakeholders to seek out potential U.S. partners and reach out to them.

Policy Options for the West

For the United States, it would make sense, in principle, to work with Russia where the two countries' interests are sufficiently close, from non-proliferation to regional conflicts to counter-terrorism. Energy and education; climate and cyber; the Arctic and Asia-Pacific offer other areas for productive interaction. This would certainly advance U.S. national interests and the collective interests of the West. Yet, such cooperation would demand a degree of strategizing within the U.S. government that is now hard to imagine. It would also place severe requirements on U.S. foreign policy, which are difficult to meet. The United States would have to take account of Russia's security concerns vis-à-vis U.S. military power, even though these may appear exaggerated to Americans. Washington would have to treat Moscow as a co-equal even if Russia is not America's equal in terms of power and influence. And Americans would need to leave the Russians to sort out their domestic issues themselves, resisting the temptation to interfere in Russia's murky politics.

A degree of cooperation, of course, is possible even if the above requirements are not fulfilled, but this will still leave the relationship in the present unstable condition. The potential for arms control to serve as a stabilizer in U.S.-Russian relations has been essentially exhausted with the New START treaty. Russia will not agree to new cuts in strategic nuclear weapons without U.S. commitments on missile defense and non-nuclear strategic systems. The hope that closer economic ties can provide a safety net for the relationship largely depends on Russia becoming more attractive to U.S. investors. This, however, does not look likely absent substantial changes in the Russian business climate. Even similar threats to both countries do not guarantee close collaboration between them, as Syria, Afghanistan and international terrorism have demonstrated. Being essentially unstable, the current situation is more likely to become adversarial, especially as a reaction to Russian domestic political developments. The United States will need to focus on managing conflicts with Russia, which have the potential to damage U.S. interests.

The European Union will need to recognize that the 20-year-long period when it basically looked at Russia as an extension of Europe -- even if Russia was never seriously considered a candidate for EU membership -- is over. In the future, Russia will have to be approached as a neighbor with its own agenda. This has important implications for European policies toward Russia.

The idea of pan-European (i.e., in this context, EU-Russian) common spaces based on the notion of "sharing everything but the institutions" has probably run its course at this stage. In the present circumstances, there is no need for a new overarching EU-Russian Partnership and Cooperation Agreement to replace the one that expired in 2007. Russia and Europe will have no common future. By the same token, a free-trade area between the EU and Russia is not a priority before 2020. The EU needs to focus on its Transatlantic partnership with the United States, while Russia faces the task of founding the Eurasian Economic Union and making it work. Given these fundamental changes, the EU-Russia semi-annual summitry should be scaled down.

This should not mean, of course, ending partnership and cooperation. But the emphasis should be on specific EU-Russian arrangements and agreements facilitating economic relations: technical standards or streamlining customs procedures, for example. There is also a need for facilitating scientific and technological cooperation and educational and cultural exchanges between Russia and the EU countries. The visa regime needs to be eased gradually at first, facilitating exchanges between Europeans and Russians. With the introduction of new security measures, visas could be abolished by 2020.

Close observers of the Russian scene as they are, Europeans should stop asking the question of what they should do for Russia in order to help it become more like the EU. Rather, they should ask the question, what does Europe need from Russia? The answer includes: assuring stable peace across the European continent, which the EU shares with Russia; pursuing economic opportunities in Russia, to the extent that they are attractive enough; and making Russian citizens appreciate Europe's historical and more recent achievements, as well as its way of life, in order to foster a degree of social compatibility between the European Union and its biggest neighbor. Europe's soft power remains its most effective tool vis-à-vis Russia.

The Japanese will have an opportunity to normalize relations with Russia by the end of the current decade; reach some of their national objectives; and improve their country's geopolitical position. Essentially, they could work with President Putin to resolve the territorial dispute on a compromise basis, and turn the dispute resolution process into a means of positively transforming relations with Russia. A Japan-Russia rapprochement is entirely in the interest of the United States, as it furthers its strategy in the Asia-Pacific region. It gives Japan's foreign policy additional strategic depth vis-à-vis China, and it allows for a more diversified Russian foreign policy in the region.

- Annex -

THE WALL STREET JOURNAL.

OPINION EUROPE
July 20, 2014 5:40 p.m. ET

Uniting for Ukraine Independence

By PAULA J. DOBRIANSKY, ANDRZEJ OLECHOWSKI, YUKIO SATOH AND IGOR YURGENS

The downing of Malaysia Airlines Flight 17 is a tragic reminder of the international community's vital interest in the future of Ukraine. The ability of Ukrainian President Petro Poroshenko to promote national unity and chart an independent course for his government will depend on the country's economic stability.

As co-chairpersons of the Trilateral Commission's Russia Working Group, we believe that Ukraine's dire economic situation calls for the establishment of a Friends of Ukraine task force.

The international task force, comprised of independent leaders from North America, Europe, Asia and Russia, should promote Ukraine's sovereignty, encourage economic reforms, and coordinate efforts with governments and nongovernmental organizations that seek to help Ukraine at this critical time in its history.

Monitoring groups on the ground determined that Ukraine conducted a free and fair presidential election on May 25, 2014. More than 80% of voters had the opportunity to cast a ballot, and turnout reached 55%, even amid security threats in Ukraine's two eastern regions. As noted in a preliminary statement by the Organization for Security and Cooperation in Europe, Ukraine held "a genuine election largely in line with international commitments and with a respect for fundamental freedoms in the vast majority of the country."

Unfortunately, Ukraine's financial outlook is less encouraging than its political developments, even with all the uncertainties that lie ahead. The country hasn't seen economic growth for more than two years. Thirty-seven billion dollars disappeared from state coffers during former President Viktor Yanukovych's tenure, a glaring manifestation of the country's entrenched corruption at all levels of government. Transparency International ranks Ukraine 144th out of 177 in its Corruption Perceptions Index. Currency reserves are dwindling. The budget deficit stands at 8% of GDP.

Nor is there a national consensus on how to address Ukraine's economic challenges. An International Republican Institute (IRI) poll revealed that 66% of western Ukrainians consider short-term economic pain an acceptable price for long-term improvements; just 17% of their eastern counterparts concur. Recent polling by an EU association showed similar regional differences.

In this environment, a Friends of Ukraine contact group could facilitate the country's economic transition in three distinct ways.

First, by promoting an international agenda that recognizes Ukraine's sovereignty, desire for economic development, and ability to choose its own regional and global trade partners. The Friends of Ukraine task force should support Ukraine's right to make its own domestic and foreign-policy choices.

Second, by encouraging economic reforms. In his inaugural address, Mr. Poroshenko challenged Ukraine to build a European economy, which he defined as an "economy of new ideas, business initiative, hard work, [and] constant self-improvement." The Ukrainian government has taken steps to address an array of economic challenges such as corruption, unsustainable energy prices and debt, which merit the international community's assistance. Supporting Ukraine's anticorruption efforts would lower the risk of economic downturn for both Russia and the European Union, as would a focus on developing an international compact to restructure the country's debts, providing an institutional foundation for economic reforms, and ensuring access of Ukrainian products and workers to Eastern and Western markets.

Third, by expanding nongovernment initiatives in Ukraine. Despite the compelling strategic and moral reasons for foreign governments to support Ukraine, the unity and sustained commitment to put Ukraine's economy on a positive trajectory will need to come from nongovernmental actors. Ukraine shouldn't be a battleground between countries of widely diverging national interests. The task force would provide a vehicle through which western NGOs and their Russian counterparts could strategize and collaborate as part of a unified effort to assist Ukraine's transition.

In delivering a landslide victory for President Poroshenko, the Ukrainian people cast a broader vote of confidence in the values of freedom and democracy. The international community has an interest and a responsibility to deliver on Ukraine's aspirations. A Friends of Ukraine task force, leveraging nongovernment resources, would be an indispensable participant in getting this done.

Ms. Dobriansky is a former U.S. undersecretary of state for global affairs. Mr. Olechowski is a former foreign minister of Poland. Mr. Satoh is a former Japanese ambassador to the U.N. Mr. Yurgens is chairman of the Institute of Contemporary Development.

http://online.wsj.com/